STUDIES
IN INTERNATIONAL LAW
AND RELATIONS

T0384609

STUDIES
IN INTERNATIONAL LAW
AND RELATIONS

by

A. PEARCE HIGGINS
C.B.E., K.C., LL.D.

*Whewell Professor of International Law in the University
of Cambridge; Fellow of Trinity College and Hon.
Fellow of Downing College, Cambridge;
Lecturer on International Law at the
Royal Naval War and Staff
Colleges; Membre de
l'Institut de Droit
International*

CAMBRIDGE
AT THE UNIVERSITY PRESS
1928

CAMBRIDGE
UNIVERSITY PRESS

University Printing House, Cambridge CB2 8BS, United Kingdom

Cambridge University Press is part of the University of Cambridge.

It furthers the University's mission by disseminating knowledge in the pursuit of education, learning and research at the highest international levels of excellence.

www.cambridge.org
Information on this title: www.cambridge.org/9781107586796

© Cambridge University Press 1928

This publication is in copyright. Subject to statutory exception and to the provisions of relevant collective licensing agreements, no reproduction of any part may take place without the written permission of Cambridge University Press.

First published 1928
First paperback edition 2015

A catalogue record for this publication is available from the British Library

ISBN 978-1-107-58679-6 Paperback

Cambridge University Press has no responsibility for the persistence or accuracy of URLs for external or third-party internet websites referred to in this publication, and does not guarantee that any content on such websites is, or will remain, accurate or appropriate.

CONTENTS

PREFACE

THIS volume contains a selection of studies on special points relating to International Law and International Relations. Many of these have already been published in legal and other periodicals, but they have all been revised and in some cases re-written. Notes are appended showing the original place of publication. Some of the studies had their origin in public lectures and the lecture form has been preserved.

The first three chapters are closely related to each other and deal with the interdependence of international relations and international law. The first chapter is a general discussion of the subject, while the second shows the difficulties which exist in state intercourse and some of their causes. The third chapter deals with the need for a greater emphasis being placed on the duties of states, rather than on their rights. The position of the Papacy from the point of view of international law is examined in the fourth chapter, and the question whether the Pope has an international legal personality is discussed. Chapter v is an attempt to sketch the history of the development of the Monroe Doctrine during the first century of its existence. The chapter on the work of Grotius and the modern international lawyer (Chapter vi) was written in the year of the celebration of the third centenary of the publication of his famous work on War and Peace. In Chapter vii I have traced the attempts made since the war to produce a greater feeling of security in Western Europe, and I have examined the Locarno treaties in some detail. I have to thank the *Law Journal* for permission to reproduce articles which appeared in that periodical on this subject. Chapter viii, on "The Law of Nations and the War of 1914," is reproduced by the kind permission of the Oxford University Press, who originally published it as one of the Oxford Pamphlets in 1914. I have, however, appended a postscript reviewing the situation in August, 1914, in the light of material which has since become available. Chapter IX is largely a commentary on the Sixth Hague Convention, 1907, relating to enemy ships in port at the outbreak of war. At the same time it affords striking evidence of its failure to produce the results for which it was intended. The chapter on Submarine Cables in time of war owes its origin to the provisions of the Treaty of Versailles dealing with the captured German cables. Chapter XI is a historical examination of the British practice of condemning captured enemy warships in the Prize Court, a practice which appears to be unique, and due to the grants of prize by the Crown. In Chapter XII I have discussed the subject of Retaliation in naval warfare: it is based on a lecture which I was asked to deliver before the United States Naval War College. I take this opportunity of expressing my great appreciation of the honour of being invited to address the officers of that famous institution on a question on which the British and United States Governments were not in accord. The last two chapters deal with the position in international law of defensively armed merchant ships. The note prefixed to Chapter XIII sufficiently explains the origins of these chapters; they are necessarily also concerned with some of the fundamental principles of the laws of naval warfare.

I am indebted to a former pupil, Mr Ifor Evans, Fellow of St John's College, for his kind assistance in reading the proofs and for many suggestions.

A. PEARCE HIGGINS

Trinity College, Cambridge
22 March, 1928

I

INTERNATIONAL RELATIONS AND
INTERNATIONAL LAW [1]

IT is always difficult for men and women of any
generation to understand fully the events which
are taking place in their own times, and in their
own country; it is still more difficult for them to corre-
late them with those that are happening in foreign
countries, for close interrelation between home and
foreign affairs is often not fully appreciated till after
the events have happened. Since the year 1914 there
has been in progress one of the great crises in the world's
history, and its reactions have by no means ceased.
Whether we look to the Balkan states of Europe, to
the great Chinese Republic or to Central America we
see evidences of the continued unrest and disturbance
which may, I think, be in no small measure attributed
to forces let loose and to doctrines enunciated during
and immediately after the close of the World War.

In every direction, political, social and economic, we
see evidences of the great changes which have been in
progress since the eventful days in the summer of 1914.
Not only internationally, but nationally these changes
have been felt, far more in the Old World than it is
probably realized in the New, for in addition to the
political changes caused by the war—alterations of
boundaries and the establishment of new states—there
has been a series of internal wars in many states, of
class against class. That an improvement has been
witnessed in the pacification of Europe generally I
think is undoubted. The work of the League of

---

[1] Based on a lecture delivered at the London School of Economics and published in *Economica*, January, 1922.

Nations, often belittled by its opponents or over-estimated by its fanatical supporters, or damned with faint praise by the cynics who are sitting on the fence, has undoubtedly been productive of much good, but there is a long road to be traversed before the goal of the idealist is in sight, before states are prepared in all matters of international interest to subordinate purely selfish interests to the general good, and to submit all disputes which cannot be settled by ordinary diplomatic means to the decision of a World Court.

If we ask what caused the stupendous changes which have taken place since 1914, changes which have rendered old maps useless so far as the political configuration of the world is concerned, it is easy enough to provide some sort of an answer. It may be said that the immediate cause was Austria-Hungary's declaration of war against Serbia, and Germany's unprovoked attack on Belgium and France in that year. But this would not be a wholly satisfactory reply to one who was seeking to probe the matter to its roots, and who asked for explanations of Austria's ultimatum, and Germany's action. It is not my intention to attempt an answer to these and many other questions which would at once spring into being. To provide anything like an adequate reply we should have to enter on a study of the diplomatic history of Europe for more than half a century. Dr G. P. Gooch in his Lowell Lectures in the spring of 1927 has endeavoured in a course of lectures on eight prominent European statesmen to get behind the scenes and explain some of the causes which were at work, but he would be the last to assert that his series of lectures, admirable and judicious as they were, gave the whole story.[1] A study such as that suggested would demonstrate the closeness of the connection between the internal and external policies of

[1] See also Dr Gooch's *Recent Revelations of European Diplomacy* (1927).

the states of the world; we should find politics and economics closely intermingled.

In the past, the people of most countries knew little, and probably cared less about the foreign policy of the Government than about any other department of state life. It is time that a change took place in this matter. It is, I believe, the duty of those who are engaged in educational work to emphasize this interdependence of the states of the world, and, in particular, to endeavour to awaken in the minds of students a living and active belief in the certainty that the well-being of one state cannot be considered apart from that of others. If we fail to realize this, our ignorance will be a constant source of danger not only to ourselves but to the world. Many domestic troubles, such, for instance, as that which is most insistent in many countries to-day—unemployment, must be envisaged from an international point of view in order that they may be fully understood. When the fact of this interdependence is grasped, we shall see that it involves the fundamental doctrine of the Christian ethic, that no state and no man liveth to itself or to himself; that not only in the Christian body but in the whole Family of Nations we are members one of another. Each is necessary to the other, and there is a real solidarity of interests. We are our brother's keeper. International relations are in truth and in fact the concern of every citizen of every state, and it is a citizen's duty to take a living interest in them.

Some years ago I read somewhere that the foreign policy of a state consisted in the normal everyday application of armaments in international affairs, just as war is their abnormal and exceptional application: that diplomacy is the paper money which saves the inconvenient use of gold in large transactions, the armaments being the gold reserve on whose existence the value of the paper depends. Diplomacy of that type, conducted without armed strength behind it, was compared to inconvertible paper money, always at a discount and entirely valueless at a crisis. This definition is based on the doctrine of Clausewitz, the well-known German writer on strategy, and it describes the foreign policy of some states in the past, in which the gold reserve was very frequently disclosed. "Shining armour," "mailed fists," "swords rattling in their scabbards," are the language of this policy which results in "Chauvinism," or "Jingoism." It is sometimes called "Realpolitik," and it has just this much only to be said in its favour, that it emphasizes the principle that when a state has adopted a definite line of policy it should count the cost, and be prepared to maintain the needful means of carrying it into effect. It has a truth underlying its grotesque and hideous appearance, and members of the League of Nations cannot afford to ignore the element of truth which it contains. Article 10 of the Covenant of the League, under which the members undertake to preserve as against external aggression the territorial integrity and existing political independence of all the members of the League, is a reminder that there must be the gold reserve behind the memoranda and despatches of the League.

All heresies live by reason of the germ of truth which they contain, and the view of foreign policy I have been discussing, though untenable as a guide for ordinary use, since it represents a policy of pure force and militarism, has enough of truth in it to be at the same time useful and dangerous. As an ideal for the conduct of international relations it is to be rejected. We must have ideals for these as for other aims in life, and we do well to consider them; but we cannot forget that we are not living in an ideal world, neither shall we ever be until the men and women who compose the states of the world themselves live ideally. In considering the principles which should guide statesmen in the conduct of international relations, we shall do well to remember the wise words of Francis Bacon and thus avoid the danger he indicates in that "philosophers make imaginary laws for imaginary commonwealths, and their discourses are as the stars, which give little light because they are so high."[1] Let us follow the advice which he gives and turn to statesmen and diplomatists who have to deal with the hard concrete facts of state life, where they are faced with the conflicting desires and ambitions of the representatives of other states. A speaker at a meeting of the Assembly of the League of Nations, in reply to the complaint that the progress of the League was slow, said that it was easy enough to go fast as long as abstractions only were being dealt with, but that when concrete cases came for consideration, the rate of progress was necessarily slow. It is well that we should be reminded of this truth.

As examples illustrative of practical statesmen's ideals let us consider some solemn declarations made at different times at meetings of representatives of the Powers, on the subject of the principles of international intercourse. It would be difficult to frame a more exalted statement of the basis of international relations than that laid down in the pact of the Holy Alliance of September 26th, 1815, between the Emperors of Russia and Austria, and the King of Prussia, which was subsequently adhered to by nearly all the monarchs of Europe, except the British King. After stating their intention of settling the steps to be taken by the Powers in their reciprocal relations upon the sublime

---

[1] *Advancement of Learning*, xxiii, 47.

truths of the Christian religion, they solemnly declared

the present article has no other object than to publish in the face of the whole world their fixed resolution, both in the administration of their respective states and in their political relations with every other Government, to take for their sole guide the precepts of that holy religion, namely, the precepts of Christian charity and peace, which, far from being applicable only to private concerns, must have an immediate influence upon the counsels of princes, and guide their steps, as being the only means of consolidating human institutions and remedying their imperfections.

Three years later, at the Congress of Aix-la-Chapelle, 1818, the Great Powers signed a declaration in which they solemnly recognized the Law of Nations as the basis of all international relations, and pledged themselves to act in accordance with its rules.

We know that the practice of the Holy Alliance fell very short of its ideals, and that the policy of supporting existing Governments led to frequent interventions in the internal affairs of states, but we must not fail to note this high standard of international conduct set forth under the inspiration of the Tsar, Alexander the First. This declaration was a personal expression of the views of monarchs who failed to live up to their ideals; let us therefore turn to more modern and more democratic times. Representatives of the Powers met at the Hague Peace Conferences in 1899 and 1907, and approved a Convention for the pacific settlement of international disputes, in the preamble to which we read:

The High Contracting Powers [16 in 1899, 44 in 1907, of which 21 were Republics] animated by the sincere desire to work for the maintenance of the general peace; Resolved to promote by their best efforts the friendly settlement of international disputes; Recognizing the solidarity uniting the members of the Society of civilized nations; Desirous of extending the empire of law and

of strengthening the appreciation of international justice....
Sharing the opinion of the august initiator of the international
Peace Conferences [in each case a Tsar] that it is expedient to
record in an international agreement the principle of equity and
right on which are based the security of states and the welfare of
peoples,

resolved on the Convention in question.

Turn now to the latest pronouncement on the subject
of the basis of international relations contained in the
Preamble to the Covenant of the League of Nations
which forms part of all the Treaties of Peace signed in
1919.

The High Contracting Parties [in the Treaty of Versailles there
were 28 Powers, not counting the British Dominions and India
separately, 19 being Republics, and now more than 50 States are
parties to the Covenant] in order to promote international co-
operation and to achieve international peace and security,

by the acceptance of obligations not to resort to war,

by the prescription of open, just and honourable relations
between nations,

by the firm establishment of the undertakings of international
law as the actual rule of conduct among Governments, and
by the maintenance of justice and a scrupulous respect for
all treaty obligations in the dealings of organized peoples
with one another,

agreed on the Covenant.

"Christian charity and peace"; "equity and right,
on which are based the security and welfare of peoples";
"open, just and honourable relations and scrupulous
respect for treaties"—these are the principles which,
at different times during the last hundred years, statesmen and diplomatists have laid down as those which
should be their guides in international relations. The
Act of the Holy Alliance cannot be summarily dis-
missed in Castlereagh's words, as a "piece of sublime
mysticism and nonsense." It was the result of a
scheme which had been in the mind of the Tsar for at

least ten years. In 1804 he had written in his instructions to Novosiltsov:

> It is no question of realizing the dream of perpetual peace, but one could attain at least to some of its results if, at the conclusion of the general war, one could establish on clear precise principles the prescriptions of the rights of nations....On principles such as these one could proceed to a general pacification, and give birth to a league of which the stipulations would form, so to speak, a new code of the law of nations which, sanctioned by the greater part of the nations of Europe, would without difficulty become the immutable rule of the cabinets, while those who should try to infringe it would risk bringing upon themselves the forces of the new union.[1]

The similarity of this view with that of the founders of the League of Nations is striking. It was a larger conception than that of either of the two Hague Conferences. It lacked, however, as Professor Alison Phillips points out, a central legislative authority, a central executive and a common armament to enforce its decrees; these are to some extent being provided for by the League of Nations, but its organization is not yet complete.

I have not cited the extracts from the Act of the Holy Alliance and from the preamble to the Hague Conventions in any spirit of cynicism or irony, neither do I wish you to draw the conclusion that because, hitherto, the acts of statesmen have fallen below the standards to which they have collectively assented in the name of their respective states, their successors will, in the future, do as has been done in the past. They may; that is a possibility which must not be overlooked; it is a warning which must not pass unheeded. But if they do, the results will be productive of far greater disasters than any in the past; they will imperil civilization itself.

[1] Cited by W. Alison Phillips, *The Confederation of Europe*, p. 144.

The efforts of statesmen, diplomatists and jurists in the past have failed, as we have seen, to prevent the outbreak of war from time to time, and worse than that, the events of the late war showed that rules for its conduct were ineffective and grossly violated. Notwithstanding the noble ideals of monarchs and diplomatists expressed in international declarations, after all the great wars of the past the old vices have reappeared, the old bad methods have reasserted themselves. After a great war which has produced intense suffering, the common conscience of the nations of the world has been quickened. Men look back with horror, as to some dreadful nightmare through which they have passed, in which they have seen the fundamental laws of humanity and the most elementary principles of morality violated, and rules of international law cast to the winds. They awake to a renewed sense of the community of the interests of mankind, and an increasing acknowledgment of the principle that purely national interests must be subordinated under a regular system of law to the well-being of all nations. It is well to recall the words of one of the most distinguished English jurists, the late Mr W. E. Hall, who, in the Preface to the third edition of his classical work on International Law, published in 1889, said: "There can be very little doubt that if the next war is unscrupulously waged, it also will be followed by increased stringency of the law," and he adds: "In a community, as in an individual, passionate excess is followed by a reaction of lassitude, and to some extent of conscience."

The war of 1914–18 was unscrupulously waged, and excesses in all departments were committed. The international conscience was aroused as it had never been aroused before. Nations reached the highest points of endeavour under the influence of an exalted ideal of duty. And then, when fighting ceased, there was heard on all sides the resolve that what had happened, both before and during its course, must never be allowed to take place again. Reaction set in in most of the countries which had been engaged in the long years of war, in Great Britain, France, Italy, Germany, and Austria. The long delays of the Paris Conference, the disappointment of the Allies and of France especially over the action or rather the inaction of the United States in not implementing the Peace treaties; the internal troubles economic and others, in many states, caused the mass of the war-wearied countries after they had become accustomed to the silence of the guns and the absence of air-raids, to fall for a time into a state of lassitude and irritability, with a disinclination for constructive thought or action. These are passing, the general outlook is brighter, but there is the danger which arises from forgetfulness, and it is essential that people of all the states which were at war should realize that they cannot entirely rid themselves of all blame for the evils of the past, and that failure to take an active interest in matters outside the borders of their own state was one of the causes of their sufferings and disasters.

The states of the world have, with scarcely any exception, adopted some form of democratic government. Democracy, therefore, has now a great opportunity of showing that it can avoid the errors of the past, and of proving that under its *régime*, the system instituted by the Covenant of the League of Nations, which is based on the recognition of the mutual rights and interests of all the states of the world, will not share the fate of the old and less complete attempts to establish a world organization. But no covenant, no written declaration of the Rights of Man, no formal change of government, will suffice. The clash of con-

flicting interests between states governed on democratic principles is not necessarily less serious than
between those under less popular forms of government.
Economic pressure, the growth of population, the
desire for territorial expansion, the trade competition
in the markets of the world, the attraction of uncivilized
or backward countries, the difficulties attending on
emigration and immigration, not to speak of other
and more subtle, but not less powerful forces, such as
greed, ambition and jealousy, which in the past have
been fruitful sources of international disputes, will still
have to be reckoned with in international relations.
Neither do I think that it has yet been clearly demonstrated that democracies are, by their nature, less
quarrelsome or less prone to desire accession of
territory at the expense of their neighbours than other
forms of government. Uncontrolled selfish passions
may sweep a democratic state into war, as well as a
great inspiration or a sudden revelation of duty. The
student of international affairs cannot ignore these
facts. Only the future will reveal whether the modern
democracies will conduct their international relations
on the basis of, and in accordance with, the ideals which
their representatives have proclaimed, and whether they
will show a willingness, even a desire, to submit such
of their differences as they cannot settle by negotiation
to the decision of an impartial international tribunal.
If conflicting group interests in various countries refuse
to arbitrate their differences, stubbornly resist mediation, and resort only to the arbitrament of industrial
war, the outlook for the future of international relations is not bright. If, on the other hand, they are
prepared to submit their disputes to impartially con-
stituted tribunals, and honourably to carry out their
awards, there will be sound reason for hoping that the
future will avoid the failures of the past. States, like

individuals, can only progress to liberty under the existence of a rule of law.

There is, however, an international morality which exists alongside international law, and like municipal law and morality they are seldom absolutely identical. This has been brought out in lines which may be familiar to all:

> Thou shalt not kill, but need'st not strive
> Officiously to keep alive.

But in international relations there is less of the letter of the law than in the civil law of a state, where a conflict may well arise between the spirit and the letter. As Westlake has well said:

There is little of the letter, little of express convention of authoritative formula, to enter into the problem of determining the duty of a state towards its neighbours. If anyone says that the technical duty of a state is to take or to abstain from taking a certain course, but that in the given circumstances it may justifiably act otherwise, we may be pretty sure that he had no sufficient reason for laying down the technical duty in the terms which he has chosen.[1]

This is not to say that there are not rules of International Law which must be construed in a legal manner, but it brings me to the point that if the spirit underlying international intercourse is one of mutual goodwill, co-operation and confidence, there is good ground for hoping for success. But this is by no means all that is necessary for a new orientation on international affairs: we need to study the trend of political and economic movements in other countries and to endeavour to understand the mentality and objectives of their people. This is essentially a matter of international education, and all Universities can do much to forward the growth of a true international spirit. By that I do not mean that in all cases where your own

---

[1] *Collected Papers*, p. xx.

state has a difference with another state you should at once conclude that the other state is in the right, and proceed to belittle the actions of your own statesmen because they are not of your political party. No; by the international spirit I mean that "we must do our best to lift political discussion, both national and international, up out of the mire of personality and unseemly controversies between individuals and private interests on to the high ground of principle."[1] Principles in international relations are greatly needed to-day. President Roosevelt well put this in addressing an American audience when he said "Let us build a genuine internationalism, that is, a genuine and generous regard for the rights of others on the only healthy basis—a sound and intense development of the broadest spirit of American nationalism."

Furthermore, there must be a spread of knowledge amongst all classes. We need to have the facts and the real position of affairs made plain. These may sometimes be grim and unpleasant to face, but it will generally be best to have them.

I have said that this is a matter of education, and there is need to begin in the schools, and to encourage the upper classes to study the history of their own time, and of that immediately preceding.

Much can be done by the press in all countries to disseminate a real knowledge of international affairs. But there is a great need of impartial presentation of the facts, and though the newspaper press may be a great instrument in advancing international co-operation, there are, unfortunately, many examples of its influence to enflame popular prejudice and encourage a narrow-minded nationalism.

Apart from newspapers, however, the number of articles in quarterly or monthly journals and maga-

[1] N. Murray Butler, *The International Mind*, p. 112.

zines both in Great Britain and the United States which have a great educational value from the international standpoint is quite remarkable. The numerous foundations and institutions which exist for the encouragement of work on international relations, and the societies which exist to hear experts and to discuss foreign policy are useful methods for the advancement of a knowledge of these important topics.

An instructed electorate and a body of legislators who make a careful study of foreign affairs, are of great value to the state: they can assist the Government of the day in its most difficult task, that of formulating its foreign policy, and indicating the principles which are to guide it. It is, however, only through the Ministry of Foreign Affairs in each state that the policy of the Government can be carried into execution.

All the public services of the state need to be constantly and wisely watched. Criticism of the departments responsible for the Army, the Navy or the Air Force is legitimate, and the public is wise in seeing that those responsible for the defence of the state should not be allowed to become antiquated in method or hidebound by tradition. But public criticism should begin a stage higher. The Army, Navy and Air Force are the nation's weapons of defence, and they are only called into use, as a rule, when Foreign Offices and diplomatists have failed to maintain a state of peace. It is even more important that the department which conducts the business of the state on which peace and war depend should be the subject of a vigilant and intelligent criticism. Failures in diplomacy in the past have too often been the result of the public ignorance and neglect. The electors have approved a policy without counting the cost. I am not advocating the intermeddling of the public in the conduct of diplomacy—far from it. When a policy has been settled, its actual working out must be left to the duly accredited agents, who have been trained in the most delicate of all tasks, that of international negotiation. "Secret diplomacy," as I understand this expression, means secret policies and secret treaties which, in time of peace, are the antitheses of popular government. But the conduct of business negotiations must generally be secret; little progress would be made if at every stage in the transaction public reports had to be made. Open diplomacy of that kind would mean not fewer, but more wars. The ignorance and negligence referred to are in relation to the formulation of the foreign policy of the state, not as regards the conduct of diplomacy. It is in the early stages that the fullest information should be given to the public. The pursuit of a given line of foreign policy may involve the expenditure of vast sums of money, and, in some cases, great effusion of blood. If those on whom the burdens will ultimately fall do not take the trouble to make themselves acquainted with the policy proposed in all its bearings, and do not insist on being furnished with the necessary information on which to base their judgment, they are neglecting to fulfil their duty as citizens.

But even with full information it is by no means easy to appreciate all the difficulties which arise in international relationships, and democracies have always been liable to be swayed by a plausible phrase or an attractive catchword. Much has been heard of "making the world safe for democracy," of "the freedom of the seas," and of the right of "self-determination" by peoples. Those to whom these phrases are addressed have the right to require from those who use them the fullest explanation, and are under the duty to endeavour to ascertain whither they are being led under banners bearing these vague inscriptions. Are we not now learning that "self-determination" is not always a safe guide in the settlement of territorial frontiers, and that economic needs and inordinate aspirations of nationalism are not always capable of being reconciled?

We must now turn to another aspect of international relations and consider the law applicable to them. Differences which arise between states are due sometimes to political matters, but at other times involve points of law. We cannot ignore the latter in our treatment of international affairs.

It has been well said that "the amount of regulation which a society requires will be in proportion to the closeness of contact between its members and the complication of their mutual dealings."[1]   International Law has come into being to govern the business relations of states who form the international society; it consists of the rules of action which states feel themselves bound to observe in their relations with other states, and of which they expect the observance from other states. Many of these rules can be traced to that part of the Roman Law which was deemed to be common to all nations, the *jus naturale*, or *jus gentium*; many have gradually been evolved by the practice of states. Modern international lawyers base them either on custom, that is the general practice of states, or on convention, i.e. on treaties or contracts between states. Nearly all relations which arise between states sooner or later involve the application of some rule or rules of International Law. And when disputes arise between states, both sides rely on these rules to support their claims. If a knowledge of the facts of state intercourse is necessary, how much more is a knowledge of the rules of the law which apply to state transactions? International disputes are, of course,

[1] J. Westlake, *Collected Papers*, p. 50.

frequently of a complex character, and the law applicable will only emerge when the facts are fully ascertained. Take such a case as the dispute between Great Britain and the United States over the Panama Canal in 1912, where the conflict turned on the interpretation of the terms of a treaty between the two states. To understand it, it was necessary to ascertain certain historical facts, and to appreciate their bearing on the words of the article of the treaty.[1]

A knowledge of the rules of International Law has a steadying influence on public opinion when an international dispute arises. In such cases an instructed public will keep calm, and thus render the greatest assistance to those who are conducting the arguments, which they will be able to follow intelligently. There are many examples that might be adduced showing the need for education on this important matter. We might go back to a case where a question of International Law was involved, which for the time being produced the greatest tension between Great Britain and the United States, and cite the case of *The Trent* in 1861, but it is unnecessary to accumulate examples. From time to time international incidents are bound to arise, involving questions of International Law, and it is of the greatest importance that there should be a widely extended knowledge of its principles so that the rights and wrongs of a case may be properly apprehended by the nation as a whole.

We have dealt with International Law in relation to international relations because of their intimate connection. Internationally the ideal is that there should be a Court administering the Law of Nations, and before which any state, believing itself to be aggrieved, should be able to summon the wrong-doer. This does not yet exist in the world, but there has come into

[1] See L. Oppenheim, *The Panama Canal Conflict* (1913).

being a Permanent Court of International Justice where right is to be done to all nations who bring their disputes before it on the basis of International Law. The establishment of the Court is a sign of progress on sound lines of legal principles. It has not introduced compulsion into the sphere of international litigation, though members of the League of Nations on signing or ratifying the Statute may declare that they recognize the jurisdiction of the Court in all or any of certain classes of legal disputes as compulsory *ipso facto* in relation to any other members accepting the same obligation. This is a step in the direction of the compulsory settlement of international disputes by judicial decision, but apart from this acceptance of the Court's jurisdiction one state cannot compel another with which it has a difference to bring it before the Court. The body of jurists who prepared the draft statute desired to make it compulsory, but the Assembly of the League of Nations has decided otherwise. The world is not yet ready for this. The new Court is, however, a great advance on the Hague Tribunal established in 1899, which is left in existence with the new Court. It is permanent, and in session at stated times, and there is no special procedure necessary for the parties to bring it into operation. Its establishment is another reason for there being a supply of duly qualified international lawyers, and for the existence of a public capable of appreciating the decisions of the Court. Clearly the establishment of this Court is only a stage in the development of International Law, but it marks a forward movement in the acceptance by states of a rule of law as the last resort in their disputes, instead of the recourse to threats of violence and self-redress by war.

No Court of Law, no League of Nations, can ensure the final abolition of war between states. Progress towards a condition of international relations which can be accepted as worthy of reasoning and reasonable beings lies in the gradual evolution of a law-abiding instinct, in a growth of respect for the Law of Nations, and in the elevation of the moral standards of men. The pessimist (and who of us is not inclined at times to take a hopeless view of the future of the world?) says of the League of Nations and the Permanent Court: You cannot change human nature; what has been, will be. This is only another futile attempt of men to administer to themselves an anodyne which will enable them to forget their troubles. Here is another quack medicine, but the old evils will again reassert themselves when states have had time to recuperate after their recent excesses. But is this true? Does it not fundamentally deny the possibility of improvement in every department of human life by identifying human nature with its lower parts, and excluding those which are essentially the attributes of a divinely created man? To Grotius, writing at a time when one might have been excused for taking a low view of mankind, human nature was the Mother of Right. But Grotius took human nature as a whole, with its impulses of kindness, pity and sociability, as well as its desires of individual pleasure and fear of pain.[1] He thus founded Law and Morality upon the whole compass of man's nature, human and social as well as his animal and individual nature, and we can do no less. Progress lies along the line of the development of the human and social side of our nature, carrying with it a sense of personal responsibility for social wrongs done in the name of the society of which we are members, and a determination to maintain in international intercourse as high a standard of morality as obtains among men in their private relations.

[1] Whewell's Grotius, pp. vii, xxvii.

We must not be led astray by the contrast too sharply drawn between the state and the human beings who compose it. Rousseau, for example, treated states and men as things of a different nature between which no true relation could be fixed, and consequently he affirmed that "a state can only have for enemies other states, and not men."[1] For each of us to-day the dictum "L'Etat, c'est moi" should have an individual application. This principle of individual responsibility has been admirably expressed by the late Professor Westlake. He points out that to lay the emphasis on the abstract state and to ignore the action of those within it, who help to guide it either in a public capacity or by the expression of opinion,

allows us to forget that not only is the action of our state that of ourselves, but that those towards whom it is taken are also men like ourselves, though they may be veiled from our eyes by the interposition of another artificial entity. I do not say this in the interest only of those improvements in International Law, which the future may have in store, although the condition of their being worked out is that we shall think more of what is human in the matter and less of what is technical. Nor do I wish only to hold up to your eyes the physical and moral suffering caused by war to individuals, though these are important enough. I deprecate the ignoring of personal responsibility quite as much with a view to the effect which the conduct of a great state may have on the destinies of other populations, especially of those which, as possessing less power or a lower civilization, are exposed to be most seriously affected by our action or by our abstinence from action, while least able to help themselves. There can neither be sound International Law nor sound international politics, nor sound treatment of inferior races, without a sense of duty; and a sense of duty will not be roused towards abstractions, nor by looking at abstractions.[2]

Personal responsibility means constant watchfulness, and the price of peace is unceasing vigilance in the field of foreign relations.

[1] *Contrat Social*, Bk. i, cap. 4.   [2] *Collected Papers*, p. 411.

II

SOME DIFFICULTIES IN
INTERNATIONAL RELATIONS[1]

IT is doubtful if the ordinary citizen of any country, should his mind ever revert to the problem, realizes the difficulties of those who are concerned with the conduct of the international relations of his state. He will probably repeat the criticism of the foreign policy of his Government contained in his newspaper, but he will rarely place himself in the position of the ministers who have to make decisions and to take action. It requires a breadth of vision and a graphic power of imagination to visualize an international situation. Knowledge of the economic, political and cultural conditions in the foreign state is requisite, as well as the fullest information regarding the position in his own state, so that its interests may be adequately protected.

It is particularly difficult for the citizens of the states of America to realize the complexities of the problems which face those responsible for the conduct of foreign affairs in the Old World. The American continent has lived under the aegis of the Monroe Doctrine, propounded by Presidents and Secretaries of the State Department for over a century. The United States is undoubtedly the most powerful and influential of the states in the American continent. Whatever else this Doctrine may be or may connote, it has proved in the main to be a doctrine conducive to the maintenance of peace in the Western Hemisphere.

The American continent has vast natural resources and wealth, there is no question of over-population in

[1] A lecture delivered before the University of Illinois, 1927.

the several states into which it is divided. These peoples tend to fall into only three or four well-marked ethnological groups; the problem of nationalism or self-determination is not one with which any of these states is faced. But, in order to get a faint idea of the difficulties of Europe, it is only necessary for a citizen of the United States to consider what would be the condition of affairs if Canada were Russia, Mexico—still remaining Mexico, Colombia Jugo-Slavia, Brazil France, the Argentine Germany, and so on. Let him suppose also that Australia, New Zealand and South Africa were colonies or territories of the United States. Would the American critics of Europe find the situation as to international relations or disarmament as simple as it sometimes appears to be regarded by them?

Great Britain is a small island with a population of over 40 millions to support, it is dependent on its overseas trade for the maintenance of its people and for its food supplies. In this outlook it is not in terms of a continent that British statesmen have to think, but theirs must be a world-wide vision. They are constantly being reminded how events in a continent thousands of miles from London may have their repercussion and reactions among the hundreds of millions of human beings for whose well-being and protection in India, or other distant parts of the Empire, they may in the last resort be responsible. France is still not without fears of her next-door neighbour from whom twice within half a century she has suffered heavy blows. Italy, having recently undergone severe internal troubles, is busy with a new experiment in government, and, under the guidance of the master-mind of her Premier, is reaching out to positions of still greater influence and jealous of movements which appear to have as their ultimate aim the imposition of limits to her expansion or control of adjacent waters or lands which may seem to threaten her safety or economic development. The new Turkey is still an object of suspicion by adjacent states. Many of the succession states of the Austro-Hungarian Empire are realizing some of the defects of a too strongly applied doctrine of nationalism or are chafing at its incomplete application. Germany remains dissatisfied with her Eastern frontier and the Polish corridor, and her relations with Poland, her Eastern neighbour, are not of an enthusiastically friendly character, though the Locarno settlement is a good augury for the future. And in the East stands Russia with its new experiment in government and its agents for disseminating its explosive doctrines throughout, not only the adjacent countries, but all countries of the world.

This may appear a disturbing and disquieting picture, but it is worth while to have sketched it in outline in order that the dangers and difficulties of European statesmen, especially in such matters as security and disarmament, may be the better realized.

It will be said that all of these European states except Russia and Turkey are members of the League of Nations, and therefore the difficulties are those of the imagination, unless the League of Nations is a valueless institution. A picture, even a sketch, needs for its proper portrayal a judicious admixture of light and shade; we have had the shade, we must also see the light which comes from Geneva. The League of Nations has effected great improvements in the relationships between its members which have made for the maintenance of peace and the promotion of international good understanding. It has enabled many of the states, by a friendly discussion round a table, to see better each other's points of view, and in an atmosphere of the highest type of internationalism, to adjust their differences and obtain impartial examinations into their grievances. The economic, social and intellectual labours of the various Commissions of the League are working for the simplification of customs and the removal of barriers to intercourse, and have in every way contributed towards the growth of a spirit of toleration and understanding which could not have been achieved by years of writing of dispatches and diplomatic representations of the pre-war type. If by some international catastrophic event the existing League were dissolved to-morrow, states would be compelled to proceed to the erection of another, for all statesmen have learned the value of the assistance of the highly-trained and organized permanent civil service of the League, which, since its inception, has been of growing importance.

But having said so much of the League and its great value as an instrument both for the preservation of the peace of the world and for the promotion of international co-operation, it is important to remember that it is still incomplete as a means for fulfilling the former purpose, since the United States, Russia and Turkey remain outside its circle. It is a substitute, and at present the only working substitute, that has been found for the ideal of the Family of Nations. This should be an international society in which every state is prepared unequivocally to fulfil its own legal and moral obligations as a member of that society, and to recognize the rights of every other member. But this ideal can only be attained when an answer has been found to the enquiry which Lord Bryce has propounded: "The prospect of improving the relations of states and peoples to one another depends ultimately upon the possibility of improving human nature itself...can it be raised to and sustained at a higher level than it has yet attained?"

When that question has been answered definitely in the affirmative the League of Nations as an instrument for the preservation of peace will become unnecessary, though its administrative and co-operative functions will be found even more requisite than they are to-day.

The difficulties of international relations which have been so far referred to may be summarized as those which are inherent in human nature as it exists, as flowing partly from the passions of jealousy, hatred, envy and love of aggrandizement and power, partly from the desire for self-preservation, security and the need for self-realization. In municipal or national societies these passions are restrained and limited in their evil consequences, and the legitimate aims of human existence are furthered by law, enforced by the power of the community. In the international society with which we are now concerned the relations of the members are also largely regulated by the rules of international law. The chief constraining force of these rules is the collective public opinion or morality of the members, and the limitations on their freedom of action to which they have voluntarily subjected themselves by their adoption of treaties of compulsory arbitration or by their acceptance of the provisions of the Covenant of the League of Nations. The difficulties which are now to be approached may be classed as those due to the inherent condition of certain of the states forming the international society, and those which are due to the defective state of the rules of the law governing their relationship, i.e. of International Law or the Law of Nations.

We have only to run over the names of the states in the world to-day which are recognized as "sovereign independent states" to realize at once that there is a very great inequality in their influence, size, and population, as well as in their intellectual, moral and economic development. It is as untrue to the facts to say that all states are equal as it is to say that all men are equal, unless one is at great pains to explain the sense in which the word "equal" is used. Equal in what? Equal, so far as states are concerned, in that they are all equally protected by law in the rights which they possess; equal in so far as they are entitled to enforce such rights as they have; equal in so far as they are all interested in the vindication of law. But they are not all equal in the sense that every rule of law applies equally to every one of the states forming the international society. Their inequality of development renders the relationship of states in a backward condition of civilization to states of a more highly developed nature one of difficulty, and is often productive of friction and serious conflict. No state and no individual is willing to confess to a lower standard of development than others with which it is in communication or relationship. But certain states emerging from a condition of isolation, or possessing religious or intellectual traditions which have hitherto kept them apart from close intercourse with those which are the inheritors of the traditions of Western Europe—of that portion of Christendom where international law first came into being—have, as a condition of their entry into the international society or Family of Nations, accepted certain limitations which are not in existence as between the older members of that society. Even amongst some of the inheritors of the old tradition, owing to conditions arising from social upheavals and civil disturbances, there are states which from time to time are incapable of fulfilling their international duties, and in whose affairs other states have found it necessary to interfere. These interventions have taken place by reason of the fact that continued civil war and the absence of effective government on their borders had become a serious danger to the welfare of other states; or that the lives and property of their citizens within these backward states were imperilled; or that they suffered injustice at the hands of the corrupt and inefficient body of men who purported to exercise the judicial functions; or by the unequal laws which were passed by their legislatures. It is wholly unnecessary—it would be invidious—to endeavour to give concrete examples of the conditions to which I am referring or to name states to which these remarks may apply. They have existed in the past, nay, they exist at the present. They constitute a grave danger to international harmony because they offer an opportunity to an unprincipled state to take undue advantage of the internal weakness or maladministration of such a state to increase its own power. This it may do either by acquiring a *de facto* protectorate while protesting that its intervention is in the interests of humanity; or by acquiring such a predominant interest in the affairs of the state by means of financial assistance, accompanied by the nomination of certain of its own citizens as advisers in the internal reorganization of the state and as supervisors of the proper application of the funds provided, that a relationship is established which is little removed in effect from annexation. The danger is not one for the backward state only, it is a danger to the peace of the world owing to the effects which the act of intervention may have on other states. Should a state intervene from disinterested motives, in a spirit of pure altruism, it would be difficult, unless such intervention were undertaken at the request of and under the auspices of the League of Nations, or some other combination of the Powers, to convince other states of its purity of motive. The continued existence of backward states is, therefore, another of the difficulties of international relations.

The constitutional arrangements which exist in some states in regard to the conduct of international relations and the ratification of treaties is another source of misunderstanding. In the greater part of the states of the world the conduct of international business is in the hands of a member of the Government who occupies the position of Minister or Secretary for Foreign Affairs. He, with the assent of his Government, negotiates and signs treaties and, in the majority of cases, the ratification by the organ of state charged with this function generally follows as a matter of course. In some, such as the United States, matters are not so simple, and the chances of a treaty which has been negotiated and signed by the responsible agents of the United States receiving the sanction of the necessary majority in the Senate are dependent on local political factors which cannot always be appreciated at their true value by the people of the state with whom the treaty has been negotiated. It is true that the legal position of the plenipotentiaries is, or ought to be, well known to the world, and, in particular, to the Government of the other contracting state; but it cannot always be expected that it will be as fully understood by the people of that state. Hence when there was a failure of the United States to ratify the Anglo-American guarantee treaty with France in 1919, and the other treaties negotiated and signed at Paris at the close of the World War, there was a wide and deep feeling of disappointment and resentment on the part of the people of other states at what they deemed to be nothing less than a breach of good faith on the part of the United States.

So too, springing out of the same constitutional cause there is, in countries with a federal system, a difficulty in executing treaties which they have both signed and ratified owing to the rights which are possessed by the States forming the federal Union. I need only refer to the trouble which arose in regard to the schools in California under the American treaty with Japan.[1]

This leads to another, and what will probably be in the future one of the gravest difficulties with which many of the states of the world will be confronted, namely racial discrimination as regards privileges of immigration. It is not a topic which can be dealt with as merely incidental to so great a subject as that with which we are now concerned. It concerns every part of the British Empire as well as the United States of America. For the British Empire it is possibly even more serious than for the United States, owing to the number of different races in allegiance to their common King-Emperor. Western states will have to reckon with Oriental states like China and Japan and, it may be, with other states in Asia or Africa whose nationals are of another ethnological stock and of different social and economic traditions from those of the nations of European descent. It is not possible to appeal to clearly defined rules of International Law for the settlement of questions which such a clash of interests may arouse.

It is generally admitted that in many important fields of international activity there are serious gaps, and in other respects there are divergences of practice in International Law itself. Law is not coterminous with all the activities of human life, but it should provide solutions for questions which arise from conflicting claims in the exercise of the normal functions of men, such as self-preservation and legitimate development.

On many topics of normal state activity, the rules of the Law of Nations are not as clearly defined or as

[1] See *American Journal of International Law* (1907), vol. i, p. 273.

capable of ascertainment as is desirable. It must be realized that International Law is a comparatively new body of rules which has come into being to meet the exigencies of circumstances as they have arisen. The generally accepted sources of these rules are the custom, or practice of states, and, in some cases, treaties in which states have embodied definite rules for the guidance of their international intercourse. There are not infrequently divergent sets of rules dealing with similar sets of circumstances. Certain states or combinations of states adhere to one set of rules, while others have a different solution for the same problem. An example may be afforded by the rules applied by states to events occurring on foreign merchant ships within their harbours, or in regard to the jurisdiction exercised in a state's territorial waters. In point of fact, however, the difficulties which arise from such variation are not great in practice. If the two systems are both of such a character that wrongs done to individuals are ultimately redressed, it is a matter of indifference to most states which set of rules is observed so long as there is consistency and certainty in such matters. From time to time these divergences may be found to cause inconvenience to those whom such laws concern. In such cases, either through the medium of international conferences of interested persons, such as shipowners and business men, or through a Commission of the League of Nations, or by a diplomatic conference of the representatives of states, a thorough examination of the practices is made and methods are sought whereby such uniformity may be produced as will best suit the circumstances and conditions of those interested.

But in dealing with questions of International Law it will be found that the systems of law in which men have been trained and under which they live exercise a very marked influence on their outlook and methods of treatment. It is not sufficiently realized even by lawyers, much less by the mass of mankind, how much their outlook on all matters involving legal principles and methods is influenced by the legal atmosphere in which their special national civilization has developed. There is a marked divergence of outlook and method of treatment between lawyers of the Anglo-American school and those trained in the continental schools of law. The former are in the habit of dealing with facts by the aid of principles extracted from a long series of cases decided by their courts administering the Common Law or that branch of law which originally came into being to modify its too great rigidity and to which the name of Equity is applied in England and the United States. The states of the continent of Europe and the peoples of the New World who derive their jurisprudence from them, have been brought up under the system of codified rules of law, primarily those of the Roman Law, and in more recent times the codes which they have respectively enacted. France, Germany, Switzerland, Italy, and Austria, to name a few of such states, are in this position, and the tendency of such peoples is to seek for clear-cut definitions and concise statements in the code for the guidance of judge and people. It is because of these recognized differences of approach and mentality which these systems produce that the jurists who prepared the Statute of the World Court laid emphasis on the necessity of the Court being provided with judges whose training and equipment would enable them to bring to bear on cases submitted for their decisions the combined results of these different systems of jurisprudence.

There are other difficulties which may be occasioned by the geographical position of states. These arise very largely when there is a question of the statement or enforcement of the laws of neutrality in time of war. The needs of purely continental states and maritime states are frequently found not to be conformable to the same standard, and war invariably brings into conflict the interests of belligerent and neutral states, especially as regards naval operations. Rules resulting from a compromise of these conflicting interests have been evolved on such matters as contraband, blockade, unneutral service and the rights and duties of neutral states, but they are far from being perfect and in many of the details show a serious divergence of opinion and practice. They lay too great stress on neutral rights without the corresponding emphasis on neutral duties.

There is also a striking difference of approach to questions relating to naval warfare in general between that of maritime and continental states. The latter too often fail to realize what all sea-Powers such as Great Britain, the United States and Holland have recognized, that the principles of naval warfare are in many important respects different from those of land warfare. The Hague Conference of 1907, when it endeavoured to base a Code of Naval Warfare on the Regulations adopted for Land Warfare, had to confess that there were so great and fundamental differences between them that progress on those lines was not practicable.

It must not be thought that I desire to minimize the value and importance of international law which states observe as a guide in their intercourse. For the purpose of showing the difficulties which exist in international relations the emphasis has been expressly laid on those divergences which produce friction in the mutual relations of states. The Law of Nations has undoubtedly made great progress since the beginning of the nineteenth century, and in all departments there is every reason to look forward with hope to further developments and improvements. "There is clear evidence that the international society is gradually transferring into the jural sphere the moral principles of sharing the common burdens of humanity and extending the application of the principles of justice to increasing areas of state activities."[1]

But there are still a number of these areas which are not yet brought within the realm of law, and the customary rules of International Law are not concerned with many matters which states generally regard as of supreme importance. The growing body of treaty law dealing with such questions as international communications, the protection of human lives, the improvement of health and the economic and social advancement of members of the international society, though many of these matters may have occasioned friction in the past, does not touch the interests of states in a vital degree. There are departments of state intercourse which contain the greatest danger to the peace and well-being of the world for which rules of International Law are lacking, and in these matters there is need for the most careful adjustment of ideals to the potentialities of international life.

It is in the area of international activities to which the name of "Policy" is generally given that International Law is wanting, and in the formation of which ethical principles are required. International Law does not play the part that it should in the really great affairs of international life, and in its extension to them, "justice, equity, convenience and the reason of the thing"—to use Lord Mansfield's phrase—must all operate. Experience alone after the adoption of new rules will enable states to decide whether their national interests are prejudiced, to the ultimate detriment of the international

[1] See my article on "International Law and Moral Ideals" in *The Contemporary Review*, March, 1925.

society. The new rules must be rules of international right, which states will not only observe because they have bound themselves to do so, but because of their value as aids to the fuller realization of international life.

One of the important subjects which has so far failed to be brought within the domain of Law relates to the economic competition between the more powerful states for the control of the countries from which are drawn the raw materials of the world's commerce; another relates to the equally severe competition between the industrial states for the disposal of their wares. The rivalry of governments in the economic competition of their nationals has in the main been unrelated to legal considerations. Competition increases as states formerly agricultural become industrial, and "concession-hunters" in undeveloped countries rely on and are aided by their states as a fundamental principle of policy. From time to time attempts have been made to deal with particular cases by means of international treaties. The Berlin Act, 1885, saved the world from war over the scramble for Africa; Great Britain and Russia came to terms in 1907 over their spheres of influence regarding concessions of a political and commercial nature in Persia, and their political activities in Afghanistan and Thibet. Various treaties, the most recent being that signed at Washington in 1922, have been made governing the relations of the Powers with China, whose entry into the sphere of the world's commerce promised much both in the way of raw materials and commerce. Other examples might be given, but the foregoing afford evidence of the means which have so far been taken to deal with such questions in regard to which it was difficult to find rules of International Law.

At the most, all that can be said to emerge from the specific attempts to grapple with individual cases is that the principle called "the open door" is increasingly

finding favour, and has received further support from
the enunciation of the principle of equality of opportunity in trade and commerce to all the members of the
League of Nations contained in the mandates which it
has approved. Beyond this principle, which affords a
sound starting-point, other rules binding on states in
their commercial rivalry are yet to seek, and in the
search sound economic principles are as important as
purely ethical considerations.

There was another sphere of policy of an equally
serious character into which International Law formerly
did not enter, namely, those problems which every
state has to consider which affect its security, self-preservation and legitimate expansion. In the past it has
been left to each state to pursue such a policy of protection as seemed best suited to its needs. This often
consisted in preventing a condition of affairs arising in
which a state might find that it was too late to protect
itself, and the maintenance of armaments was a consequence. Some states have met the position by making
unilateral declarations of their views and policy, as was
done by the United States in the Message of President
Monroe of December, 1823. The Monroe Doctrine was
originally confined to the Continents of America, but
it has in effect been extended to large portions of the
Pacific Ocean. British statesmen have adopted a somewhat similar doctrine in regard to India, and British
policy with reference to Turkey, Egypt, Afghanistan,
Persia and Thibet has been guided by it. The alliances
of the groups of European states before the World
War were based on a desire of the Powers concerned
to obtain security and an insurance of their own
continued state existence. It was to meet this
situation, which it was realized would be fraught with
continued danger to the peace of the world if it were
allowed to revive after the war, and also to enable

states to adjust their differences of a political nature, that the League of Nations was founded, each member on entry being required to abandon all engagements contrary to the spirit of the Covenant. The founding of the League was at the same time a recognition that a world organization is a necessity for the fuller realization of the social duties of the members of the Family of Nations, and should provide the means of adjusting disputes which arise between them. The establishment of the Permanent Court of International Justice, one of the most noteworthy of the League's achievements, marks an important step towards that end.

It will be appreciated that international relations are involved in difficulties of the greatest complexity, and it follows that the conduct of international business demands that those who are engaged in it should possess abilities of the highest order. For their success, statesmen and diplomatists should be able to rely on the intelligent understanding of those for whom they are acting, and this can only be acquired if their citizens will take the necessary trouble to make themselves acquainted with the problems which they are endeavouring to solve.

The greatest and the most permanent of all the difficulties in international relations are those which arise from the imperfections of human nature, and we are again brought back to Lord Bryce's crucial question "Can human nature be raised to and sustained at a higher level than it has yet attained?" When that has been answered satisfactorily, and there is an affirmative answer to be found, most, if not all, of the other difficulties will find themselves in a fair way of solution.

III

THE DUTIES OF STATES[1]

IT is a commonplace to say that to nearly every question there are generally at least two sides, and it is certain that the side from which any problem is approached must influence the person who is engaged in dealing with it. This is particularly true of international relations, and it constitutes one of the great difficulties in the intercourse between states. In the past it has nearly always been taken for granted that International Law consists in my country's rights and in your country's duties,[2] but there are reasons which appear to me to make it worth while to see whether another point of view is not more likely to lead to better results than have followed from this traditional view of the subject which places the emphasis on the rights rather than on the duties of states.

I believe it to be the duty of international lawyers to assist not only in enunciating what they believe to be the existing rules of law which obtain amongst states but to do more than this. If International Law is to be treated as a science, the lawyer's work is not limited merely to the ascertainment and interpretation of its positive system; he has to go further and consider all the circumstances which bear upon the problems which may arise in the application of law between states, whether they be political, economic, historical or social. In doing this he will find that he has to get down to foundations, to the fundamental principles which are the basis of the positive rules, and rationalize them in

[1] An address delivered before the American Society of International Law, Washington, 1927. Printed in the *Proceedings* of the Society for 1927.
[2] See *British Year Book of International Law*, 1925, p. 234.

the sense of endeavouring to find some sound reason underlying them which will show that they are just and therefore worthy of observation.[1]

In the approach to the subject of International Law there has been a tendency on the part of writers to follow the beaten track of their predecessors, and in many ways this has not been altogether a bad plan. This is true especially in terminology, where words have acquired a well-recognized and technical meaning. But it is not in every respect a satisfactory method of procedure. There is no doubt that, basing ourselves on positivist principles, we shall, in endeavouring to formulate the rules of International Law as reflected in the facts of state life, arrive at the conclusion that the emphasis is nearly always laid on the rights which a state possesses. The ultimate foundation of International Law, says Hall, is an assumption that states possess rights and are subject to duties corresponding to the facts of their postulated nature.[2] But both he and Westlake formulate the position that International Law consists of the rules of action which states feel themselves bound to observe in their relations with other states, and of which they expect the observance from other states. In this view it will be seen that the emphasis is on the obligation or duty to observe the rules of action prescribed by law, for only when its duty is fulfilled can the law-abiding state feel itself in a strong position in requiring the corresponding observance of the law from states with which it is in relation. Duties and rights are generally correlative. It is because I think that an emphasis on the duty of states rather than on their right may lead to a better understanding between states and a juster application of the rules of International Law that I ask for the consideration of this

[1] This topic is more fully discussed, p. 101.
[2] *International Law* (8th ed., p. 50).

point of view. Circumstances of important international consequences in different parts of the world
to-day appear to me to make the exploration of this
subject one of immediate practical value. In approaching the question I shall have to leave the sphere of
purely jural relations and commence by drawing attention to the latter part of the definition of Mr Hall which
I have already quoted. He refers to the rights and
duties of states corresponding to the "facts of their
postulated nature."

It has hitherto been assumed, and I think rightly,
that men can attain to their highest development only
in society. The doctrine that man is a social animal is
the basis of the sciences of ethics, politics, economics,
and law. The nation or the state, I do not stop to distinguish between them, is an aggregation of families;
the group, not the individual, is the basis of modern
civilization. The influence of the evolutionary doctrine
in formulating and in moulding the state and the laws
for individuals within it, as well as the laws between
the states themselves, has, in recent times, been very
prominent, often causing mankind to acquiesce in and
to resign themselves to a condition in which things
should work themselves out (as it is sometimes loosely
expressed), or in which men are considered as the
victims of some inexorable cosmic process.[1] But it is
necessary to realize that man is himself a part of this
process, that he is a moral being capable of ideals and
possessing a will to work towards their fulfilment. In
this he can exercise the creative powers of mind and
through the energizing force of his intelligence proceed
to mould both himself and the society of which he is a
member towards the attainment of his ethical idea of
the just and the good. Morals and politics cannot be

[1] Cf. W. McDougall's *Ethics and some Modern World Problems*
(1924), Lecture v.

divorced, and legislation in any given state represents the combined results of these two forces by which the collective public opinion is enshrined in enactments whose enforcement is deemed necessary for the advancement of the social ideals of the state.

There is at the present time another ideal which is struggling hard for realization and causing much of the trouble and unrest in the field of international relations, namely—the achievement of the ideal of a world-state in which all ties of nationality are abandoned and a communistic cosmopolitanism takes the place of nationalism; such internationalism would see the end of International Law as it is understood and has been understood for the past three centuries. The League of Nations has come into being on the basis of the existing social order and from its very nature represents an antithesis of the ideal for which Soviet Russia is working in every country of the world. Believing, as I do, that the realization of this Soviet ideal would be fraught with incalculable harm to the rest of mankind, both physically and morally, I confine myself to the examination of the principles of International Law on the present basis of national state life.

There exists to-day a society of sovereign independent states whose relations to each other are governed by rules which are recognized by them as having a binding force comparable to that of the municipal law in each of the states forming this society. But it will be at once recognized that these states are unequal in influence, size and population, as well as in intellectual, moral and economic development; and though it may be predicated of all of them that they are equally protected by International Law in the rights which they possess, this is not the same as saying that they have legal equality. They are all equally entitled to assert such rights as they have, they have all an equal interest in the vindication of law, just as individuals have in all well-organized states. In other words, though every rule of law does not apply to every person or state, yet every rule of law does apply equally to every person or state governed by it. It is in this way that the so-called doctrine of state equality appears to be capable of accurate statement.[1] Much harm has been done by loose statements of this principle, as a wrongful emphasis has been laid upon alleged rights which follow as a deduction from false premises. States are under a duty to give to all other states the equality of treatment according to their condition, but if such states are not in a condition to fulfil the duties which their membership of the international society entails, are they, nevertheless, entitled to assert the rights which they possess by International Law?

For a complete enjoyment of these rights I submit that a state from its postulated nature is under certain obligations or duties. (1) In its internal government a state must, by efficient legislation and administration of its laws, protect all persons within its jurisdiction and provide that justice shall be fairly administered to them. Each state must possess a government capable of fulfilling its international obligations effectively, since the welfare and stability of the whole family of nations is dependent on the welfare and stability of each member of that family. (2) A state must be prepared to co-operate in the moral evolution and social advancement of the whole society of states of which it forms a part. The fulfilment of this international duty is an essential part of the terms of its enjoyment of the benefits of International Law.

---

[1] This subject has been exhaustively examined by E. D. Dickinson, *The Equality of States in International Law* (1920); see also P. J. Baker in *The British Year Book of International Law*, 1923–4, p. 1. See also *ante*, p. 26.

If states were purely isolated units, living of and to themselves alone, their internal development would be no concern of any other state; but this is impossible in the existing condition of the world. All states of the world are to-day increasingly interdependent, no state can live to itself alone, and each state has serious responsibilities to every other state. Sooner or later this is painfully brought home to every state which attempts a purely individualistic career, and indulges in experiments that have reactions outside its own borders.

In practice these differences in the degree of development of the internal governments have resulted in inequality of treatment. There could be no justification for demands for extraterritorial jurisdiction over the subjects of one state within the territory of another, or for some of the treaties for the protection of minorities, or for the intervention by states to protect the lives and property of their nationals imperilled by civil disorders or corrupt administration, if these states were in a position to fulfil their international duties, for such demands are limitations on the internal sovereignty of such states. In many of these cases the limitations have been the price which backward states have paid for the privilege of admission into the Family of Nations or for an increase of territory. When the other members of the international society have been satisfied that the state from which such grants and undertakings have been obtained has attained to a condition of political organization in which law is impartially and justly administered, and is in the position to discharge its international duties effectively, such limitations on its full membership of the international society ought to be and have been removed.

Unfortunately the progress of International Law to-day in its full application to all independent states is hindered by the continuance of the existence of these backward states whose internal conditions form an obstacle to the adequate performance of their international duties. In dealing with the fundamentals of the Law of Nations stress should, therefore, be laid on the doctrine that only those states can claim the full benefits of the law who are at the same time capable of fulfilling their corresponding obligations.

There is another side to this question of the emphasis on international duties rather than rights. If the backward state is expected to bring its internal organization into a condition for the adequate fulfilment of its duties, other states should be equally under an international duty not to take an unfair advantage of its weakness or of its incomplete development. It is for this reason that backward states may be characterized as the danger spots of the world, because they continually offer strong temptation to the more highly organized and developed members of the international community to deal with them in ways which may not only retard their development but may seriously menace their capacity for attaining to full international statehood. Moreover, when any one state takes undue advantage of the backward condition of another, it immediately produces international feelings of hatred, or jealousy, and history shows that "war and rumours of war" have been the consequence.

But it is not only as between backward states and those with a high standard of civilization and administration that there is this need for the emphasis on international duties; there is every reason for asking for it to be applied in the mutual relations of those who are most highly developed. In the Mosaic code of laws a series of commands was laid on the Jewish people which has had a most important influence on the religious and moral development of the world. These commands, as interpreted by one important branch of the Christian Church, in accordance with the teaching of its Founder, have been resolved into two sets of duties which are held to be binding on those who desire to conform to the highest ethical standards. In form, the statements in the Mosaic code were all mandatory and mostly negative, but in the interpretation to which I have referred, they have become a series of positive injunctions. So far as these commands involve duties regarding the life, limb, reputation, and property of one's fellow-men they may be taken as connoting corresponding rights vested in them, but the stress is laid on the individual's duty, not on his rights. Possibly it may be thought to be old-fashioned and reactionary to cite such an illustration, but it appears to me that to-day there is great need for the formulation of a state's "duty to its neighbour," and for the observance of these duties. I venture to think that the weakening of the force of the older set of duties by citizens in their private lives is likely to be always responsible for the slack observance by states of those of an international character. The demand now being made on all sides for the recognition of rights by individuals and groups within states and the disregard of the duties which are the correlative of those rights is symptomatic of a condition of society in which the assertion of unqualified self-interest may ultimately lead to anarchy. The modern movements which I have indicated are probably a reaction against the undue assertion of *my* rights and *your* duties in the past; it is time that attention was called to the observance of my duties if I am to be entitled to assert my rights. So with nations; a new adjustment is necessary for the improvement of international relations. Duties first, rights after; the fulfilment by states of the former before the enjoyment of the latter can be claimed is the great desideratum. This is the position which should appear with greater clearness and emphasis in any presentation of the fundamentals of the Law of Nations. And when we come to the use of the word "state," it should be made clear that when it is used to designate a "subject" of International Law, it connotes the requirement of every such community to accept as an international duty the obligation to organize itself in such a way that justice be impartially and equitably administered within its borders, and its organs of government be such as to facilitate international intercourse and the fulfilment of international obligations.

IV

THE PAPACY AND INTERNATIONAL LAW [1]

THAT states are the authors or makers of International Law is a doctrine generally accepted by all publicists, but there is not to-day the same agreement as to whether states alone are the subjects of International Law, that is, whether they only have international personality. The position of the Pope in this respect is one on which publicists even of the Positivist School show considerable difference of opinion.

English and American writers on International Law do not as a rule deal with this question at any length; in fact, by some it is practically ignored. Continental publicists give it greater prominence, and a large number of these writers deny that the Pope is an international person in the sense in which that term is used in International Law.

The position of the Papacy is exceptional; there is no institution in the history of humanity with which it can be compared. The fact that the Pope was for centuries both a temporal sovereign and the chief ecclesiastical dignitary in Western Christendom naturally raised doubts as to the capacity in which he was acting on a given occasion. When he ceased to be a temporal sovereign the tradition which had so long attached to his dual position was not easily disregarded, and it is the continuance of this tradition which a distinguished French publicist asserts to be responsible for the anomalous position which, from the standpoint of

[1] Based on a lecture delivered before the University of Cambridge. Published in *The Journal of the Society of Comparative Legislation*, 1909.

International Law, is now occupied by the head of the Roman Church.[1]

Down to the year 1870 the Pope was both the earthly head of the Roman Catholic Church and a sovereign monarch of one of the States of Europe, the Papal States. For a few years, at the end of the eighteenth and beginning of the nineteenth century, he was without territory—a dethroned temporal monarch; but on the fall of the Napoleonic Empire in 1814 he was restored to his temporal dominions and remained in possession of a diminished realm (for a large part of the Papal States demanded and obtained union with the Kingdom of Italy in 1860) until on September 20th, 1870, the Italian troops entered Rome. This action of King Victor Emmanuel was endorsed after a plebiscite by an overwhelming number of the inhabitants of the Papal States on October 2nd, 1870. By a Royal Decree of October 9th in the same year it was declared that "Rome and the Roman provinces form an integral part of the Kingdom of Italy." This Declaration appears to undermine the position adopted by one writer that as the Italian troops did not actually enter the Vatican, the Pope remained in undisturbed possession of a territory which, though minute in area, still sufficed to entitle him to rank as a territorial sovereign.[2] From the standpoint of the Italian Government their possession of Rome was complete, and though the venerable Pontiff was undisturbed, the occupation of the Papal States was effective, and the Pope ceased to

[1] See P. Fauchille, *Traité de Droit international*, §§ 370–96 (with bibliography); F. Despagnet, *Cours de Droit International public*, §§ 147–70; E. Nys, *Droit international*, vol. II, pp. 297–323; J. Westlake, *Peace*, pp. 37–9; L. Oppenheim, *International Law*, §§ 104–7. Sir R. Phillimore, *International Law*, vol. II, pp. 343–531, affords the fullest treatment of the Papacy and its relation to the various European states, though it is now out of date.

[2] G. Flaischlen, *Revue de Droit intern.* vol. VI (2nd series), p. 85.

exist as a territorial sovereign. But though his territorial sovereignty was at an end, no change was or could be effected by the Italian Government in his ecclesiastical position. For a large part of Christendom he still personifies the greatest moral force in the world, and from his exalted position it follows that his spiritual subjects of every nation wish to continue to have access to him and freely to receive his agents as in the past. Roman Catholic states therefore recognize that the Pope still occupies a special legal position, and his legates and nuncios are ranked with, and sometimes take precedence of ambassadors in these states, a precedence which even before the loss of temporal power was accorded to the Papal representative as the ambassador of the highest dignitary in the Catholic Church and not as a temporal sovereign.[1]

It is unnecessary for our purpose to trace even in outline the history of the struggles between the Papacy and the Empire, or the fight for supremacy between the Conciliar party and the Pope, though it must be remembered that in the fifteenth century Oecumenical Councils received ambassadors from the Empire and Kings, and these ambassadors took precedence of those of the Pope.[2] The Papalist cause was for the time being triumphant at the Council of Basle.

Out of these struggles there emerged the anti-papal doctrine of the Divine right of secular governments to

---

[1] Pradier-Fodéré, *Cours de Droit diplomatique*, vol. I, p. 120. Fénelon declared that the Papal Nuncio was regarded simply as the ambassador of a foreign prince, and in 1788 a distinguished lawyer, Christian Henri de Römer, maintained that the right of legation belonged to the Pope as a temporal sovereign only (E. Nys, *Droit inter.* vol. II, p. 310). The majority of modern writers hold that the Papal envoys represent the Pope in his ecclesiastical capacity (E. Lémonon, "Les rapports de la France et du Saint-Siège," *R.D.I.* (2nd series), vol. IX, p. 415.

[2] Nys, *op. cit.* vol. II, p. 288.

be free from Papal control, a doctrine which contributed in no small degree to the formation of modern views on sovereignty,[1] a doctrine which is still working in the anti-clerical movements of our own times.

The position of the Papacy down to the eve of the Reformation was a striking one. The Pope claimed and not infrequently exercised the position of arbitrator in international disputes. The good faith on which treaties were made brought international contracts within the sphere of the Canon Law. The Pope was an "independent international magistrate, head of the supreme tribunal for the settlement of international disputes, and the supervisor of engagements. With this object he used all the powerful moral forces at his command—admonition, censure, excommunication."[2]

The struggles in England between Anselm and Henry I and between Becket and Henry II were typical of those constantly recurring between the religious and civil forces in the states of Europe. Acting under Papal instructions, the clergy everywhere sought for and in some cases obtained, exceptional positions and immunities from the civil laws. Popes issued Bulls deposing and setting up kings, allotting kingdoms and dividing newly-discovered lands. With the Reformation a great change took place. The Peace of Westphalia of 1648 affords striking evidence of the existence of a new order of things. The legal equality of Protestant and Catholic states was acknowledged, the absence of the recognition of a common religious bond, which had hitherto been a bar to equality of intercourse, was thus removed, states met as secular institutions free from religious trammels, and the way was prepared for the ultimate admission of all civilized

[1] J. N. Figgis, *The Divine Right of Kings*, p. 44.
[2] R. de Maulde-la-Clavière, *La Diplomatie au Temps de Machiavel*, vol. I, p. 23, cited by E. Nys, *op. cit.* p. 300.

states, irrespectively of creed, into the Family of Nations. The treaty, furthermore, abolished a crowd of petty ecclesiastical states in Germany, dependent in no small measure on the Pope. It was in vain that Innocent X issued the Bull *Zelo domus Dei*, condemning and utterly annulling the Treaties of Münster and Osnabrück.[1] Papal protests against treaties cease henceforth to be effective and the protest of Pius IX against the Italian occupation of Rome in 1870 met with no response from the Powers of Europe.

This protest leads to a consideration of the theory of the Church as regards its temporal power. It is important to understand why the Pope attaches so much importance to the possession of temporal sovereignty, when he claims a spiritual world-empire. The Holy See has always considered that the States of the Church were a domain with which the Pope had been endowed for the purpose of assuring his independence in the exercise of his spiritual functions. The keeper of the oracles of God, the standing witness for truth and righteousness in the world, should, it was argued, be free from all physical compulsion, and this absolute freedom could only be maintained by the possession of a definite territory uncontrolled by any temporal power. The area of the temporal dominions of the Pope was never very large, but Popes and Cardinals on admission to office swore to preserve the domains intact, and sought by means of physical force and spiritual weapons to ward off all encroachments.

One important result of the view taken by the Papacy of the character of the domains of the Church and the necessity for the preservation of the temporal power is clearly dealt with by Despagnet.[2] The Church

---

[1] Phillimore, *International Law*, vol. i, p. 395.

[2] *Droit international*, § 150; P. Fauchille, *op. cit.* § 375; see also Phillimore, *International Law*, vol. i, p. 635.

contended that it was the duty of all Catholic states to protect the Pope against any change external or internal which might compromise his temporal sovereignty, and thus militate against the free exercise of his spiritual functions. Interventions in the Papal States were the result of this teaching. Napoleon Bonaparte, on the plea of better affording protection, took the extreme step of making Pius VII prisoner and removing him to France. France, Austria and Spain at different times during the nineteenth century intervened in the Papal States, and the movements in favour of popular government in these states were suppressed. For nearly the whole period between 1849 and 1870, French troops guarded the Pope. Their withdrawal led to the entry of the Italian troops and the fall of the temporal power.

The allegiance of Western Christendom to the Pope had in early times led to the growth of a regular service of Papal agents.

The earliest representatives sent by the Pope were the *Apocrisarii* or *Responsales*, who were sent first by the Bishop of Rome in the time of Constantine to reside at Constantinople; subsequently they resided at the Courts of the Frankish Kings. They were sent as spiritual agents and it is not improbable that at first their presence was required by the Emperors, who to some extent were enabled to supervise the doings of the Bishop of Rome. But the decay of the Roman Empire synchronized with the increasing power of the Bishops of Rome, and their growing claims to the obedience of Christendom. It was not however until the eleventh century that the institution of legates appears.[1] The Papal envoys were sent for various purposes, of which English History affords ample illustration. Gradually they became differentiated in rank

[1] Nys, *op. cit.* vol. II, p. 303.

according to their missions.[1] *Ablegati* were those who
had no political mission, but were sent for such purposes as bearing the Cardinal's Hat to a newly elected
member of the Sacred College: *legati* with a political
mission were either *legati a latere*, who were always
Cardinals and occupied the highest rank, or *legati missi*,
who were never Cardinals but were invested with
similar powers to the former; when sent as permanent
residents they were known as *Nuntii*. These agents of
the Pope were ranked with ambassadors in the first
class in the Regulations adopted by the Congresses of
Vienna, 1814, and Aix-la-Chapelle, 1818, for settling
the precedence of diplomatic agents. Below the *Nuntii*
came a lower class called *Inter-nuntii*.

The chief reason for the institution of resident agents
from the Papal Court was the negotiation and execution of Concordats. Concordats have been described
as agreements between the Holy See and the governments of states, the inhabitants of which are either
wholly or in part Catholic, not on questions of faith or
dogma but on matters of ecclesiastical discipline, such
as the organization of the clergy, the boundaries of the
dioceses, the nominations of bishops and parish priests.[2]
Concordats resulted from the struggles between the
civil and ecclesiastical authorities in the Middle Ages;
they were compromises between Church and State.
Two or three instances will suffice to show the importance of these agreements. The Concordat of Worms in
1122 between Calixtus II and the Emperor Henry V
settled the long-disputed question of Investitures. The
Concordat of Vienna in 1448, between Nicholas V and
the Emperor Frederick III, marked the triumph of the
Papacy after the Council of Basle. The Concordat of

---

[1] Phillimore, *op. cit.* vol. II, p. 525.
[2] Fauchille, *op. cit.* §§ 390, 896–9; *Manuel de Droit International
public*, 5th ed., §§ 390, 896.

1516, between Leo X and Francis I of France, which lasted till the outbreak of the French Revolution, regulated the relations of France and the Church for nearly three centuries; and lastly the Concordat of July 15th, 1801, between Pius VII and Napoleon Bonaparte, took the place of that of 1516, and was terminated by the *Loi de séparation* of December 9th, 1905. Whether the law which thus dissolved the union of Church and State was such a denunciation as is required for the termination of an international treaty, and whether the relations between France and the Holy See are merely suspended or entirely dissolved by the recall of the Apostolic Nuncio turns entirely upon the view taken as to the international position of the Pope, and the nature of the Concordats.[1] What then is the nature of these Concordats? Are they treaties made with the Pope as a temporal sovereign and thus ranking with and governed by the rules ordinarily applicable to engagements entered into between states, or are they arrangements which a state makes for the regulation of its internal well-being entered into with the Pope as the Head of Catholic Christendom?

There appear to be two cogent reasons why Concordats cannot be viewed as treaties.[2] In the first place the parties making them are not now (since 1870) independent sovereign powers, and in the second, the object of the Concordats is foreign to that of treaties. It is contended by M. Lémonon that the absence of temporal power is no bar to the treatment of the Pope

---

[1] Ernest Lémonon, "Les rapports de la France et du Saint-Siège," *R.D.I.* (2nd series), vol. IX, p. 415. (The 44th article of the law of December 9th, 1905, repealed the law of 18 Germinal, An x, confirming the agreement made on 26 Messidor, An IX, between the Pope and the French Government.) See also Phillimore, *International Law*, vol. II, p. 428, for the history of the relations between France and the Papacy.

[2] F. Despagnet, *op. cit.* § 158; Fauchille, *op. cit.* §§ 897-8.

as an international person, that he is one by reason of his position under the Italian Law of Guarantees of 1871; this point will be discussed subsequently. The subject-matter of Concordats is however clearly not a matter of international law. Treaties are in the main concerned with a state's external policy, and its relations to other states. Concordats purport to regulate a state's internal affairs in regard to the religious worship of its own subjects. The parties to a Concordat are moreover not on a footing of equality, a breach of it involves no principles of international law, the Pope has no armed forces with which to retaliate on a state for breach of its obligations. Failure to carry out a Concordat on the part of a state appears to be merely a failure to abide by arrangements made for certain internal matters, in the regulation of which the state must be guided by circumstances. The continued maintenance of a Concordat may be incompatible with the exercise of civil authority necessarily incident to sovereignty, and it is admitted that even a treaty becomes voidable under such circumstances.[1]

Viewing Concordats as constitutional arrangements which states make to regulate the relations between the lay and the ecclesiastical authorities, they become subject to denunciation, modification or even non-fulfilment without denunciation, whenever changes in the Constitution or the political opinions of the state with which they are made render such a course advisable. The dissolution of a Concordat may be fraught with serious consequences to the internal order of a state, but this is not a matter for international law.[2]

It will now be necessary to enquire whether the Italian Law of Guarantees of May 13th, 1871, can be relied

[1] W. E. Hall, *International Law*, § 116.
[2] See Despagnet, *op. cit.* §§ 157–9.

on as giving the Pope a position of international personality. Previous to the occupation of Rome by Victor Emmanuel, Italy had made overtures to the Powers and the Pope with reference to the position of Rome, and in 1868 and 1870 the Italian Government submitted to Pius IX a scheme which left him with the sovereignty of that part of Rome known as the Leonine City, having a population of about 15,000 persons. These overtures were rejected, and the complete annexation of the city was effected on October 9th, 1870. Unlike previous drafts, the law of May 13th, 1871, was not submitted to any foreign power. It is a municipal statute of the Kingdom of Italy. It is not the result of an arrangement with the Pope, who has not ceased to protest against it. It has moreover not even the special sanctity of a constitutional law which requires special forms to be observed to modify or repeal it: it is an ordinary statute which the Italian legislature can at any time by its ordinary legislative procedure amend or repeal at will. Further, its provisions only apply so long as the Pope resides on Italian territory.

In the discussion of this law in its passage through the Italian parliament, the *Rapporteur* stated that the draft did not recognize the sovereign character of the Pope and his exterritoriality, as to do so would be an admission of its consequences, such as claims to rights of jurisdiction, and rights to conclude treaties of alliance; and a provision in the original draft which provided that the Pope should enjoy immunity from the jurisdiction of the state was suppressed.

The Law of Guarantees is in two parts[1]; the second deals with the relations between Church and State in Italy and therefore need not be considered. The first part contains thirteen articles, and is concerned with

[1] For text (in Italian) see Phillimore, *op. cit.* vol. II, p. 655; for a commentary see Fauchille, *op. cit.* §§ 377–85.

"the prerogatives of the Sovereign Pontiff and the Holy See."

By the first article the person of the Pope is declared to be sacred and inviolable; the expression probably being the outcome of long usage and reverence for the Head of the Church. This inviolability does not extend to his officials, who have on more than one occasion been proceeded against in the Italian Courts by creditors of the Holy See. The Pope is not declared to be an Italian citizen, but the death of Leo XIII was registered before the civil authority in Rome as that of "His holiness the sovereign Roman Pontiff, Vincenzo Giocchino Raffaele Luigi Pecci"; and all the formalities required by Italian law were observed in proving his will.[1] The Pope enjoys all the honours of a sovereign and the precedence allowed by Catholic sovereigns, "so that he would take precedence of the King if they happened to meet."[2] He is allowed to keep the same number of troops for a body-guard as before the annexation, but they are not his subjects; no Italian state-official may enter his palaces without his permission. The places left in the occupation of the Pope, the Vatican, the Lateran and the Villa of Castel Gandolfo, his ordinary or temporary residence and places occupied by a Conclave or Oecumenical Council, are withdrawn from Italian control unless the Pope, a Conclave or Council calls for it, but these places and the works of art and archives are the property of the Italian state. The Pope has complete liberty in the exercise of his spiritual functions; in Rome he may order notices with reference to the services of the Church and directions to the faithful, to be affixed to the churches. He has the right of free communication with the Episcopate and the Catholic world, and is entitled to his own post and telegraph

[1] E. Nys, *op. cit.* vol. II, p. 315. [2] J. Westlake, *Peace*, p. 38.

offices in the Vatican, and may appoint the clerks. He retains complete control of the educational establishments for the clergy in Rome and the suburbicarian dioceses. Envoys of foreign governments to the Pope enjoy in the Kingdom of Italy all the prerogatives and immunities which belong to diplomatic agents by international law. Offences against them are subject to the same punishments as offences against envoys to the Italian Government. The Papal envoys to foreign powers are given in Italy the privileges and immunities accorded by international law when going and coming on their missions. Lastly, the annual sum of 3,225,000 lire is provided by the Italian budget for the sacred Apostolic palaces, the Sacred College, the ecclesiastical congregations and the diplomatic service of the Church. This amount is only to be reduced in case the Government takes over the maintenance of the museums and library. No Pope has ever availed himself of this sum annually placed to his credit.

Such being the position of the Pope according to the Italian Law of Guarantees, can it be said that he is thereby invested with an international personality? Is he thereby a member of the international state society? The correct answer appears to be given by M. Brusa, who says: "the Pope is inviolable, but this is by virtue of an Italian statute; he has rights of legation under the same statute; he enjoys immunity as regards his residence, but this also is by virtue of the law of a particular state and not by virtue of international law."[1]

The law of one state cannot create an international personality any more than it can effectively neutralize a portion of the state's territory. If the Pope is not an international person apart from the Italian Law of Guarantees, that statute does not make him one. But though this statute has no international effect, it is

[1] E. Brusa, "La jurisdiction du Vatican," *R.D.I.* vol. xv, p. 134.

nevertheless a law of international interest. It concerns the relation of Church and State in Italy and as affecting the Italian Constitution forms part of the public law of Europe, though it forms no part of public international law.[1] The Italian parliament by enacting this law gave official recognition to the fact of the Pope's residence in Italy, and made provision for the honours to be accorded him there. The civil authority asserted its territorial supremacy while at the same time it made concessions for the purpose of facilitating intercourse between the Pope and the Roman Catholic world. Presumably the Catholic Powers were satisfied by the terms accorded to the Pope, as no protest was made to the Italian Government with reference to this law. Whether they would view with unconcern its modification, or even its total repeal and the subjection of the Pope and the Papal Palaces to the Italian Common Law is a matter of conjecture.

The question of the right of the Papacy to rank with temporal powers appears to have received a definite solution by the refusal of the representatives of the Powers at the Hague Conference in 1899 to receive the Papal envoy. Italy protested against his admission on the ground that he did not represent a state interested in international arbitration. Notwithstanding the fact that the Russian project had been communicated to the Pope and his moral support had been obtained for the Tsar's proposals, his representative was excluded. Similarly the Papacy has so far not been admitted to membership of the League of Nations, nor to the various conferences which followed the conclusion of the war of 1914–18.[2]

---

[1] J. Westlake, *Peace*, p. 38.
[2] Despagnet, *op. cit.* § 153. Fauchille, *op. cit.* § 396[2,3,4]. See the Memorandum presented in May, 1922, to the Genoa Conference of the Holy See printed by Fauchille, *op. cit.* § 396[4] note.

The Pope ceased in 1870 to be a temporal sovereign; but long before the Papacy was stripped of its temporal power that power was a mere accessory. The Papacy was concerned not with temporal aggrandizement but with a spiritual propaganda, and it may well be contended that the Papacy, by becoming a purely spiritual institution free to devote itself to the furtherance of religion, has increased in authority since the Pope ceased to be the temporal sovereign of a petty Italian state.

Sovereignty in the sense in which that word is used in political philosophy is generally associated with bodies of men banded together for political objects on a definite territory. The Pope is no longer such a political sovereign as is contemplated by international law, he is no longer the head of a state. But in all countries where there are congregations belonging to the Roman Catholic Church his authority is supreme over the consciences of the members. It is impossible for statesmen and publicists to ignore the difficulties which ensue when religious and civil duties are found to be in conflict, and states in which an important portion of the inhabitants are members of the Church of Rome frequently find it to their interest to enter into communication with the Roman Curia for the purpose of adjusting difficulties as they arise. Politics and religion are frequently closely allied; national interests are involved, Church and State at times form two opposing camps, an internal dispute may pass beyond the mere territorial frontiers and become an international one. It is enough to recall the fact that the Catholic party in several of the states of Europe, especially in Germany, France and Belgium, has an influence which on occasion may prove decisive in matters of home or foreign policy.

Early in June, 1908, the riotous behaviour of the

students in the University of Innsbruck and their refusal to attend lectures, a refusal which spread to other
Austrian Universities, resulted in the closing of the
Universities of Vienna, Innsbruck and Gratz. The in-
fluences producing these results afford further striking
evidence of the power of the Papacy in the internal
politics of Catholic countries. The Professor of Canon
Law in the University of Innsbruck had published a
pamphlet which the Catholic party considered to be
offensive. The Papal Nuncio at Vienna demanded the
dismissal of the Professor, and although the Austrian
Government did not take this extreme step, the Professor was compelled to abandon his lectures, and, as
before stated, the Universities were closed. The dispute
spread from the Universities to the general political
world and produced a cleavage in the political parties
in Austria.

Many states, Catholic, Protestant and Orthodox,
find it to their advantage to have agents at the Papal
Court. The number has increased considerably since
1914. Great Britain at the outbreak of the war
established an extraordinary mission at Rome which
has since been maintained, and France, who withdrew
her representative on the eve of the passing of the *Loi
de séparation*, in 1905, resumed relations in 1921. In
some Catholic states, an honorary precedence is sometimes accorded to the Papal envoy by the *Corps Diplomatique*.[1] But the fact that some states find it an aid in
the art of government to treat directly with the official
head of the religion to which a large number of

---

[1] Fauchille, *op. cit.* § 386. See Pradier-Fodéré, *Cours de Droit
diplomatique*, vol. I, p. 249, for an interesting account of a discussion at Lima in 1878 when the majority of the *Corps Diplomatique* refused to recognize the Papal Envoy as Doyen. The
Doyen, however, with the consent of the members of the Body,
expressed the desire to yield the precedence to the Nuncio.

their subjects belong, carries with it no consequence of importance in international law.

It has been suggested that resort to the fruitful field of legal fictions may result in the discovery of institutions bearing features of international personality analogous to those claimed for the Pope, and that therefore the Papacy, if not a "natural" person in international law, may yet be ranked with "artificial" or "juristic" persons. Creations of the Powers such as the European Commission of the Danube, the Postal Union and other similar international institutions, may possibly be compared to the artificial or juristic persons of private law; but even here the analogy appears strained. The Papacy has not been erected into an artificial person of international law by reason of the fact that Roman Catholic states have continued their intercourse with the Holy See on the same footing as before its loss of temporal power. The tacit acceptance of a situation, or the continuance of a practice by a certain number of states is not sufficient to create a position legally binding on other states. The international Commissions and Unions neither send nor receive envoys; no state accepts their Presidents as monarchs. They are express creations of the Powers for the better fulfilment of certain special purposes for the common benefit of all.

The Papacy is unlike these international commissions in all respects. He is a "sovereign Pontiff" who enters into personal relations with states by means of agents assimilated in their treatment to those sent on purely diplomatic missions. He makes agreements with states which are akin to treaties in form, but different from them in subject-matter. He is a sovereign Pontiff, whose subjects are in no one land and yet in all lands, at whose commands statesmen have trembled and ministries fallen. The Papacy, like the King, never dies;

on the death of a Pope the agents of the Holy See need no renewal of their powers.[1] The Church of which he is the earthly head and whose unity he personifies was old before any of the states which make up the Family of Nations were in existence, and before the rules which they are evolving and have evolved to regulate their mutual intercourse commenced to take shape. Outside all states and yet working within all are the forces personified by the Pope, and guided by the Roman Curia, forces with which most Christian states have to reckon.[2]

"The Papacy is a unique phenomenon in history," says Geffcken. It refuses to fall into any tabulated arrangement of states or sovereignties. In some departments of its activities legal analogies are valueless but in others they are extremely useful. The principles of

[1] Pradier-Fodéré, *Cours de Droit diplomatique*, vol. i, p. 251.

[2] The influence of the Holy See in international politics is still manifested, says the late Professor Despagnet, in three directions. (1) It determines in certain countries the formation of a Catholic party, such as the Catholic centre in the German Reichstag. Leo XIII gave a powerful impulse to the action of the Church in political and social questions (see the Encyclical of January 10th, 1890, *De praecipuis civium christianorum officiis*: and that of May 15th, 1891, *De conditione opificum*). (2) The Pope disposes of an important means of influence in non-Christian countries by the protectorate of the Catholics there, as in the Ottoman Empire. (3) The Pope has in quite recent times acted as mediator and arbitrator, even in disputes to which Protestant Powers were parties: e.g. Leo XIII mediated between Germany and Spain in 1885 on the subject of the Carolines; in 1895 he arbitrated between Hayti and San Domingo; and in 1898 he offered to mediate between the United States and Spain (*Cours de Droit international*, § 153, note). It must not be forgotten that His Holiness Pope Benedict XV addressed to the Heads of the Belligerent Peoples on August 1st, 1917, proposals for peace, but these were not found to be acceptable to all the belligerents. (For these proposals and correspondence relative thereto see Parl. Papers, Misc. No. 7 (1919), Cmd. 261.)

international law relating to the treatment and privileges of diplomatic ministers appear to be applicable to Papal envoys, though they may not be capable of enforcement by the Pope. Most of the states which, before the fall of the temporal power, received Papal envoys have continued their intercourse with the Holy See, and by implication have guaranteed to such envoys a continuance of treatment similar to that which they received when the Pope was a temporal sovereign whose right of legation had been recognized by the Congresses of Vienna and Aix-la-Chapelle. It would be nothing less than a breach of good faith to give these agents less favourable treatment than they have by long usage received without due notification to the contrary. But they cannot claim more favourable treatment than diplomatic agents, and therefore a Papal envoy guilty of acts of interference in local politics has no ground of complaint if the state resorts to the extreme step of expulsion. The French Government expelled Mgr Montagnini, who had been Secretary to the Papal Nuncio, from France in December, 1906.[1] Diplomatic ministers have received similar treatment for serious violation of the laws of the state to which they were accredited. It is an extreme step to take, and one which has rarely been taken. More usually his passports are handed to the minister and he is requested to depart within a fixed time. On his departure the minister's hotel and papers are either left in charge of a subordinate official, or if there be none, an inventory of the effects is taken, and the archives and effects are sealed by the agent of some friendly Power. In the case of Mgr Montagnini, the agents of the French Government took possession of the papers in the Nunciature. The legality of the expulsion of Mgr Montagnini is admitted, but the action

[1] E. Lémonon, "Expulsion de Mgr Montagnini," *R.D.I.* vol. IX (2nd series), p. 90; *Rev. Gén. de Droit int.* vol. XIV, p. 175.

of the French Government in entering the official residence and searching for and seizing the papers therein calls for examination. When Count Gyllenborg, the Swedish Ambassador in London in 1717, contrived a plot against George I, he was expelled from the Kingdom, his cabinet opened and his papers, which furnished proofs of his guilt, were seized. The papers of Count Cellamare, Spanish Ambassador to France in 1718, who was expelled for similar reasons, were also searched and seized.[1] In the former case the *Corps Diplomatique* protested against the seizure but withdrew the protest when the facts were laid before them. It is certain that the seizure of papers at a minister's residence can only be justified by the existence of very exceptional circumstances. The French Government in this case entered the house which had formerly been the official residence of Mgr Lorenzelli, the Apostolic Nuncio. In July, 1906, France handed his passports to Mgr Lorenzelli and recalled her ambassador from the Vatican. Relations with the Holy See were broken off. In Rome a subordinate member of the French mission was left in charge. Mgr Montagnini had been left in charge of the archives at the house where Mgr Lorenzelli had formerly resided. The Government suspected him of engaging in correspondence with the French bishops, and several of the local clergy, with a view to preventing the carrying into execution of the *Loi de séparation*, and having arrested him and escorted him across the frontier, the *juge d'instruction* accompanied by an official of the Foreign Office took possession of the whole of the papers of which Mgr Montagnini was in charge. They examined them, with the view, it was said, of separating those which were of a date anterior to the rupture of relations from the papers of Mgr Montagnini, and transmitting the former to Rome, or to the agent of a

[1] Ch. de Martens, *Causes célèbres*, vol. i, p. 154.

friendly Power, using the others for evidence of the culpability of Montagnini. The Pope addressed a note to his representatives at foreign Courts, on December 21st, 1906, strongly protesting against this violation of the privilege of inviolability of the official residence of his agent. By making the distinction between the two sets of papers France appears to have in a manner recognized the inviolability of the Nuncio's archives; but had the Nuncio been a diplomatic agent, it is hardly conceivable that the Government would have taken such a step unless it was prepared for war. When in 1887 the archives of the French Consulate at Florence were violated by a local magistrate, the French Government sought and obtained reparation from the Italian Government, and the position of a Consul is far less privileged than that of a diplomatic minister.[1] Nothing but the gravest offence on the part of a minister could justify such a step; it is never resorted to even when an ambassador is withdrawn on the outbreak of war. But war with the Papacy in the literal sense is impossible, and nothing remained for the Pope but a protest. The occurrence brings out in the strongest relief the anomalous position of the Holy See in its relations with temporal powers. The violation of the Papal archives cannot have been a breach of International Law, for reasons already stated; but unless there was a necessity approximating to self-preservation, it appears to have been a breach of the tacit understanding on which France had for so long conducted her relations with the Papacy. A Papal Nuncio, when he is received in his official capacity, should receive the treatment of a diplomatic agent. In the strict meaning of the term he is not such an agent, for like the Pope whom he represents he is a "unique phenomenon."

[1] *Journal du Droit International privé*, vol. xv, p. 53.

V

THE MONROE DOCTRINE[1]

ON December 2nd, 1823, President Monroe, the fifth President of the United States, addressed to Congress a message which for a hundred years has formed the very bed-rock of the foreign policy of that great Republic. Few pronouncements have received so much attention from statesmen and writers. The literature on the subject would fill scores of yards of shelf-space. The message has been so often cited, appropriately and inappropriately, by Presidents and Secretaries of State in varying terms and under varying circumstances, that it becomes necessary to go back to the texts to ascertain the meaning and appreciate the circumstance of the original message.

It is right that we should endeavour at this time, on the occasion of the hundredth anniversary of the Monroe message, to understand it, for one part of it was prepared after communications had passed between the American and the British Governments, though the two Governments have by no means always been in agreement as to its application. The doctrine laid down has exercised a profound influence not only in the hemisphere to which it originally applied but over a far wider area. For a century it has kept the New World free from attempts to impose on it the political system of the Old, and although the past century has by no means been a century of peace in the whole of the Western Hemisphere, there can be no doubt that the maintenance of the principles enunciated has been justified by the result.

[1] A lecture delivered before the University of Cambridge, December 3rd, 1923. Published in the *British Year Book of International Law*, 1924.

With these preliminary remarks it is necessary to turn back to the year 1823 and see what President Monroe actually said, to consider the circumstances which led him to make so momentous and so far-reaching a pronouncement, and then to examine some of the constructions subsequently put upon it.

There are two declarations of policy contained in President Monroe's message of December 2nd, 1823, separated widely in the order of the message as well as by the circumstances which gave rise to them. These have often been combined as if they were one, but they must be kept separate and distinct as dealing with separate and distinct situations. These two declarations enshrine two principles which may be described as (a) non-colonization, and (b) non-intervention. The whole of the message relating to these points is not cited, but the following are the essential paragraphs:

(a) The occasion, said Monroe, has been judged proper for asserting, as a principle *in which the rights and interests of the United States are involved, that the American continents, by the free and independent condition which they have assumed and maintain, are henceforth not to be considered as subjects for future colonization by any European Powers.*[1]

This is the non-colonization principle.

(b) *In the wars of the European Powers, in matters relating to themselves, we have never taken any part, nor does it comport with our policy so to do.* It is only when our rights are invaded or seriously menaced that we resent injuries or make preparation for our defence. With the movements in this hemisphere we are of necessity more immediately connected, and by causes which must be obvious to all enlightened and impartial observers....We owe it, therefore, to candour and to the amicable relations existing between the United States and those Powers to declare that *we should consider any attempt on their part to extend their system to any portion of this hemisphere as dangerous to our peace and safety.* With the existing colonies or dependencies of any European Power we have

[1] § 7 of the message.

not interfered and shall not interfere. But with the Governments who have declared their independence and maintained it, and whose independence we have, on great consideration and on just principles, acknowledged, *we could not view any interposition for the purpose of oppressing them, or controlling in any other manner their destiny, by any European Power, in any other light than as the manifestation of an unfriendly disposition towards the United States....*

It is impossible that the allied Powers should extend their political system to any portion of either continent without endangering our peace and happiness; nor can any one believe that our southern brethren, if left to themselves, would adopt it of their own accord. It is equally impossible, therefore, that we should behold such interposition in any form with indifference.[1]

This is the non-intervention principle, but as will be seen, in the policies of some administrations the two principles have tended to merge into each other.

I

The circumstances giving rise to the two separate pronouncements were different in their character. The reasons which led to the non-colonization doctrine were several, but it was primarily an order of the Tsar of 1821 which brought the question into prominence. The only Powers in North America in 1823 other than the United States were Great Britain and Russia, the latter Power having the sovereignty of Alaska. The Tsar by an ukase of September 4th, 1821, had asserted exclusive territorial right from the extreme northern limit of the continent to the fifty-first parallel of latitude.

By a treaty of 1818 between Great Britain and the United States these two Powers had agreed to a joint occupation for ten years of all the country that might be claimed by either on the north-west coast, westward of the Rocky Mountains, without prejudice to the rights of either party. These rights it was realized would

[1] §§ 48 and 49 of the message.

turn on questions of discovery, occupation and settlement, and it was to guard against such claims on the
part of Russia that this part of the doctrine was founded.
Early in the summer of 1823 John Quincy Adams, in
a letter to Mr Rush, United States Minister in London,
propounded the principle that the entire continent was
closed against the establishment by any European
Power of any of the colonial systems which had
restricted commerce, navigation, trade and fishing.
Mr Rush was not successful in obtaining the assent of
Great Britain, the Government of which denied the
correctness of the facts, especially the statement that
the whole of the continents were occupied by civilized
nations and that they would be accessible to Europeans
and each other on that footing alone. Great Britain
considered the whole of the unoccupied parts of
America as being open to her future settlement as before, that is by priority of discovery and occupation.
These instructions of J. Q. Adams were the germ of
this portion of Monroe's message. As Dana says of this
part of the message: "the question presented was one
of political geography."[1] It was accepted neither by
Great Britain nor by Russia, neither can it, in my
opinion, be justified by the facts of the case, that is as
facts of political geography. But what it did here was
similar to what it did in the non-intervention portion.
It gave notice to the world that there was to be
no "scramble" for the Americas, North, Central or
South. Future colonization would be viewed as a
menace to the United States and would involve their
rights and interests. In the second part of the message
it is intimated that there is no intention to interfere

---

[1] Dana's note in his edition of Wheaton's *International Law*
(1866), pp. 97–112, is one of the most valuable expositions of the
subject, and has been of much assistance in the preparation of
this paper.

with existing colonies. It is true that the words of the message refer to the "free and independent" condition which the continents had assumed, which was certainly open to question, but the essence of this part of the message is the same as that of the other part, viz. the protection of the interests of the United States. It also did more; it made for peace in the whole hemisphere. "Colonization" only is referred to, and Mr Calhoun, who was a member of Monroe's Cabinet, stated in 1848 that this portion of the message was never before the Cabinet, that the statement regarding the continents having asserted and maintained their freedom was inaccurate, and that it gave such offence to England with whom the United States was acting in the other portion of the message, that she refused to co-operate in settling the Russian difficulty.

The meaning of the non-colonization principle soon came into question. At first, in 1825 and 1826, President Adams announced that it was for each state to defend its own territories. For the moment the United States seemed afraid of the magnitude of its task, and Mexico was told that the Government of each state must see to the enforcement of the non-colonization principle. This is in accord with its principle: there is no reason why each state should not announce a Monroe Doctrine for itself. It cannot be a Pan-American doctrine.

But with President Polk came an extensive interpretation. The Monroe Doctrine was invoked to assist the United States in the annexation of Texas and to warn off European Powers from intervening, and in his message of December 2nd, 1845, while purporting to reiterate the Monroe Doctrine against colonization, the President proceeded to extend it to the acquisition of any dominion by any European Power without the consent of the United States. This, in effect, was a prohibition of transfer by any means by any European Power of any of its colonies to any other European Power without United States sanction. In 1848 Polk took the further step, in regard to the possible transfer of Yucatan to a European Power, of declaring that it could in no event be permitted. With the internal politics of the United States which led to this attitude we cannot deal; already in 1848 there were the rumblings of the coming storm which was to break in 1861 on the question of slavery. Polk's doctrine was reiterated by President U. S. Grant in 1870, when it was rumoured that Italy was in negotiation with Sweden for the transfer of the island of St Bartholomew. In the previous year President Grant had stated in his annual message that the dependencies of Spain could no longer be regarded as the subject of the transfer from one European Power to another: "When the present relation of colonies ceases they are to become independent Powers, exercising the right of choice and of self-control in the determination of their future condition and relations with other Powers."

This idea of preventing colonization on the American continent received still further expansion in the matter of Magdalena Bay. An American company had secured from Mexico rights over a tract of land surrounding Magdalena Bay in lower California. The venture was unsuccessful and the mortgagee foreclosed and was in negotiation for the sale to some Japanese private purchasers. But before concluding the bargain he consulted the United States State Department. Its view was unfavourable, and the matter was brought before the Senate. On August 2nd, 1912, that body, on the proposition of Mr Lodge, passed a resolution:

That when any harbour or other place in the American continent is so situated that the occupation thereof for naval or military purposes might threaten the communications or safety of the

United States, the Government of the United States could not see without great concern the possession of such harbour or other place by any corporation or association which has such a relation to another Government not American as to give that Government practical power of control for national purposes.[1]

As an abstract proposition based upon the principle of self-defence there is a good deal to be said for the doctrine embodied in the resolution, but as applied to the facts it appears to be strained. This resolution purported to be based on the doctrine of self-defence, on which a state must be allowed to judge for itself. There is no need in such a case for the Monroe Doctrine. Opinions may differ as to the merits of the case, but the basis relied on is a universally accepted principle.

In the previous year (1911) President Roosevelt had added a corollary, as it has been called, to the Monroe Doctrine, by holding that whenever it was necessary to throw a South American state into the hands of the receivers, it was necessary for the United States to act as receiver. If a foreign Power came in it might lead to territorial acquisition, and so the United States claimed to keep such foreign creditors out as a legitimate extension of the Monroe Doctrine.

President Wilson carried this extension yet further in his famous Mobile speech on October 27th, 1913, when he protested against certain concessions which Colombia had made or was proposing to make to a British syndicate. He said the time had come when South American states must stop making such concessions, because foreign interests might dominate the internal affairs of states granting them. The negotiations in question were broken off, whether *propter hoc* or merely *post hoc*, I do not say. And in September, 1919, President Wilson increased the vagueness of the doctrine by saying that "the United States means to play big

---

[1] *American Journal of International Law*, vol. VI (1912), p. 937.

brother to the Western Hemisphere in any circumstances where it thinks it wise to play big brother."[1]

By a long series of extensions beginning with that of
President Polk a position has been reached whereby
the doctrine of the non-colonization principle has become hardly distinguishable from the non-intervention
principle. But the application of these principles has
been by no means uniform, and this is to be expected,
bearing in mind what the doctrine is, namely a statement
of policy. What one administration considered to be an
infringement another did not. Thus Great Britain
occupied the Falkland Islands in 1833 and the United
States declined to accede to the Argentine's view that
this was a violation of the doctrine. The making of the
Clayton-Bulwer Treaty in 1850 was scarcely in accord
with the doctrine, though subsequently, on the ground
of its being a violation of the Monroe Doctrine, the
United States declined arbitration on points arising
out of it. Yet the United States left the final determination of the Oregon boundary to a European monarch,
but intervened to take the side of Venezuela in the dispute with Great Britain over the boundary question.
At one time the transfer of the island of St Bartholomew
from Sweden to a foreign Power was, as we have seen,
viewed as a violation of the principle, but later no
opposition was raised when, in 1877, Sweden transferred it to France. It would appear that to-day this
part of the message has been interpreted to mean that
the United States asserts a right to oppose the acquisition
of any control over any part of the American continent
by any non-American Power, by any means whatever,
and even to protest against grants to non-American
citizens of any concessions which might ultimately lead
to intervention by a non-American state to enforce the
claims of its nationals. But it does not follow that the

[1] *American Journal of International Law*, vol. xiv (1920), p. 207.

claim will always, in all circumstances, be advanced. Political expediency is the guide, and expediency here means the resultant of varying forces based on, or deemed by popular opinion to be based on, the principle of self-defence. Mr Root has put it thus:

> Undoubtedly as one passes to the south and the distance from the Caribbean increases, the necessity of maintaining the rule of Monroe becomes less immediate and apparent. But who is competent to draw the line? Who will say "to this point the rule of Monroe shall apply: beyond this point it should not"?[1]

The answer clearly is that no one can settle these points before a case arises.

II

The non-intervention doctrine falls into two parts: (a) non-intervention of the United States in European affairs; (b) non-intervention of European states in American affairs.

The doctrine of non-intervention of the United States in European affairs had already been laid down by Washington in 1796 and emphasized by Jefferson. As propounded by Monroe it is not an absolute doctrine of non-intervention, but it was, with few exceptions, steadfastly observed until the closing years of the nineteenth century. The possibility of American rights being invaded led to the participation of the United States in the Conferences of Berlin and Brussels to settle the difficult questions raised in the scramble for Africa, and again the United States took part in the Conference of Algeciras in 1906 over Morocco. The work of the United States delegation at both of the Hague Peace Conferences is too well known to call for any further comment.

The New World has twice in the century been called in to redress the balance of the Old, but the second

[1] *Proceedings of the American Society of International Law*, 1914, p. 20.

time it entered voluntarily. It was no violation of the Monroe Doctrine when the United States entered the conflict raging in 1917, for American rights had been invaded and seriously menaced, and in accordance with Monroe's doctrine the time had come for the United States to resent injuries and prepare for defence. Slowly but surely there entered the minds of the American people the knowledge that, quite apart from any other reasons, and there were potent ones, the history of German policy in the New World showed there was danger ahead. The longing eyes of German statesmen were cast on the great unpeopled spaces of the rich South American continent, and these desires could not be satisfied till the Monroe Doctrine had been blown to atoms by a successful war. The declaration of war by the United States against Germany in April 1917 was in an important sense an intervention in defence of the doctrine. Of the abstention of the United States from participation in the League of Nations there is not space to speak in detail. To attempt to do so in a few words would be to do injustice both to President Wilson and to his opponents. The United States is still opposed to alliances and this must account for the refusal to accept the Anglo-American-French treaty of guarantee, a refusal which has cost Europe much.

But having taken the step of non-ratification of the Treaty of Versailles with the League of Nations Covenant, and of the French guarantee treaty, the American Government still reserves to itself the right to act in European affairs when its co-operation can be the means of advancing peace and the re-establishment of sound economic conditions. Fortunately for millions of starving and homeless people in Europe, the Monroe Doctrine of non-intervention in Europe has not applied to the generous hearts and purses of the American people.

The principle of non-intervention of European states in American affairs was enunciated with the goodwill and approval of Great Britain under the following circumstances.

The Holy Alliance had been formed in Europe after the close of the Napoleonic wars. Russia, Prussia, Austria and France had intervened in several European countries to put down movements for free constitutions. In 1823 France invaded Spain to suppress the constitutional Government of the Cortes and to restore Ferdinand VII. French intervention was successful and there were signs that the Holy Alliance intended to assist Ferdinand to recover his lost possessions in Central and South America. The intervention of France in Spain was particularly hateful to Great Britain, who, only some ten years previously, had by brilliant victories driven the French forces from the Peninsula. France, as a way of undermining English influence with the United States, hinted that England had designs of her own on Cuba, then torn asunder by civil war. At this juncture Mr Rush, the United States Minister in London, informed Canning that the United States could not view with equanimity the possession of Cuba by any European state other than Spain, and informed him of the rumours which had reached the United States. Canning at once disclaimed any intention to interfere in Cuba, and added that he could not view the passing of Cuba into the hands of either France or the United States with indifference. He proposed an agreement on this head with France and the United States which the latter Government left to him to arrange. Canning, too, was averse from the intervention of France or of any European Power on behalf of Spain's revolted colonies. He was not, as yet, prepared to recognize their independence, and he proposed to Mr Rush a joint declaration with the United

States that they had no aim to possess any portion of the Spanish colonies for themselves, but that they could not view with indifference the intervention of any foreign Powers. The joint declaration was never made, but before making a pronouncement Monroe took the opportunity of consulting Mr Jefferson—who was then in retirement—on the subject of Canning's proposal. His reply was an elaborate letter of October 24th, 1823, the original of which, as I learn from a telegram which appeared in *The Times* on October 29th, 1923, has just been brought to light. This letter, which is of great interest for us to-day, contains the following sentences:

Our first and fundamental maxim should be never to entangle ourselves in the broils of Europe; our second never to suffer Europe to intermeddle with cis-Atlantic affairs. America, North and South, has a set of interests distinct from those of Europe, and peculiarly her own. She should therefore have a system of her own, separate and apart from that of Europe. One nation most of all could disturb us in this pursuit; she now offers to lead, aid and accompany us in it. Great Britain is the nation which can do us the most harm of any one or all on earth, and with her on our side we need not fear the whole world. With her, then, we should most sedulously cherish cordial friendship, and nothing would tend more to knit our affections than to be found fighting once more side by side in the same cause.

When we remember that less than ten years before this the two countries had been at war, this statement is the more remarkable. Jefferson agreed to the proposed declaration and sent a draft of the words to be used, but this draft was not accepted, and Monroe's declaration, under the strong influence of John Quincy Adams, took a different form, much more lengthy but less minatory. Jefferson had suggested that the President should say—

that we aim not at the acquisition of any of those possessions; that we will not stand in the way of any amicable arrangement between the colonies and their mother country; that we will oppose with all our means the forcible interposition of any other Power as auxiliary, stipendiary, or under any other form or pretext, and most especially their transfer to any Power by conquest, cession or acquisition in any other way.[1]

Monroe used the less aggressive form of saying that the United States would consider any attempt on the part of foreign Powers to extend their system to any portion of the hemisphere as dangerous to the "peace and safety" of the United States, and further that it was impossible for them to behold European interposition in any form with indifference. There is no indication of the steps which the United States would take should any European Power intervene. Monroe's message on this subject was received by English statesmen with great satisfaction. It strengthened Canning's hands in his negotiations with France; it put an end to further schemes of the Holy Alliance to interfere in America. The message drew from Sir James Mackintosh the eulogy that—

This coincidence of the two great English commonwealths (for so I delight to call them; and I heartily pray that they may be for ever united in the cause of justice and liberty) cannot be contemplated without the utmost pleasure by every enlightened citizen of the earth.

This part of the Monroe Doctrine has, like the other, been the subject of expansion, and President Polk's tenure of office is again the starting-point. At first, in 1845, he spoke of it in terms applicable only to North America, but later, in 1848, he declared it applicable to Central America. The original doctrine spoke of intervention for the purpose of "oppressing or controlling" the destinies of the states of America, but Secretary Blaine in 1881 stated that by virtue of the Monroe Doctrine no European state could be allowed

[1] Dana's note to Wheaton's *International Law*, p. 107.

to exploit or construct or finance any transcontinental canal. In the Venezuela boundary discussion the United States relied on and quoted Monroe's message, and claimed a right to protect Venezuela against the claims being advanced by Great Britain in regard to the disputed boundary between British Guiana and Venezuela. Of the dispatches of Secretary Olney on the Venezuela boundary question it is as well, perhaps, to say little now. His claim, in a restatement of the Monroe Doctrine in his correspondence with Lord Salisbury, put the United States in the position of supreme arbiter in the affairs of the whole of the American continent. In an extraordinary spirit of Caesarism he wrote: "To-day the United States is practically sovereign on this continent, and its fiat is law upon the subjects to which it confines its interposition."[1] Lord Salisbury's reply was a refusal to accept the Monroe Doctrine in this sense, or as being applicable to the question, and he showed that the circumstances of the controversy had very few features in common with those prevailing in 1823.

III

Anything like a detailed examination of the applications of the Monroe Doctrine in its original or extended meaning in the century which has just closed since it was first promulgated would involve a very large portion of the diplomatic history of the United States. It is only possible to take a rapid survey and to endeavour to reach some conclusions.

All that is claimed in the Covenant of the League of Nations (Art. 21) is that the Monroe Doctrine is a "regional understanding" (a curiously ambiguous phrase) which makes for the maintenance of peace. On the whole I believe the claim is justified if we limit

[1] J. B. Moore, *Digest of International Law*, vol. VI, p. 553.

the expression somewhat. The message enunciated a policy which in the opinion of the President should be the guide of American statesmen. It is one of the remarkable things about the Monroe Doctrine that it is no part of the law of the United States; it has never been promulgated by Act of Congress or Resolutions of Congress, though Congress has recognized it often. It is in no sense legally binding on any Government, but it has been reaffirmed time after time and applied by successive Ministries according to their perception of the national requirements. By its reiterated assertion the American continents, except for the French expedition to Mexico in 1863, have been preserved from any attempts on the part of non-American Powers to acquire forcible possession of any part of the territories, or to introduce the political schemes of European statesmen.

This doctrine, whether in its original or in its expanded form, is not a doctrine of American altruism. As Senator Lodge has put it concisely, and Mr Root in a more detailed manner: "The Monroe Doctrine rests primarily on the great law of self-preservation." British statesmen had enunciated a doctrine not dissimilar in regard to India, and have brought within its scope countries as near and as far as Afghanistan, the Shan States, Persia and Egypt. The problem of the Pacific raises similar questions. The first century of the Monroe Doctrine has witnessed an immense expansion of the territory of the United States, and the methods employed have by no means always been such as present-day writers can justify. Few states with widely extended territories have a perfectly clean record in this respect. The Monroe Doctrine has been invoked more than once in this expansion, and Mr Bushnell Hart in a recent work has drawn attention to "the contrast between the principle that foreign nations must not annex American territory and the equally well-established principle that the United States may annex what she pleases."[1]

If the states of Europe have sometimes taken umbrage at the manner in and occasions on which the Monroe Doctrine has been asserted, the states of South America have often been no less antagonized. And yet some of them have, by its invocation, been more than once saved from the just punishment of their breaches of International Law, and their very existence is, in no small measure, due to its enunciation. Some of the more backward have been prevented in the past from reforming their international manners in a way which would have brought them into line with more advanced states. The Big Brother has sometimes done them harm by preventing them from getting a wholesome spanking. The leading states of South America, Argentina, Brazil and Chile, have in modern times, by the mouths of highly esteemed writers and statesmen, protested against the assertion of the Monroe Doctrine as a suggestion of the primacy of the United States on the American continent. President Polk's statement that "we have withdrawn the rights to conquer colonies and intervene from European states, but we have reserved them to ourselves to exercise without respecting the other states of the New World" has rankled in the memories of many of the states, especially as they have seen certain evidence of this from time to time in Central America. The policy of the United States in regard to the South American states has undergone an important change in recent times. President Roosevelt's famous message to Congress on December 5th, 1905, recognized that there had been much suspicion engendered in certain of the southern republics lest the United States should interpret the Monroe Doctrine as inimical to their interests. He declared that the Doctrine

[1] *The Monroe Doctrine*, p. 368.

must never be used in any way to further the aggrandizement of the United States at the expense of the southern
republics, but he warned some of them that the United
States would not permit them to use the Monroe Doctrine to shield them against the consequences of their
misdeeds—a necessary warning. But in order to prevent foreign Governments from territorial occupation
with a view to the collection of their lawful debts, he
put forward the view that the United States must themselves undertake such arrangements as would ensure
the collection of such debts as were really due. The
more recent attitude of the United States to the
smaller Latin republics has been generally characterized by the principle which Roosevelt propounded,
and on the whole it has been for the benefit of these
defaulting states as well as for that of their creditors.

The South American states remain, however, suspicious of the Monroe Doctrine, the "definition, interpretation and application" of which is in the hands
of the Washington Government. Twice within six
months in 1923, Mr Secretary Hughes emphasized the
view that the Monroe Doctrine is no infringement of the
sovereignty of other American states, who have become members of the League of Nations and who appear to prefer to rely on the Covenant. There seems to
be no contradiction between such membership and
Pan-Americanism, but in the latter the South American
states appear to see looming too close the great power
of the United States, making against the equality of
states as some of the South American lawyers and
statesmen interpret that doctrine. But things are what
they are.

The Doctrine of Monroe was the enunciation of a
principle of policy, and is not an obligation of International Law. The whole of the American continent is
certainly now no longer open to colonization—whatever

may have been the position in 1823—and in its literal sense this portion of the message no longer has any application. It is in the interest of the peace of the world that no part of the continent should be made the object of intervention or domination by any foreign Power, whether European or Asiatic. On the other hand, attempts such as have been sometimes suggested to limit the free play of economic forces in the republics of South America will be met by the assertion by non-American states of a right to equality of opportunity and treatment there; and to invoke the Monroe Doctrine to prevent capital from flowing freely into all parts of these countries, the richest in natural resources of all the world, would provoke opposition and be a misreading of the principle of self-preservation, the basic doctrine of the non-intervention section of Monroe's message. The United States have introduced and asserted a policy of the "Open Door" in other parts of the world; they cannot consistently refuse to recognize it on the American continent.

It is frequently pointed out by some of the more thoughtful American statesmen and publicists that it is an error to speak of certain extensions of the Monroe Doctrine by Presidents and Secretaries of State under the pressure of great popular movements as being applications of that Doctrine. It is well that this should be done, but from the very nature of a political doctrine such as that which we are considering, interpretations of it must vary from time to time. The Doctrine, from its elastic interpretations, has been described by a South American President as a "gutta-percha" doctrine. Many acts which have been done in its name might have been justified on other principles provided by the rules of International Law and there was often no need to relate them to the Monroe Doctrine. But when a political movement is taking place and the people are under the stress of a mass-emotion the use of the phrase "the Monroe Doctrine" becomes a far simpler means of supporting a policy than the use of more involved expressions of greater accuracy taken from the texts of books on International Law. It becomes a useful slogan for the politician who knows the value of catchwords, whether it be "the Monroe Doctrine," "Self-determination," or "Your food will cost you more." And it is largely for this reason that American politicians have made use of the Doctrine for acts which strictly speaking did not fall within its content. When, as has happened, this same Doctrine is made use of to justify either interference with the internal affairs of a Latin American republic, or to warn off some too insistent creditor (in both cases probably, in the long run, to the advantage of both), or to cover some phase of imperialism either political or financial (for republics no less than empires are liable to severe attacks of chauvinism), the historians may well complain that the Monroe Doctrine is misapplied or misunderstood; but that complaint will not prevent its use on similar occasions in the future. Only a well-instructed people can distinguish between the true and the false doctrine.

I have said that attempts are made from time to time by distinguished American statesmen and lawyers to recall the world to a more accurate understanding of President Monroe's message. I cannot do better than quote an extract from such an attempt by Mr Elihu Root, a former Secretary of State, in a valuable address to the members of the American Society of International Law in the Spring of 1914. I should add that Mr Hughes, the present American Secretary of State, in an address before the American Bar Association on August 30th, 1923, and again on December 1st, 1923, spoke in very similar language. We may take it that in its negative aspect Mr Root's words which follow

give us the present view of the Monroe Doctrine as held
by responsible American statesmen:

A false conception of what the Monroe Doctrine is, of what it
demands and what it justifies, of its scope and of its limits, has
invaded the public press and affected public opinion within the
past few years. Grandiose schemes of national expansion invoke
the Monroe Doctrine. Interested motives to compel Central and
South American countries to do or refrain from doing something
by which individual Americans may profit invoke the Monroe
Doctrine. Clamours for national glory from minds too shallow
to grasp at the same time a sense of national duty invoke the
Monroe Doctrine. The intolerance which demands that control
over the conduct and the opinions of other peoples which is the
essence of tyranny invokes the Monroe Doctrine. Thoughtless
people who see no difference between lawful right and physical
power assume that the Monroe Doctrine is a warrant for interference in the internal affairs of all weaker nations in the New
World. Against this supposititious doctrine, many protests both in
the United States and in South America have been made and
justly made. To the real Monroe Doctrine these protests have no
application.[1]

On its positive side the Monroe Doctrine sums up the
traditional policy of the United States for the past
century, namely, that there shall be no intervention or
domination by any non-American state in, nor any
attempt to extend the European system to, any portion
of the Western Hemisphere. This is the real Monroe
Doctrine, which is the basic principle of the foreign
policy of the United States, which has deserved and
enjoyed from the citizens of the United States "a
popular affection and admiration which are hardly
accorded to any other policy, save to the first principles
of the Republic itself."[2]

[1] *Proceedings of the American Society of International Law*, 1914, p. 21.
[2] *The Times*, December 1st, 1923.

VI

THE WORK OF GROTIUS AND OF THE MODERN INTERNATIONAL LAWYER[1]

I

ASTRIKING feature of the literature of to-day on the subject of International Law is the great emphasis which is laid on the defects, short-comings, and lacunae in the rules governing states in their mutual relations. On the third centenary of the publication of the great work of Grotius, the *De jure belli ac pacis*, we find a demand for a re-examination of the principles of the Law of Nations and a call for another Grotius to co-ordinate divergences of national practice and lay down principles for international relations which shall accord with the altered conditions which have taken place both in states and in the international society in recent years. On the other hand there are those who, while admitting that gaps undoubtedly exist in the rules of International Law, would have us get back to the Grotian doctrine, not necessarily in the express form in which it was stated by him in 1625, but in its fundamentals. In much the same way that the argument that Christianity had failed because it did not prevent the outbreak of war in 1914 was countered by the reply that the teaching of Christ had not been practised, so there are to be found those who contend that the weakness of International Law to-day is due to the non-observance of the fundamental teaching of Grotius, whose claim in a very real sense to be the founder of the Law of Nations of the modern world is almost universally admitted.[2]

[1] Published in *Cambridge Legal Essays* (1925).
[2] See C. van Vollenhoven, *The Three Stages in the Evolution of the Law of Nations* (1919).

It is unnecessary to recapitulate the events of the life of Hugo Grotius (1583–1645) or to discuss in any detail the numerous contributions to all branches of literature which came from the pen of this remarkable man, but it may be well before considering the present position of the Law of Nations to notice a few facts concerning the famous treatise published exactly three hundred years ago, almost to the very day on which these words are being written.[1] There have appeared up to the present time forty editions in Latin and twenty-four editions in translations of the *De jure belli ac pacis*, the most recent being the Leyden edition of 1919 (edited by Dr Molhuysen), and the Washington edition with an English translation by Professor Francis W. Kelsey, published by the Carnegie Endowment in the present year.[2] These facts are striking testimony to the value of the work of Grotius, the publication of which marked an epoch in the history of jurisprudence as well as "in the philosophical, and we might almost say the political history of Europe," to use the language of Hallam. This is the more remarkable as it is not an easy book to read; the multitude of quotations from ancient writers of all kinds renders it sometimes difficult to follow the thread of the writer's argument and disturbs "the didactic clearness and convenient brevity which we wish to find in a philosophical work."[3]

[1] The book came from the press in July, 1625, and Grotius in a letter to his brother William, dated from Paris, July 4th, promises to send copies to him (C. van Vollenhoven, *The Land of Grotius*). I should here state my indebtedness to several interesting monographs from the pen of Professor van Vollenhoven on Grotius.

[2] Reference to the earlier works of Grotius must not be omitted, since one of them has exercised considerable influence on the development of the doctrine of the freedom of the seas. The earliest was *De jure praedae commentarius*, written between 1604 and 1605, but not published until 1868, the other was the famous *Mare liberum*, published in 1609.

[3] Whewell's Grotius (1853), editor's preface, p. vi.

The book is not simply a treatise on International Law; civil law, jurisprudence, ethics, philosophy and history are all drawn upon by the author in the fulfilment of his aim "on behalf of justice."[1] The rules which nations should or do observe in war and peace are not set apart from the principles which bind, or should bind, men living together in states; the analogies between the laws of a single state and those which have received an obligatory force from the will of all or nearly all nations are constantly before the writer. This is in the line of his basic idea that just as law governs the relation of individuals within states, so it should govern the relation of states *inter se*. The book is thus a compilation of laws applicable to individuals and states. This is especially noteworthy where Grotius is making a comparison between the coercive power of municipal law and International Law. For the writer had to deal with a strong body of pacifist opinion, and he thought it necessary to devote the whole of his second chapter in the first book to an examination of the question whether war is ever just. Nearly the whole of the second book relates to matters which are the foundation of much of the modern law obtaining between states in time of peace. These principles are introduced after a discussion of the causes of war of which the first given is that of self-defence and defence of property or territory. Modes of acquisition and loss of property largely based on the principles of the Roman law (*jus gentium*), obligations, treaties and rights of legation are dealt with as involving possible causes of war, municipal and international activities being compared.[2]

[1] "This work presumes to inscribe your revered name in dedication because of confidence not in itself nor in its author, but in its theme. For it has been written on behalf of justice." Dedication to Louis XIII of the edition published in 1646.

[2] Marriage and intestate succession are fully dealt with in Book II, chaps. v and vii.

This is followed by an elaborate examination of the theories of punishment and then the writer returns to the subject of unjust and doubtful causes of war. War is viewed partly as a punishment, and a chapter[1] is devoted to warnings to sovereigns not to go to war rashly even for just causes. In the concluding paragraphs on this subject, after shrewdly stating that then only is the time for war when we have right on our side, and, what is of the greatest consequence, might also, Grotius adds:

> When we consider that God forbad His temple to be built by David, who is related to have carried on pious wars, because he had shed much blood...how can anyone fail to see, especially any Christian, what an unhappy and disastrous thing, and how strenuously to be avoided is a war, even when not unjust?[2]

The last book is concerned with what is lawful in war, and here Grotius enumerates the brutal practices current in his day as the positive Law of Nations. But this does not satisfy him, and so he makes an appeal for *temperamenta*, ameliorations of the existing practices, basing his arguments on the judgment of the most moral times and peoples, the rule of mercy, equity and natural justice. The appeal is from the positive Law of Nations to the higher Law of Nature.

There are few passages better known than that in the Prolegomena in which Grotius gave his chief reason for writing on war.

> For I saw prevailing throughout the Christian world a licence in making war of which even barbarous nations would have been ashamed, recourse being had to arms for slight reasons or no reason; and when arms were once taken up, all reverence for divine and human law was thrown away, just as if men were thenceforth authorised to commit all crimes without restraints.

[1] Book II, chap. xxiv.
[2] Book II, chap. xxiv, 3.

The concluding paragraph of the last book is no less impressive and characteristic:

> May God write these lessons—He who alone can—on the hearts of all those who have the affairs of Christendom in their hands; and may He give to those persons a mind fitted to understand and to respect rights, divine and human; and lead them to recollect always that the ministration committed to them is no less than this: that they are the governors of man, a creature most dear to God.[1]

These extracts show us Grotius the man, with a wonderful breadth of charity and a toleration far removed from the bigotry which characterized the great mass of both the Protestant and the Catholic leaders of the day. In his work on Capture there is a striking tribute to a Spanish author (Vasquius decus illud Hispaniae), and this after all that the Netherlands had suffered from Spain, and while war was still in progress.[2]

There remains to be considered the most important element in his work, that in which undoubtedly lay its chief attraction for the men of the age, for Grotius was the offspring of his time, and accurately reflected its thought in his philosophic outlook. His fundamental appeal was to the Law of Nature, and in it he sought for immutable and eternal rules independent of individuals. Above the rules of positive law, those which originated in custom or legislation, there was another law ascertainable by all reasonable beings, and this was the Law of Nature, the common creed of the theologians, philosophers and lawyers of the period. He admits in his system the *Jus Voluntarium*, those customary rules which states observe, but his main emphasis is on the *Jus Naturae* which made a universal appeal, and from these two sources he derives the Law

[1] Book III, chap. xxv, 8.
[2] W. J. M. van Eysinga, "Grotius," *Rev. de Dr. int.* 3rd ser. vol. VI, p. 279.

of Nations—the *Jus Gentium*. So great was his influence in the philosophical world that he appeared to many as the father not only of the Law of Nations but also of the Law of Nature.[1] Here was the strength of Grotius' position. Christendom, Catholic and Protestant, acknowledged the same moral order. Grotius made the appeal to apply this moral order, hitherto acknowledged to be applicable to individuals, to the kings and governors of the states of Christendom in their international relations, and the appeal was so far successful in that it produced the acceptance of a body of rules which were soon acknowledged as the basis of the Law of Nations, and to which in international controversies appeal long continued to be made.[2] But the co-ordination of states under a system of legal rules required a jurisprudential basis at a time when the claims of both the Pope and the Emperor to overlordship of the states of Europe were being everywhere called in question or rejected. It was this juridical plan which Grotius traced with no small success.

The Reformation had produced the modern state, but the Reformation had by no means run its course in the age of Grotius. The wars of religion known as the "Thirty Years' War" had been raging for seven years when the *De jure belli ac pacis* was published. Breaking out in the eastern part of the Empire, it soon spread so that in the end civil wars raging in Italy and the United Provinces, the rivalries of the Scandinavian Powers, the struggle between the United Provinces and Spain, and the strife between France and Spain in

---

[1] Sir F. Pollock, *Journ. of Soc. of Comp. Legislation*, N.S. vol. III (1901), p. 206.
[2] The Entente Powers in their dispatch to the Netherlands Government of February 14th, 1920, regarding the extradition of the ex-Emperor William II, cited Grotius (Book II, chap. xxi, sec. 5), in support of their request.

Italy all gradually merged into the great European struggle.[1] If ever there was an age of unrest in Europe (and the reactions were felt in the New World), it was the period of the Thirty Years' War. In Holland there was civil war, caused by religious differences, but the contending parties were opposing Protestant sects. The rigid Calvinists were led by Prince Maurice of Orange, while the more liberal party was led by the Grand Pensionary Oldenbarnevelt. The fall of the latter in 1618 sent Grotius to perpetual imprisonment, from whence he escaped in 1621 in a book chest with the assistance of his devoted wife. Three years after the death of Grotius the great European settlement was made by the Treaties of Münster and Osnabrück (the Peace of Westphalia), and not only was the principle of equality between the recognized religious confessions assured, but the doctrine of a common superior to the independent states of Europe received its *coup de grâce*. It is well known that Grotius' hero, Gustavus Adolphus, constantly carried a copy of his work with him, and in 1661 the Elector Palatine appointed to a newly founded chair of Natural Law in the University of Heidelberg, Samuel Pufendorf, who had already written studies on the work of Grotius. "The great Dutchman had not lived in vain, when within sixteen years of his death *Jus Naturae et Gentium* had won a place as a subject of systematic University study side by side with the texts of Justinian."[2] But Pufendorf exceeded the devotion of his master to the Law of Nature, and abandoned or denied the claim of the positive Law of Nations founded on custom or treatises to the name. Meantime another contemporary of Grotius, Richard Zouch (1590–1660) while not denying the existence and value of the Law of Nature laid the emphasis of his *Jus inter Gentes* on the

[1] *Cambridge Modern History*, vol. III, p. v.
[2] T. A. Walker, *A History of the Law of Nations*, vol. I, p. 337.

positive or customary part of the law. The basis of the Positivist school was the custom of states, and to-day it is the predominating school, but though several distinguished writers in the eighteenth century adopted this standpoint, the Grotian school continued to flourish; the followers of Pufendorf, the pure Naturalists, are, however, but little in evidence in modern times.[1] An interesting set of replies to a questionnaire on the present position of the Natural Law doctrine as a basis of International Law recently issued by Professor Th. Niemeyer of the University of Kiel reveals the fact that there are still to be found followers of all three schools to-day, though it would appear from an examination of the works of English and American writers that they have almost without exception adopted the positivist standpoint.[2] But even with many of these writers there are appeals to reason which in Professor Manley Hudson's opinion differ but little from those formerly made to "nature."[3]

II

The age in which the work of Grotius was done, and in which it had so far-reaching an influence, differed in many respects from our own, but there are also noteworthy points of similarity. It was a period of wars, national, religious, and civil. Europe had emerged from the middle ages, kingdoms and states were consolidating, religion was a mighty force. The mass of human

[1] For a valuable sketch of the three Schools of International Lawyers, Naturalists, Grotians and Positivists, see Oppenheim, *International Law*, vol. i, secs. 55–9.

[2] *Jus Naturae et Gentium. Eine Umfrage zum Gedächtnis des Hugo Grotius. Sonderabdruck aus Band XXXIV. der Zeitschrift für internationales Recht* (1925).

[3] For examples see Manley O. Hudson, "The Prospect for International Law in the Twentieth Century," *The Cornell Law Review*, vol. x (1925), p. 428.

beings composing the various states were as yet little concerned with affairs of government, politics being handled by rulers and their ministers. But there was a feeling of vigour and self-reliance in the air, and men were thinking, and thinking to a purpose. The seventeenth century was, especially for England, the age in which the work of the sixteenth century in both religion and politics was approved, developed, and placed upon a footing so stable that it endured in practically the same form for some two centuries. On the continent of Europe this political development was delayed for a century, and the effects of the French Revolution, in the genesis of which philosophers played no small part, have not ceased in the world of the twentieth century. The government of states to-day is now almost universally on a democratic basis, but there are other organizations of men of an economic order which cut across the political. Interstate relations are still conducted through the medium of foreign offices, but there exist other international organizations of a very different character and concerned with the economic conditions of large and compact groups of people in many states whose interests are controlled by leaders selected by the groups and not by the majority of the electors. There are national interests and group interests, and these two are tending in some stages to paralyze each other, and in this way to hinder international state activities. Furthermore, there is the increasing pressure on the occupants of the lands of the Old World caused by the growth of population. Lastly there is now a new organization of the Society of States in the League of Nations, and an important aspect of economic international life has come under the operation of the International Labour Bureau.

The situation to-day in many of its aspects is due to the results following on a long and exhausting period of war and the ignorance of demagogues posing as statesmen. A picture of modern society has just been painted in very dark colours by one of the few striking personalities which the time has produced:

Scepticism, criticism, irony and negation have forced faith into the background, man has become uneasy, inconstant, restless, nervous; through his very energy, often artificially increased, he has fallen into Utopianism; through his continual searching and enterprise he has been deceived again and again; the idealist has plunged himself into gluttony, but has not found satisfaction; pessimism, not only theoretical, but also practical, has become widespread—as also joylessness and anxiety, hate and despair, and from these exhaustion, nervousness, psychism and suicide. Modern society is pathologically irritated, torn, disintegrated—always in one transition after another....The internal disintegration and disharmony of the modern man and his life, the disintegration and disharmony of society and the general spiritual anarchy, the contest between the present and the past, between fathers and children, the war between the Church and science, philosophy, art and the state, these penetrate the whole of modern culture. We are seeking for the peace of our own souls—how and where shall we find it? In our effort to attain spiritual freedom we fell into an excessive individualism and subjectivity, which were the source of this general spiritual and moral anarchy. Many of us gave ourselves up to materialism and mechanics. We have cultivated intellectualism one-sidedly, and have forgotten the harmonious cultivation of all our spiritual and physical powers and qualities.[1]

Whether this be accepted as a true, or as only a one-sided, view of the present situation, it draws attention to important factors which must be taken into account by the international lawyer of to-day.

The appeal of Grotius was to the rulers of his day, emperors, kings, grand-dukes, electors and others whose wills were those of the states they governed. The appeal of the international jurist to-day is less to individual rulers, and more to the various group interests

[1] President T. G. Masaryk, "Reflections on the Question of War Guilt," *Foreign Affairs* (New York), July, 1925, pp. 529–40.

which ultimately control the destinies of states. Is the appeal of to-day likely to have a speedier or more complete success than that which Grotius made? Democracy is everywhere installed as a system of government with varying degrees of efficiency and power. Politics and economics are almost universally intermingled in the problems of states. The appeal therefore has to be made to masses, groups, collectivities, and these tend to have a lower ethical standard, and to act on a lower moral plane than the individuals composing them. The ignorance both of the groups and of their leaders is a real danger in international affairs. But at times these groups are capable of being moved by a great ideal, at others they easily fall victims to a current catchword. It is difficult to estimate the effect of appeals made on moral grounds such as those which Grotius made, but I believe that there has been progress made in the ethical standard of states during the centuries since Grotius, though it is slow and intermittent. At times it seems to take a leap forward, spend itself and return almost to its starting-point. As the result of a great mass emotion the states collectively saw a great vision when the League of Nations was brought into being; the difficulty is to maintain the position won in a moment of insight. The disquieting feature to-day from the international standpoint is the apparent enthusiasm of certain sections in states for the compulsory settlement of international disputes by pacific methods, and their reluctance to resort to similar methods for the settlement of disputes between the groups within the state. Unless the same system can work in internal and international disputes, the peoples will perish, for they will cease to have the necessary vision to carry through to its fulfilment a great ideal.

There is a curious and interesting interdependence between reasonableness and sanity in the conduct of domestic politics on the one hand and kindly feeling and generous sympathy in our attitude towards foreign relations on the other....Political progress, whether national or international, must depend upon trust in the better instincts of the people, and cannot rest upon their appetites and their passions, their envies and their animosities.[1]

The picture drawn by President Masaryk has this much of truth in it, that it emphasizes the impossibility of real progress in the realization of the international society, and the development of its law, while the peoples of the world remain a prey to "their appetites and their passions, their envies and their animosities." But the picture is a very partial representation of the facts of to-day, and even if it should be accepted as wholly true, what was the state of Europe when Grotius lived and wrote? There is no need to give a detailed answer to this question, it was the age of the "Thirty Years' War." Grotius was in his day a *Vox Clamantis*, and the success which has attended his work must not blind us to the fact that his appeals to the highest standards for International Law are still far short of fulfilment. Law and morality are inseparably interwoven, and the law reformer inevitably starts with higher ideals than those of the masses of his time. To effect any result he is invariably compelled to compromise, to reason with men to obtain the Good while still holding before them the Best. All improvements in law to be effective and such as will not bring law into evil repute by their non-observance invariably fall below the highest ethical standards. Progress in the elevation of human conduct is obtained by the gradual recognition that only by subordination of self-interest within certain limits can there be an advance to the general good. One of the important functions of all

---

[1] N. Murray Butler, *The International Mind* (1913), p. 111. Cf. also Ch. Dupuis, *Le Droit des gens et les rapports des Grandes Puissances avec les autres États* (1921), p. 529.

law is that of a schoolmaster, and this is true of International Law. Its very defects when realized constitute a stage in the progress of the education and illumination of states.

III

"A lawyer must be orthodox, else he is no lawyer," says Maitland, and this is true of international as of other lawyers. His prime duty is to know the law and, if he be a teacher or writer, to expound it as he finds it. Grotius did this when he laid down the positive rules of the Law of Nations prevailing in his day, evidenced by numerous precedents, drawn, it is true, from far distant times, and supported by authorities as ancient as Moses. The modern international lawyer has a similar task to perform in dealing with the existing rules of International Law, and for him the evidences of the positive rules of law whose basis is the consent of states will be precedents showing their application (custom) and agreements which states have entered into between themselves (treaties). In dealing with specific rules relating to international intercourse he is bound to take cognizance of the general jurisprudential ideas underlying the system. Juristic speculation lies behind the great mass of the rules of International Law, and many of these have passed into realities on which the present rules have been based.[1] The orthodox international lawyer will have, therefore, to expound certain fundamental principles on which the science rests. He will speak of the notion of states, and of the meaning of law in their mutual relations; he will be met with claims based on states' sovereignty, independence and equality. But the international lawyer of to-day will also, in stating the positive rules which obtain, be led to

[1] Roscoe Pound, *Philosophical Theory and International Law*, Bibliotheca Visseriana, vol. I, p. 88.

examine many of the traditional commonplaces of the text-books and the shibboleths of the politicians to see how far they conform to the standards of his time. With some of the views which to-day are current under the name of political or social philosophy and jurisprudence, I am unable to agree, because I am unable to understand them. This is particularly the case with some of the modern expositions of the idea of the state. Without accepting all that the new social philosophy and the new sociological jurisprudence may have to say in relation to International Law, but realizing the truth of the view that the measure and test of law is not to be found in the shifting sands of philosophical fancies which are subject to the inroads of each recurring tide,[1] even the orthodox lawyer will have to face the position that the facts of everyday international intercourse do not warrant the full deduction from some of the fundamental principles which were made by the writers of an older generation. It is as true of International Law as of the Common Law that "the life of the law has not been logic; it has been experience,"[2] and by this experience the jurist will test the alleged philosophic or jurisprudential bases. He will find that doctrines of sovereignty taught by many jurists and enunciated by statesmen are in need of revision, and that independence is often too strongly emphasized to the loss of the growing sense of interdependence.[3]

I have elsewhere drawn attention to the fact that the danger spots in the world lie with the backward

[1] J. B. Moore, *International Law and some Current Illusions*, p. xiv.
[2] O. W. Holmes, *The Common Law*, p. 1.
[3] "In the present state of the development of International Law and international relations it cannot be admitted that states are bound by their own wills when their conduct affects other states or their nationals." J. W. Garner in *American Political Science Review*, February, 1925, p. 1.

nations. Rights and duties are correlative terms in law, and in general, the emphasis of all writers is on state *rights*. The demand for the recognition of rights by individuals and groups within states to-day and the disregard of their duties is symptomatic of the condition of society portrayed in the extract from President Masaryk's article just quoted. In international relations a similar condition may be observed. A recent writer has very wisely emphasized the need that jurists in dealing with International Law should lay more stress on the *duties* of states. He points out that good government within a state is essential to progress, and for this to be obtained every department of the administration must reach a high level of efficiency. I am in hearty accord with his statement that "International lawyers can help materially in the progress of the world if they will inculcate the doctrine that the extent to which a state can expect to achieve recognition of its rights depends on the extent to which, and the success with which, it fulfils the purposes for which states exist."[1]

The undue emphasis placed by most international lawyers on a doctrine of the equality of states ignores this point of view, and Lorimer was right when he pointed out that while all states are entitled to be recognized as such, they are not all entitled to be recognized as equal, simply because they are not.[2]

[1] *British Year Book of International Law*, 1925, p. 234.

[2] "No principle has been repeated more frequently or authoritatively than the equality of states and their absolute independence, except perhaps their counterparts, the balance of powers, and the *status quo*; and all of them may now, I think, be safely said to have been repudiated by history, as they always were by reason." J. Lorimer, *Institutes of the Law of Nations*, vol. i, p. 44. For an examination of the doctrine of state equality, see P. J. Baker, *Brit. Year Book of Inter. Law*, 1923, p. 1, and E. D. Dickinson, *The Equality of States in International Law* (1920).

But the international lawyer, besides stating the present rules of law and examining their bases, has work before him also of the kind which Grotius undertook. He will find that on many points there are divergent practices and views, and also that there are large areas of international activity for which there are no rules of International Law. The harmonizing of divergent usages and the making of new rules can only be done by states themselves, but the lawyer can and should put forward proposals for those ends, and in so doing he will have to bear in mind the extremely complex conditions of modern societies and the existence of the new organs for international co-operation. International lawyers can never rest satisfied with their subject until in every department of state life, economic and political, there are rules accepted whereby states can obtain justice within the law.[1] Just as when in examining the existing rules he will from time to time step aside to point out wherein they subserve and wherein they conflict with the objective solidarity of the interests of the international community, so in formulating proposals to meet new cases he will be guided by similar principles. So far as the appeals of Grotius succeeded, they did so because he based them on standards of morality of general acceptance, his appeal to the Law of Nature was an appeal to the educated reason of mankind of his time. This appeal is necessary to-day as regards both the expository and the constructive work of the international lawyer, but it is not an easy task to undertake. Lawyers, English and American, trained in the school of the English Common Law, have an outlook on many important branches of jurisprudence which differs in fundamentals from that of their continental brethren, and under this

[1] I have more fully dealt with these matters in "International Law and Moral Ideals," *Contemporary Review*, March, 1925.

designation we have to include the growing number of jurists of the South and Central American continents, whose material requirements often differ from those of their own Latin kinsfolk in Europe. Further, the needs of purely continental states and maritime states have not always appeared to be conformable to the same standard. There is, however, a unifying force at work which must not be left out of consideration, as it may in time prove strong enough to weld together even these divergent schools, namely, the influence emanating from the League of Nations. Already international legislation on no small scale is being affected through its various organs and commissions. It is remarkable that among the subjects already dealt with have been those in support of which Grotius and his school prayed in aid the doctrines of the Law of Nature, and to which he and other jurists have given the name of "imperfect" rights, such as the freedom of intercourse for the citizens of all states by land and by water.[1] A reasonable appreciation of the needs of the whole international society has achieved successes here which centuries of lip-service to the Natural Law theory had failed to produce.

The chief expository work of the international lawyer of to-day in dealing with the large body of rules generally accepted by states is to place them on a rational basis, to give such explanations of the positive law as will appeal to the reasonable man of the day. From premises which to-day are denied or rejected by the current social or legal philosophy many sound rules of law have been evolved and observed as meeting the needs of states. The reasons given for a rule of law by one generation often fail to satisfy another, yet the rule itself is accepted as necessary. In saying that the first duty of the international lawyer of to-day is to rationalize

[1] Hall's *International Law*, 8th ed. p. v.

the existing rules of International Law I believe that I am stating in simpler terms the demand which others are making for the application of philosophical principles to the Law of Nations. It will only be when this reasonableness of the law is accepted that the strongest motive for its observance will have been generated.

So the work of the international lawyer of to-day is in the first place to use the large amount of material to his hand, to expound it and commend it to the instincts of reason, justice, and humanity of states; and secondly, where rules are uncertain or lacking, to propose those which will enable states in their modern complex social relations to fulfil their highest ends. Reason is thus both a check on the customary rules of International Law and a source of rules for the seeker after international right.[1]

Wherever there is a deep-seated and widespread national sentiment of justice and right which demands satisfaction in regard to other states, the Law of Nations must answer to the call, and the international lawyer who can suggest the appropriate method by which this desire can be satisfied is in the direct line of succession from his spiritual ancestor, Hugo Grotius.

[1] J. Westlake, *International Law*, vol. I, "Peace" (1910), p. 14.

VII

THE LOCARNO TREATIES[1]

IN order fully to understand the genesis of the treaties signed at Locarno on October 16th, 1925,[2] it is necessary to note the stages which led up to the settlement.

Ever since the end of the late war practically all the political events of Europe have turned on the question of security, and on that the future peace of Europe ultimately depends.

At Paris, 1919, there was negotiated the Three Powers Guarantee Treaty between the British Empire, the United States and France, for it was recognized that it was due to France that steps should be taken to safeguard her land from the invasions of an enemy who three times within a hundred years had devastated her territory. This Treaty failed by reason of its non-ratification by the United States. The course of Anglo-French negotiation turned thereafter on this question of a Guarantee Pact. At Cannes in January, 1922, Mr Lloyd George proposed a new pact whereby all states undertook mutually to refrain from attacking each other. This failed and M. Briand resigned. Then came the Genoa Conference where Mr Lloyd George's attempts were again rejected and in July, 1922, came a temporary break in the negotiations. Meantime the question of Reparations became pressing and the Dawes scheme was ultimately the result.

The League of Nations was also concerned with the question of security in combination with disarmament,

---

[1] Based on two articles in *The Law Journal*, November, 1925.
[2] Parl. Papers, 1926 (Cd. 2525).

and in September, 1922, the Assembly (Resolution 14) resolved that states should disarm, but must render military aid to a disarmed state if it were attacked. After lengthy discussion by Committees of the League the *Treaty of Mutual Assistance* was submitted to the Assembly in September, 1923. The principle of Resolution 14 was elaborated and recognition was given to the necessity of regional treaties and alliances as the chief means of providing assistance to a disarmed state when attacked. Mr Ramsay MacDonald's government pronounced against it, rejecting the principle of regional agreements and demanding a universal treaty. Thereupon a new approach was made on a threefold basis of limitation of armaments, guarantees for security and compulsory arbitration. Out of these developed the *Geneva Protocol* of 1924 declaring aggressive war to be a crime and demanding the unconditional submission of all disputes to arbitration. After the fall of Mr MacDonald's government British opinion set against the Protocol in which it was considered that too much stress was laid on the forcible sanctions contained in it. At the meeting of the Council of the League at Rome in December, 1924, Mr Austen Chamberlain announced the refusal of Great Britain to accept the Protocol in its existing form. Other states, and in particular, France, still sought to bring it into force, but France was willing to substitute something for it temporarily, while still asking for the whole. Great Britain looked to the principle of guarantee pacts between the states chiefly interested and especially sought to bring Germany into such a scheme, provided that the Pact was under the control of the League of Nations. In March, 1925, the British Government definitely pronounced against the Protocol, Mr Chamberlain laying it down that His Majesty's Government did not regard a general application of the principle of arbitration as acceptable and wished to reserve the possibility of settling disputes by other means. It was further stated that the obligations imposed on the British Empire under the Protocol were too heavy, as they might well be understood to involve a guarantee of the preservation of peace in Eastern Europe.

Meantime Germany, while protesting against the occupation of the Ruhr by France under the Poincaré government, saw in it a bid for security and not merely a sanction for the enforcement of the Treaty of Versailles. In December, 1922, the American Secretary of State, Mr Hughes, transmitted to France an offer from Germany that the Powers interested in the Rhine should guarantee peace for thirty years, i.e. that none of the Powers would declare war against each other without such declaration being preceded by a vote of the people. This was rejected by M. Poincaré and neither Great Britain nor the United States showed any indication of joining. A second proposal, made by Herr Stresemann in May and September, 1923, to settle all questions with France by arbitration was rejected. It appeared to be a part of the scheme for getting France out of the Ruhr. Meantime the League was at work, as has been seen, in preparing the Treaty of Mutual Assistance and the Geneva Protocol. In December, 1924, came the new proposal by Germany for a guarantee pact and in January and February, 1925, speeches of M. Herriot and Chancellor Luther advanced matters, and on February 9th, 1925, a Memorandum from Dr Luther put forward in detail the scheme which ultimately matured, providing for the mutual guarantee of the *status quo* in the Rhineland and the maintenance of the demilitarized zones as laid down by Articles 42 and 43 of the Treaty of Versailles and the entry into Arbitration Treaties with the neighbours of Germany on her Eastern as well as on her Western frontiers. Negotiations on this basis followed and were transferred to London in September, 1925, when the legal advisers of the interested states met and agreed on the principles for both the Rhine Pact and other Arbitration Treaties. The Delegates of Great Britain, France, Germany, Italy, Belgium, Poland and Czechoslovakia met at Locarno from October 5th to the 16th, and on the last day initialled the documents to be now considered; on December 1st, 1925, they were all signed in London and have since been ratified by all the contracting Powers. On December 14th, 1925, the various documents were deposited in the Archives of the League. On September 8th, 1926, Germany was admitted a member of the League of Nations, on September 14th, ratifications of the treaties were deposited at Geneva, and from that time the various treaties became operative.

I. THE SECURITY PACT

The texts of the various treaties are preceded by a final Protocol summarizing the work of the delegates, and stating the principles which had guided them. For the first time since the outbreak of war in August, 1914, Germany and six of her former enemies met together on terms of equality and freely negotiated agreements which they believe "will contribute greatly to bring about a moral relaxation of the tension between nations." No one of the states can claim the credit for the result, but the initiative in the final move came from Germany. After difficult negotiations and conversations between Great Britain and three of her allies it was found that there was an earnest desire to bring to an end a condition of affairs both political and economic which was grievously retarding the recovery of Europe. The acceptance in the summer of 1924 of the Dawes scheme was a preliminary step in this direction, but there was marked in it the maintenance of the spirit of the war. Germany faced her creditors as a vanquished state whose obligations imposed by the Treaty of Versailles were unfulfilled. At Locarno, though it is expressly provided that the rights and obligations of the parties under the Treaty of Versailles and the Dawes scheme remain unaffected, there was no question of victor and vanquished but a common and equal desire to arrive at such a permanent settlement as would enable the parties to arrive at a condition of security. They desired to seek by common agreement means for preserving their respective nations from the scourge of war and for providing for the peaceful settlement of disputes of every nature which might eventually arise between them. These treaties should mark the end of the war era. The documents drawn up at Locarno were eight in number. The Final Protocol has five treaties annexed. The first, and for our present purposes the most important, is the so-called Security Pact or Treaty of Mutual Guarantee (these terms do not occur in it) made between Great Britain, France, Germany, Italy and Belgium; the other four are arbitration treaties made between Germany and Belgium, France, Poland and Czechoslovakia respectively. The Security Pact and the four arbitration treaties are mutually interdependent. Besides these there are two treaties made between France and Poland and Czechoslovakia respectively providing for mutual assistance in case of unprovoked attack by Germany. They are of a purely defensive character and in accord with the spirit of the Covenant of the League of Nations.

The treaties are made within the Covenant and the League is invested with considerable authority, its intervention being provided for in numerous Articles. Without the League machinery it is hard to see how the arrangements could have been carried out. The treaties did not become operative till ratified and registered and Germany had become a member of the League. The entry of Germany is most important and must have far-reaching consequences. So long as she remained outside, its powers were obviously curtailed and the feeling common in Germany that the League was instituted as a means of enforcing the Treaty of Versailles had some colour. Moreover, so long as Germany, Russia and Turkey all remained outside the League there was always a danger of their forming an opposition League.

Germany's undertaking to enter the League was rendered possible by means of a letter signed by the delegates of the other Parties to the Pact giving their construction of Article 16 of the Covenant. Germany had contended that owing to disarmament she was unable to take part in any measures which might be decreed by the League against a recalcitrant member. The interpretation of Article 16 is to the effect that each state must co-operate loyally and effectively in support of the Covenant but only to the extent compatible with its military situation and geographical position. The necessity for interpretation draws attention to the looseness of wording of some of the Articles of the Covenant which was to be a layman's document, but like many a layman's will affords considerable scope for the ingenuity of the lawyer. The interpretation put on Article 16 appears to be reasonable and indicates that in the opinion of the Parties (and it cannot be binding on other members) Germany cannot stand aside and claim to be an impartial neutral in the former sense of the term in case of a league war or of a decree of non-intercourse against a recalcitrant member, but that her active assistance will be limited to her capacity and geographical position. Germany's emphasis on the Article, and her reference to her disarmament are not without significance. More will probably be heard of this.

Germany's presence within the League and on the Council to which she was elected shortly after admission may, of course, not work out in the way in which it appears to be generally expected. All will depend on the force of opinion in Germany; the power of the Nationalists or of the moderate parties will dictate the policy of the German Delegate. Germany's representative at The Hague in 1907 occupied a very striking position, and the diplomatic manœuvring at a large gathering such as the Assembly may well produce combinations which may paralyse action at a critical moment. This side of the matter must not be overlooked, but, having been noted, we prefer to dwell on the other and more hopeful side.

The pact is a guarantee by all the Parties of the maintenance of the territorial *status quo* resulting from the frontiers between Germany, France and Belgium and the inviolability of such frontiers as defined by the Treaty of Versailles, and also of the observance of the provision relating to the demilitarized portion of the Rhineland. The guarantee is collective and several, that is, each party is severally and all are collectively liable to perform the undertaking. In a purely collective guarantee such as that given to Luxemburg in 1867 the guarantors act as a body, but in this guarantee each state is individually under an obligation to intervene when the object of the guarantee is violated.

Not only does Germany voluntarily accept the loss of Alsace and Lorraine and the demilitarization of a large area of her Rhineland province, but each Party guarantees the other the possession of its territory. Germany had accepted these frontiers and the limitation on her user of the Rhineland in the Treaty of Versailles, but that acceptance was under compulsion; now it is a voluntary acquiescence in the *status quo*. The three Powers, France and Belgium respectively undertake with Germany not to attack or invade the others' territory—the promises are bilateral. France and Belgium respectively will not attack or invade Germany, neither will Germany attack or invade either of them. There is thus a solemn affirmation of the sanctity of treaties and a guarantee of the Western frontiers of Germany. There is, however, nothing to prevent Germany at some future time, by peaceful negotiation or through the League of Nations, obtaining modification of the terms of the Versailles treaty either in regard to frontiers or other matters. Already the possibility of colonial mandates is being suggested.

The possibility of war is not wholly eliminated. War may be undertaken (1) to resist a violation of the guarantee or breach of the Articles relating to the demilitarized zone; (2) when military operations are decreed by the League under Article 16 of the Covenant, i.e. where a member resorts to war in disregard of its covenanted obligations; (3) where military action is taken as a result of a failure of the Council to reach a decision on a matter referred to it, which decision must be unanimous, excluding the parties to the dispute (Article 15, par. 7).

All questions which the three Powers cannot settle by ordinary diplomatic means are to be dealt with either by judicial decision—in the case of questions involving legal rights, or by reference to a permanent Conciliation Commission as regards other matters of a political or non-justiciable character. If the parties do not accept the proposals of this Commission, the question is referred to the League of Nations under Article 16 of the Covenant. These matters are dealt with in detail in the Arbitration Treaties.

If, however, one of the parties alleges a violation of the Security Pact, as regards aggression or as regards

non-fulfilment of the Articles relating to the demilitarized zone, the question goes to the League of Nations.
If the Council finds the allegation is true it notifies its
finding at once to all five of the parties and each undertakes immediately to come to the assistance of the
Power against whom the act complained of has been
committed. Furthermore, if there is a flagrant violation of the Articles of Guarantee or of the Article relating to the demilitarized zone each party undertakes
at once to come to the help of the party against whom
the violation or breach has been directed "as soon as
the Power has satisfied itself that the violation constitutes an unprovoked act of aggression and that immediate action is necessary." The party aggrieved will
bring the matter at once before the Council of the
League which will issue its finding which, if unanimous (except for the party which had engaged in
hostilities), is to be acted on by the parties.

These provisions of Article 4 of the Security Pact
are vital for Great Britain and Italy and it is unfor-
tunate that there is a slight ambiguity in the language
used, at least in the English text. Each party is to come
to the help of the other as soon as "the said Power"
shall have satisfied itself of the act of aggression. No
"Power" had been previously mentioned, but "the
said Power" must refer to each of the guaranteeing
Powers, and not to the Party against whom the act of
aggression has been committed. The position of Great
Britain and Italy is, therefore, that when the League
notifies that there has been a violation of the Security
Pact as regards aggression or non-fulfilment of the
Article relating to the demilitarized zone, they undertake to come immediately to the assistance of the party
aggrieved. If the violation is flagrant they undertake
similarly at once to aid the aggrieved party as soon as,
but not until, they are satisfied that there has been an

unprovoked aggression, and that immediate action is necessary. But there is no need here to wait for a League decision. Though even here the League is to be seized of the matter and will issue its report, which, if unfavourable to the aggressor, will then bring into play the provisions of Article 16 of the Covenant, and the war will be legalized by the League.

There may be less serious violations of the Pact, as where one of the three Powers, without attacking or invading either of the others, refuses to submit a dispute to arbitration or to comply with an award. In this case the other party brings the matter before the Council of the League and the Council shall propose what steps shall be taken and all the parties to the Pact, including Great Britain and Italy, undertake to comply with these proposals.

The Pact in no way derogates from the Treaty of Versailles or the operation of the Dawes scheme, nor does it limit the action of the League under the Covenant in taking steps to safeguard the peace of the world. Its position remains intact, there is no derogation from the Covenant, and this is important in regard to Article 9 of the Pact which states that it imposes no obligation upon any of the British Dominions or upon India unless their Governments signify acceptance. The British Dominions and India are members of the League, and though they may accept no liabilities under the Pact, their liabilities as members of the League remain.

II. THE ARBITRATION TREATIES

The four Arbitration Conventions made by Germany with Belgium, France, Czechoslovakia and Poland respectively contain the machinery for determining the methods by which a peaceful solution shall be attained of all questions which cannot be settled amicably between them. The operative contents of all four treaties are identical.

The preambles of the two sets of treaties are different. The French and Belgian refer merely to their being in fulfilment of the provisions of the Security Pact; the Czechoslovak and Polish treaties refer to the desire of the parties to maintain peace by assuring the peaceful settlement of differences and declare that respect for rights established by treaties or resulting from the Law of Nations is obligatory on international tribunals, and agree that the rights of a state cannot be modified save with its consent. They further state that they consider that sincere observance of the methods of peaceful settlement of international disputes permits of resolving, without recourse to force, questions which may become the cause of division among states, and they have decided to embody in a treaty their common intentions in this respect. This language doubtless covers and conceals the difficulties which were felt on both sides. While Germany was prepared to accept the territorial *status quo* resulting from her western frontiers, she has entered into no such guarantee on the east. The Polish corridor, and the Silesian boundary are by no means acceptable to Germany, and it is the more remarkable that she and her eastern neighbours have agreed that the best way of settling their differences is in the peaceful methods indicated in the treaties. The Czechoslovak and Polish treaties are in all respects verbatim the same as the French and Belgian Arbitration Conventions; the former pair of treaties, however, contains an additional article which was rendered unnecessary in the case of the latter, as its provisions were embodied in the Security Pact. This Article provides that the rights and obligations of the parties as members of the League of Nations remain unaffected by the treaty, whose terms are not to be interpreted as restricting the duty of the League to take whatever action may be deemed wise and effectual to safeguard the peace of the world. There is no difference between the two sets of treaties, apart from their pre-ambles, but the Franco-Belgian set taken in conjunc-tion with the Security Pact reveals the fact that whereas Great Britain, Italy, Germany, France and Belgium respectively guarantee the Rhineland Settle-ment, and the parties agree not to attack each other, there is no such undertaking in the Polish and Czecho-slovak treaties. Both sets of treaties contain the under-taking to refer all matters in dispute to peaceful solution, and this would appear to go as far as was possible.

The methods for settling disputes adopted in all these treaties come under one or other of the following heads: Arbitration tribunals, the Permanent Court of Inter-national Justice, Permanent Conciliation Commission, the Council of the League of Nations.

(i) All disputes of every kind between the parties as to their respective *rights* are, failing settlement by ordinary diplomatic methods, to be submitted either to an arbitral tribunal or to the Permanent Court of International Justice; (ii) All other questions which are found to be insoluble either by diplomacy, arbitration or reference to the Permanent Court are to be sub-mitted to a Permanent Conciliation Commission. If the parties fail to agree within one month after the report of the Conciliation Commission, the question is, at the request of either party, to be brought before the Council of the League in accordance with Article 15 of the Covenant.

The meaning of the term the "rights" of the parties is not specially defined, but it is agreed that it connotes such justiciable questions as those mentioned in Article 13 of the Covenant. The four matters which are declared by this Article as generally suitable for submission to arbitration or judicial settlement are disputes as to

(1) the interpretation of a treaty;

(2) any question of International Law;

(3) the existence of any fact which, if established, would constitute a breach of any international obligation;

(4) the extent and nature of the reparation to be made for any such breach.

The Article leaves the parties to decide, after they have failed to settle a dispute by diplomatic means, what other question, if any, they will remit to arbitration or the Permanent Court. The four examples given are not meant to be exhaustive and it is certain that any question may become "justiciable," to use the term of the Covenant, which the parties choose to make so, if the question is put in a form to which a judicial answer can be given.[1]

This procedure is not applicable to disputes anterior to the Convention, nor to those for which any other form of special procedure is laid down by convention between the parties. The parties may, even as regards questions of a justiciable character, agree to remit them to the Conciliation Commission. Moreover, where a question is one which by the municipal law of one of the parties falls within the competence of its national courts, it cannot be referred to arbitration or judicial determination or the Conciliation Commission until the national court has adjudicated. When it has done so the question will then arise as to whether there has been a denial of justice.

The Permanent Conciliation Commission established by these treaties is not a new method of procedure; the Bryan Arbitration treaties signed at Washington in

[1] Sir Frederick Pollock, *League of Nations* (1922), p. 145.

1914 contained somewhat similar machinery for the purpose of investigating facts and enabling the hot blood of the disputants to cool down—hence the name of "cooling off" treaties which was applied to them. In the Dutch, Swiss, Scandinavian and German schemes for a league of nations an international conciliation or mediation body formed part of the machinery, the Scandinavian scheme being more nearly akin to that adopted at Locarno. As a result of the efforts of the Scandinavian States, Conciliation treaties were concluded in 1920 and the third Assembly of the League in 1922 unanimously adopted a resolution in favour of this procedure and since then all the Northern Powers have entered into Conciliation treaties with each other.

The Permanent Conciliation Commission provided for in the Locarno treaties is composed of five members, one nominated by each of the two parties to the treaty, while the other three, who are all to be of different nationalities, are to be nominated by common accord and the President is to be appointed by the two Governments from among the three. The Commission is to be appointed within three months after the Convention comes into operation, and if the nomination of the three Commissioners is not made within this time or within three months after a vacancy has occurred, the President of the Swiss Confederation, in the absence of other arrangements, is to make the nomination. The details of the work of this Conciliation Commission need not be pursued, but it is provided that its task shall be to elucidate questions in dispute, to collect with that object all necessary information and to endeavour to bring the parties to an agreement. It may inform the parties as to the terms of the settlement which it considers suitable and give a period within which they are to make their decision. It must finish its work within six months from the date when the dispute has been notified to it and at the end of its work it draws up a report stating either that the parties have come to an agreement, and, if necessary, the terms, or that no settlement has been effected. Its proceedings are not to be published without the consent of the parties.

There is one interesting point about the procedure of the Conciliation Commission which links it up with the work of the Hague Conferences, namely that unless there is a unanimous decision to the contrary the Commission is to act in accordance with the provisions for the procedure of International Commissions of Enquiry as laid down in the Hague Convention for the pacific settlement of international disputes, 1907. There is another link with the same Convention, as it is laid down in these treaties that in the case of questions relating to disputes as to their rights, if the parties cannot agree before the Conciliation Commission, they will submit the dispute either to the Permanent Court of International Justice or to the Hague Tribunal under the conditions of the 1907 Convention. If they cannot agree to the terms of reference, either of the parties may bring the matter to the knowledge of the Permanent Court by means of an application.

We have so far been considering the treatment of disputes as to legal "justiciable" questions, rights; *all other questions* are to go to the Permanent Conciliation Commission, and if the two parties have not reached an agreement within a month from the termination of its labours, the question shall, at the request of either party, go before the Council of the League under Article 15, as being a dispute likely to lead to a rupture. The Council can then take the steps indicated, which means that it can either keep the matter in its own hands, submit questions to the Permanent Court, take judicial opinion on special points, refer the

matter to a specially appointed committee or refer it
to the Assembly. If all these methods fail, then the
parties are left face to face, and that will probably
mean war. It may be, however, that the publicity
provided for in the public statements to be made either
by the Covenant or by any member of the League re-
presented on it will have the effect of bringing public
opinion to bear on the dispute so effectively that the
parties may even at such an advanced stage deem it
advisable to compromise their differences.

There is a general provision relating to all kinds of
disputes under which either the Conciliation Commission, the Permanent Court, or the Council of the
League, as the case may be, may lay down within the
shortest time provisional methods to be adopted.
Something in the nature of an Interlocutory Injunction
may be ordered, and the parties agree to accept such
measures and to abstain from all acts likely to have a
repercussion prejudicial to the execution of the decision or arrangements proposed, and from any sort of
action which may aggravate or extend the dispute.

Such are the methods proposed whereby disputes
arising between Germany and France, Belgium, Poland
or Czechoslovakia respectively shall be dealt with. They
appear to embody everything necessary to enable the
parties to reach a pacific settlement if they honestly
desire to do so. The scheme is not completely water-
tight in excluding every possibility of war. As in the
Covenant, so here its possibility is envisaged when in
the last resource the League fails to deal with the
matter in dispute. The problem sought to be solved is
that of international conciliation between states for a
long time very far apart from each other in friendly
feelings. They have shown a willingness to employ a
method whereby justice shall be done to each by
peaceful methods. No document, however solemn,

however perfectly drawn (and it will not be out of place to praise the skill which the draftsmen displayed), can produce a condition of permanent peace between states. If both the parties to a dispute have the will to peace, peace will be preserved.

A striking feature of the Security Pact and of the Arbitration treaties is the absence of any prominence being given to sanctions for their violation. Sanctions there are, force may be used, and the conditions under which it may be resorted to are specified. There is no attempt as in the Geneva Protocol "to close the circle drawn by the Covenant and prohibit all wars of aggression," with an emphasis on the sanctions, but as far as seems possible the circle has been closed on the western, though not on the eastern frontiers of Germany. The objects set forth are to achieve security, encourage arbitration and promote disarmament. There is no attempt to amend the Covenant; the Security Pact is an agreement within its terms. It entirely conforms to the principles of Article 21 of the Covenant which contemplates the making of international agreements such as treaties of arbitration or regional understandings for securing the maintenance of peace. It answers to both of these requirements and the participation in it by Great Britain is on the lines of the treaties entered into during the Franco-Prussian War, when she entered into treaties with France and Germany respectively for the maintenance of the security of Belgium, and undertook to join forces against whichever of the two belligerents violated the terms of the guarantee of 1839.

Great Britain found the provisions of the Geneva Protocol of 1924 inacceptable, but she could not stand aside and adopt a purely negative attitude towards a question which is of vital importance not only to Europe but also to her own position. We were told in

1914 that if only it had been made clear that we should come to the assistance of Belgium or France if they were attacked, the war would not have taken place. There was a tendency to consider the Belgian guarantee as out of date on the principle of "conventio omnis intelligitur rebus sic stantibus." The Security Pact, while it notes the abrogation of the treaties for the neutralization of Belgium, emphasizes the principles on which that neutralization was based, namely, "the necessity of ensuring peace in the area which has so frequently been the scene of European conflicts." We are as much concerned to-day as in 1831 and 1839 to ensure peace in this area and for that purpose we must take risks.

No treaties can ensure permanent peace, but the Security Pact by supplementary guarantees within the framework of the Covenant of the League of Nations and the treaties in force between the parties, and by reason of the goodwill displayed by all the parties who have accepted undertakings which they believe they can reasonably implement, is as strong evidence as can be given of the intention of the Powers concerned to live peaceably with each other. These treaties are therefore an endeavour to place international relations between the Contracting Powers on a new basis, substituting arbitration for war as a means of settling their disputes.

It is not often given to a statesman to see his wishes in regard to so complicated a question as that of the security of Western Europe completely realized in a short time. But if a comparison be made between proposals made in the speech of Mr Austen Chamberlain at the meeting of the Council of the League on March 12th, 1925, and the terms of the Security Pact it will be seen how remarkably they have been fulfilled. He then said:

His Majesty's Government conclude that the best way of dealing with the situation is, with the cooperation of the League, to supplement the Covenant by making special arrangements in order to meet special needs. These objects can be best attained by knitting together the nations most immediately concerned, and whose differences might lead to a renewal of strife, by means of treaties framed with the sole object of maintaining, as between themselves, an unbroken peace. Within its limits no quicker remedy for our present ills can easily be found, nor any surer safeguard against future calamities.

This, it is hoped, will be effected by the Locarno treaties.

We have been warned against taking the Locarno settlement as the end of a process of conciliation, and advised that it must be looked on rather as a beginning. The spirit which enabled the parties to reach a conclusion must be continued in regard to the future and extended to Eastern Europe where the greatest danger, in my opinion, exists, of a breach of the peace of Europe. It follows that one important result expected is the diminution of armaments, and so far as France and Germany are concerned there seems no reason why the vast expenditure of France should not at once be diminished. But for Great Britain what is the position? We are guarantors and we must be in a position to fulfil our guarantee. We have no guarantees under the Pact and are left to look after our own safety. Our Navy, Army and Air Forces are still necessary to enable us to fulfil our guarantees and for the protection of our Island and Empire and for the feeding of our people. If disarmament follows on Locarno, it must be of such a type as will enable us to feel that there is no grave menace for which we have to be always prepared. The real test as to whether the Locarno treaties have succeeded in their object will be afforded by the state of the armaments of European states in the next few years. If a great diminution is shown, well and good; if not, it will be evident that the security aimed at has not been felt to be achieved.

The British Guarantee of the western frontier, in effect, has made the Rhine the boundary of Great Britain. We have entered into a guarantee to go to war if it is violated and it is putting it within the power of France, Germany and Belgium to say when we shall have to go to war on the Continent. This is, of course, the practical effect of any treaty of guarantee, but the Locarno treaties are much more explicit than the guarantees of Belgium under the treaties of 1831 and 1839. As regards the eastern frontiers we give no such guarantees but it is not difficult to conceive situations in which we might ultimately be involved in case Russia attacked Poland or *vice versa*, and Germany took advantage of the occasion to endeavour to get back some of her lost eastern territory, while France was called on to aid Poland. If such a case occurred the question of the violation of the western frontier would certainly be a matter for the independent judgment of Great Britain.

Time did not permit of an Empire Delegation taking part in the Conference, and none of the Dominions nor India has acceded to the Locarno treaties. But from the point of view of International Law I think that if Great Britain should go to war to fulfil her obligations under them, the whole of the British Empire would be in a state of war. How much assistance we could hope to get from the Dominions would undoubtedly depend on the nature of the war, as in 1914. The Imperial Conference of 1926 approved "of the manner in which the negotiations had been conducted" and congratulated "His Majesty's Government in Great Britain on its share in this successful contribution toward the promotion of the peace of the world."[1]

[1] See H. Duncan Hall in *The British Commonwealth of Nations*, World Peace Foundation Pamphlets, vol. x, No. 6 (1927), p. 613.

VIII

THE LAW OF NATIONS AND THE WAR OF 1914[1]

THE German Chancellor, in his speech in the Reichstag on August 4th, 1914, said: "Gentlemen, we are now in a state of necessity, and necessity knows no law. Our troops have occupied Luxemburg, and perhaps are already on Belgian soil. Gentlemen, this is contrary to the dictates of International Law." We start, then, with a clear admission that Germany commenced the present war with a violation of the Law of Nations by entering the territory of two states the permanent neutrality of which had been guaranteed by all the Great Powers of Europe, including Germany herself. The entry of German troops into Luxemburg and Belgium was not only a violation of the treaties guaranteeing their neutrality, but was contrary to Article 2 of the Fifth Hague Convention of 1907, which forbids belligerents to move across the territory of a neutral Power troops or convoys either of munitions of war or of supplies. We might, I think, add to the violation of treaties and of the common Law of Nations the further acts of entering French territory with armed forces, and so commencing hostilities, without any previous ultimatum to France or without any previous declaration of war, in accordance with the Third Convention signed at the Hague in 1907 by Germany and France, and subsequently ratified by both Powers.[2] There is this further point that immediately war was declared Germany proceeded to lay mines in the

[1] A lecture delivered at the London School of Economics and Political Science on October 8th, 1914. Published in the *Oxford Pamphlets*, 1914.

[2] There appears to be a doubt as to this, but see Parl. Papers, Misc. No. 10 (1915), 234.

North Sea, in waters open to the traffic of all the nations of the world, and, in particular, waters in which thousands of fishermen of all the northern states of Europe earn their livelihood, and from which they provide food for millions of their fellow-countrymen.

But I prefer to deal first with the violation of International Law, which is admitted by the highest official of the German Empire, and to examine the excuse which he offers for it. The defence is necessity.

The German doctrine of Necessity put forward by Dr von Bethmann-Hollweg is no new doctrine; it is to be found in the writings of several German international lawyers and is a military maxim they have adopted. It is worth while spending a little time in examining the principle which, by making necessity a rule instead of an exception, would, if accepted, result in an annihilation of the laws of war, written and unwritten. This doctrine is stated by one German writer in the following terms:

A violation of the laws of war must be regarded as not having taken place if the military operation is necessary for the preservation of the troops or the averting of a danger that threatens them and cannot be averted in any other way, or even if it is advantageous either for the effectual carrying out of a military enterprise not inadmissible in itself or the securing of its success.[1]

"The laws of war cease to be binding," says another authority, Lueder, "when the circumstances are such that the attainment of the object of the war and the escape from extreme danger would be hindered by observing the limitations imposed by the laws of war."[2]

These views are in accordance with a German military maxim, *Kriegsräson geht vor Kriegsmanier*—"Necessity in war overrules the manner of warfare." It is justified by Lueder on the ground that commanders will act on it

[1] Meurer, cited by H. Wehberg, *Capture in War*, p. 4.
[2] Lueder, in *Holtzendorff's Handbuch*, p. 255.

whatever is laid down. "It ought to happen because it must happen, that is, because the course of no war will in such extreme cases be hindered and allow itself to end in defeat, perhaps in ruin, in order not to violate formal law," thereby, as Professor Westlake says, reducing law from a controlling to a registering agency.[1] The German theory introduces a new meaning of the term "necessity" different from that which finds acceptance in the Hague Conventions. These Conventions everywhere recognize that circumstances may occur when a commander finds himself unable to comply with the strict letter of their provisions. It was with a view of diminishing the evils of war, "so far as military necessities permit," that the Powers adopted the regulations for land warfare. But the content of this term as it is used therein may be understood from the preamble to the Convention, which admits the incompleteness of the Code and declares that in cases not included the populations and belligerents remain under the protection and rule of the principles of the Law of Nations, as they result from the usages established between civilized nations, from the laws of humanity and the requirements of the public conscience. The ordinary laws of war, with the occasional exceptions due to military necessity, are acknowledged by the German authorities, but on them they superimpose their own theory of *Kriegsräson*, by virtue of which they may all be cast to the winds. "It is not, then," as Westlake says, "a question of necessity of war, but of necessity of success"—a very different thing, and results, as he points out, in this, that "the true instructions to be given by a state to its generals are: Succeed—by war according to its laws, if you can—but at all events, and in any way, succeed." "Of conduct suitable to each instruction," he adds—and the words had surely a

[1] *International Law, War*, p. 127.

prophetic ring—"it may be expected that human nature will not fail to produce examples."[1]

The German doctrine is subversive of all the laws of warfare which have grown up during the past century in the interests of non-belligerents and of the combatants themselves: it leaves these rules mere discretionary ideals to be obeyed or broken according to the will of a government or commander determined to win by any means and at any costs.

"We are in a state of necessity," said the German Chancellor in regard to the violation of the neutrality of Belgium, but it was a necessity of the kind contemplated by the German maxim. It was a "necessity" prepared by the Germans themselves ten years ago! There is clear and irrefutable evidence that the German move was no sudden manœuvre called for by the anticipated violation of Belgian territory by France. The plan of campaign had been settled by the general staff as long ago as 1904; strategic railways were built for the purpose, the plan was set forth in a memorandum of General von Schlieffen and sanctioned by the German Emperor in 1909. It was no secret, it had been published.[2]

To justify the violation of the territory of a friendly state, said the Government of the United States in 1838—and their view was accepted by our own Government—it is needful "to show a necessity of self-defence, instant, overwhelming, leaving no choice of means and no moment for deliberation." Such a necessity as this the Germans could not show. From whatever point of view we examine the necessity for the attack on Belgium, the evidence of treachery, and complete and callous disregard for international obligations by Germany, is overwhelming.

[1] *Op. cit.* p. 128. See also L. Oppenheim, *International Law, War*, § 69; T. E. Holland, *War on Land*, p. 12.
[2] See *Spectator*, September 19th, 1914.

There is in German law a defence allowed in certain cases which are covered by the term *Notwehr*, a term which I understand cannot be properly translated. It is—according to Article 53 of the German Criminal Code—"such defence as is necessary to avert an immediate unlawful attack on oneself or another." It is not, strictly speaking, identical with self-defence or self-preservation, but approximates to it. The meaning of the speech of Dr von Bethmann-Hollweg seems to be clearly this: We have guaranteed the neutrality and inviolability of these two small states; we find that the observance of the guarantee would inconvenience us in a course of action on which we have decided; it is therefore necessary for us to ignore this word "neutrality," and to disregard this "scrap of paper," for if we do not, France will. Self-preservation stands as the first law of individuals and states; our existence may be irreparably threatened unless we take this step, therefore International Law must on an occasion such as this be broken.

I take, then, the German standpoint for the moment— let us assume the German Chancellor had consulted some English text-book on International Law to see what was said there on the subject of self-preservation.

"The right of self-preservation," says Hall, "in some cases justifies the commission of acts of violence against a friendly or neutral State, when from its position and resources it is capable of being made use of to dangerous effect by an enemy, when there is a known intention on his part so to make use of it, and when, if he is not forestalled, it is almost certain that he will succeed, either through the helplessness of the country or by means of intrigues with a party within it."[1]

Grotius, also, the founder of the science of modern International Law, allows the occupation of neutral territory in certain cases under his law of necessity.

[1] *International Law*, § 85.

Hall, however, to illustrate his proposition, discusses the British operations against Denmark, and the bombardment of Copenhagen, in 1807.

Can these violations of Luxemburg and Belgium be in any degree compared with the British action in 1807? In July 1807 Canning received information that, by secret articles of the Treaty of Tilsit, Denmark, Sweden, and Portugal were to be compelled by France and Russia to join in the war against Great Britain, thereby largely increasing the French fleet. Napoleon was in great need of ships for his proposed invasion of England. Denmark was certainly powerless to resist the demands of France, the possession of her fleet would have been of the greatest assistance to Napoleon, and would have provided him with the means of making a descent on the British coasts. Such were the facts which came to Canning's knowledge, and it was evident to his Government that Napoleon had to be forestalled. He therefore instructed his agent to demand from Denmark an explanation of their policy, a treaty of alliance with Great Britain, and the deposit of the Danish fleet. Denmark was offered the most solemn pledge that if the British demand was complied with every ship would, at the conclusion of the general peace, be restored to her "in the same condition and state of equipment as when received under the British flag." Denmark, acting within her undoubted right, treated the British demand as a hostile act, and only after the bombardment of Copenhagen did the Danes decide to surrender their fleet. This high-handed proceeding of Great Britain against a small state has naturally been severely criticized, and is condemned by many continental writers. I am unable myself to join in this condemnation. I agree with Hall that the occurrence is a matter for extreme regret, but that "the emergency was one which gave good reason for the general line of conduct of the English Government." That being so, I have to ask whether the action of Germany can be justified for similar reasons.

In 1807, Great Britain had been at war with France for more than ten years. Napoleon had overthrown Austria, crushed Prussia, and for the moment obtained the alliance of Russia. His methods were severe and unscrupulous. It was known that he would be deterred by nothing which stood in the way of the achievement of the object dearest to his heart—the overthrow of Great Britain. It is now held that Canning acted on imperfect evidence, but the information he received was well in accord with the plans which Napoleon might have been expected to form, and Canning took a step which to the other neutral Powers seemed a violation of the principles of neutrality, which it must be remembered were not so well established then as now. But even so, England's proceeding was at the time "regarded as little better than piratical," and the attack on Denmark was followed by a loss of reputation which for the moment outweighed the material gain to her navy.[1] We know to-day more of the inner diplomacy which caused Canning to take this step than was known to his contemporaries, and the circumstances surrounding the seizure of the Danish fleet and the violation of Denmark's neutrality by Great Britain are, I submit, far removed from comparison with the outbreak of the present war.

To-day, Great Britain, Germany, and Russia, at the very outset of the war, issued their respective cases to the world; they entered their pleadings before the court of the public opinion of the nations. It is, therefore, no question here of secret treaties, mutilated dispatches, and imperfect information. All the Powers concerned have made public the evidence on which they rely for

[1] *Camb. Mod. Hist.* vol. IX, p. 298.

a justification of their proceedings. If we accept Hall's statement of the law and apply it to the German invasion of Luxemburg and Belgium, Germany, to obtain exoneration on the ground of self-preservation, would have to prove that there was clear evidence of the intention of her prospective enemy, France, to march across the territory of Belgium in order to gain a strategic advantage in an attack upon her territory, and that Belgium's condition rendered her too weak to resist such a violation of her neutrality by France. On these points the evidence against the German contention is clear. Denmark, in 1807, had no strong Power to whom to turn for defence against Napoleon, she lay at his mercy; but Belgium was not dependent solely on her own strength. Germany had in 1870 received striking proof that England would under no circumstances tolerate a violation of Belgian neutrality, for at the outset of the Franco-German War she entered into identical treaties with both belligerents, whereby she undertook to co-operate with either of them against the other in defence of Belgium, if either violated its territory. But Germany had much more recent evidence of a like nature. On July 31st Great Britain asked France and Germany for engagements to respect the neutrality of Belgium. France at once gave the undertaking; Germany replied in evasive terms. Germany therefore had the clear and definite promise of France not to violate Belgian territory in case of war; she had ample evidence that Belgium herself and Great Britain as her guarantor would resist any violation of her neutrality by France. The case against Germany is further strengthened by a statement of the Belgian Minister of War, which appeared in *The Times* of September 30th, 1914. The whole paragraph is as follows:

The German Press has been attempting to persuade the public that if Germany herself had not violated Belgian neutrality,

France or Great Britain would have done so. It has declared that French and British troops had marched into Belgium before the outbreak of war. We have received from the Belgian Minister of War an official statement which denies absolutely these allegations. It declares, on the one hand, that "before August 3 not a single French soldier had set foot on Belgian territory," and, again, "it is untrue that on August 4 there was a single English soldier in Belgium."

It adds:

For long past Great Britain knew that the Belgian Army would oppose by force a "preventive" disembarcation of British troops in Belgium. The Belgian Government did not hesitate at the time of the Agadir crisis to warn foreign Ambassadors, in terms which could not be misunderstood, of its formal intention to compel respect for the neutrality of Belgium by every means at its disposal, and against attempts upon it from any and every quarter.

The comparison between Belgium in 1914 and Denmark in 1807 breaks down on every point.

The position of Great Britain in the great European war is different from that of her allies. Germany declared war against Russia on August 1st and against France on August 3rd, though war between Russia and Austria-Hungary—for we must remember that the latter is, ostensibly at any rate, the prime cause of the whole catastrophe—did not commence till August 6th. As against Russia and France, Germany was the aggressor. But the Declaration of War, or rather the ultimatum with a conditional declaration of war, was made by Great Britain to Germany on August 4th, and a state of war commenced as from 11 p.m. on that day. Technically Great Britain took the aggressive against Germany. International Law, unlike municipal laws, is destitute of a judiciary; there is no legal court before which nations can be arraigned, it leaves it to them to decide when they must resort to force to support their demands. It cannot determine the various causes for which war may justly be waged, but it can lay down that under given circumstances there has been a violation of a rule of International Law or international obligations. Whether such violations are of a sufficiently grave character to justify resort to war is a matter for international morality, but, as I pointed out in an inaugural lecture in this place only just three years ago, situations sometimes arise in which the acceptance of peace would be felt by a nation to be an intolerable humiliation, and when a state could have no alternative but war to preserve its legitimate self-respect and dignity.[1] War is sometimes the only means by which the liberty of a people may be preserved or obtained. The Chancellor of the Exchequer (Mr D. Lloyd George), in his famous Mansion House speech during the Agadir crisis in 1911, emphasized the fact that Great Britain had more than once in the past redeemed continental nations from overwhelming disaster and even from national extinction. That is the position to-day.

"We are at war to-day," said the German Chancellor in the now historic interview with Sir Edward Goschen in Berlin on August 4th, "just for a word—'neutrality,' a word which in war time has so often been disregarded —just for a scrap of paper." But this scrap of paper represents the very fundamentals on which the Law of Nations is based. It represents a treaty of guarantee entered into by the Great Powers of Europe for a small state whose position as a buffer between two Great Powers, France and Germany, would necessarily have been precarious without a guarantee of the Powers. It represents an obligation "which," as the Prime Minister has said, "if it had been entered into between private persons in the ordinary concerns of life, would have

[1] *War and the Private Citizen*, p. 8.

been regarded as an obligation not only of law but of honour, which no self-respecting man could possibly have repudiated." The manner in which the violation of a solemn pledge is viewed by the parties to this dispute is the measure of the spiritual and moral forces on both sides; war becomes a struggle between these forces, and as Clausewitz, perhaps the greatest of all writers on military strategy, says, "in war such a struggle is the centre of all."[1]

Underlying the observations made by the German Chancellor, both in his interviews with the British Ambassador and in his speech in the Reichstag, there is a principle which, if accepted, would shatter not only the whole fabric of the Public Law of Europe but of Public International Law in general. This principle, too, is the groundwork of the basis of the policy which has been systematically pursued by both Austria and Germany since the former with the latter's assistance in 1908 tore to shreds a large part of the Treaty of Berlin without the assent of their co-signatories, and entered on the path which led direct to the Austrian ultimatum to Serbia, an ultimatum launched with the connivance of Germany by a Great Power which denied to the smaller the elementary rights of an independent sovereign state. Ever since the close of the Russo-Japanese War in 1905, when the balance of power in Europe was for the time disturbed to the advantage of the Powers forming the Triple Alliance, Germany and Austria have acted in defiance of the principles which normally underlie the whole code and system of international intercourse. The visit of the German Emperor to Tangier in 1905, the Congress of Algeciras, the annexation of Bosnia and Herzegovina in 1908, the visit of the *Panther* to Agadir in 1911, were all steps downward from the standard of international ethic which

[1] See S. L. Murray, *The Reality of War*, p. 13.

deems force to be but the last resort of nations, and only to be appealed to when diplomacy has failed. These acts afford evidence of the application of the doctrine that war is "politics par excellence," and lead direct to the enunciation of the principle that "might is right"; that the Society of States or Family of Nations based upon equal justice and legal equality before the Law of Nations is a useless and unworkable fiction; that there is no room in the world for International Law to regulate the mutual intercourse of sovereign independent states. They show the increasing insistence on the part of Germany for a dominating and supreme control in European politics.

For what are the presuppositions on which International Law is based? They are the principles (advanced by Grotius in 1625, acknowledged by the Peace of Westphalia in 1648, and extended and applied by subsequent generations of statesmen and jurists) that the independent sovereign Powers of the civilized world form a Family or *Societas*; that all the mutual intercourse of these Powers is conducted under, and their relations to each other are governed by, rules which they regard as being binding on themselves with a force comparable in nature and degree to that binding the conscientious person to obey the laws of his country. Further, that, notwithstanding the great differences which exist in size, population, wealth, and other qualities, all are, as subjects of the Law of Nations, equal. It is not contended that as regards the influence which accompanies physical strength or a highly developed civilization all states are or ever will be equal to each other, but that their equality is a legal consequence of their independence.[1] Further, it follows that all these independent states have a moral nature, that the statesmen who conduct their business of mutual

[1] The doctrine of equality is more fully dealt with, *antea*, pp. 26, 40.

intercourse must conform to certain ethical standards, that they are actuated by a sense of right, and feel themselves under an obligation to act in accordance with it, and therefore that good faith is predicated of all their dealings. Consequently, the contracts or treaties which states make with each other they recognize as binding, and only to be terminated according to accepted rules. When several states are parties to the same transaction, any modification must be made with the assent of all. "We cannot recognize the right of any Power or state to alter an international treaty without the consent of the other parties to it," said Sir Edward Grey on October 7th, 1908, on the occasion of the annexation of Bosnia and Herzegovina by Austria, "because if it is to become the practice in foreign politics that any single Power or state can at will make abrupt violations of international treaties you will undermine public confidence with all of us."

The treaties, the breach of which Germany acknowledges, are Treaties of Guarantee, and it must be admitted that treaties of this nature have not always been enforced by the guarantors by force of arms. The interests of the guaranteeing states have always been the determining factor in their political action. All treaties of this character are made for particular political purposes, and that fact has perhaps been one of the reasons why statesmen, and text-writers dealing with the acts of statesmen, have often pointed out their weakness. Some of the guarantors must of necessity nearly always be unable to interpose by force in defence of a guaranteed state, and must limit their aid to the exercise of their influence on behalf of a state whose independence, integrity, or neutrality they have guaranteed. The cynical view of Frederick the Great that "All guarantees are like filigree work, made rather to please the eye than to be of use" reads very like the view of the

German Chancellor. Gentz takes a different view:
"I know well," he says, "that guarantees on paper are
feeble means of defence; however, one would be wrong
to neglect them, for they furnish, at least to those who
wish to do their duty and fulfil their engagements, a
legal means of action when circumstances call them to
it." "However," says Geffcken, a distinguished German writer who quotes this authority, "the interest of
the guarantor will always be a great weight in the
balance. The guarantees of the neutrality of Belgium
and of Switzerland have stood the test, that of the
integrity of Turkey has not."[1] This statement of Gentz
is important: "They furnish to those who wish to do
their duty and fulfil their engagements a legal means of
action when circumstances call them to it." This is the
British position to-day. We have interposed to defend
a state whose neutrality we have guaranteed; we step
in, and do our duty by so doing; we take part in the war
by right; it is a war in defence of justice and good faith
in international dealing; it is a fulfilment of a legal
engagement.

It is contended, however, with some authority, that
treaties which in their origin and from their nature
were clearly intended by the contracting Powers to be
perpetual are all entered into on the tacit condition
known as *rebus sic stantibus*, that is, if vital changes in
circumstances occur, the parties shall be exonerated
from any further compliance with their terms. In
other words, "they were concluded in and by reason
of special circumstances, and when those circumstances
disappear there arises a right to have them rescinded."[2]
The German Chancellor did not take this ground,
though his fellow-countryman Bernhardi does in reference to the treaty guaranteeing Belgium's neutrality.

[1] A. G. Heffter, *Das europäische Völkerrecht der Gegenwart* (ed.
F. H. Geffcken), § 97.   [2] J. Westlake, *Peace*, p. 295.

Dr von Bethmann-Hollweg distinctly recognized the neutrality of Belgium and Luxemburg, and in his overtures to Belgium promised to restore her condition if she accepted his terms for the violation of her territory. Belgium rejected the overtures, and Great Britain, recognizing both the fundamental principle of *pacta servanda sunt*—treaties must be kept, and the other doctrine of *rebus sic stantibus*—circumstances have not changed, took the only step open to her and declared war on Germany.

But we may ask, Have the circumstances changed since the Treaty of Guarantee was entered into? Would not Germany be justified in appealing to the doctrine of *rebus sic stantibus*? This involves the further question, What led to the treaties whereby Belgium's neutrality was guaranteed, and what is the special interest which calls for British intervention in the war? Why did Great Britain in 1831 and again in 1839 solemnly pledge herself to a treaty which her statesmen must have foreseen would at some time, sooner or later, lead to our having once again to take part in a war on the Continent of Europe? The answer to this question brings us to a doctrine which, if not a fundamental principle of International Law, is nevertheless, in one form or another, "a political principle indispensable to the existence of International Law in its present condition."[1] I mean the need for the maintenance of a balance of power among the states of Europe.

In 1813 the Powers allied to overthrow Napoleon, and with a view to limiting the power of France and its expansion to the north, and having, as they subsequently stated in a protocol of December 20th, 1830, "the object in view of forming a just equilibrium in Europe, and assuring the maintenance of the general peace,"[2]

[1] L. Oppenheim, *Peace*, § 136.
[2] C. Dupuis, *Le principe d'équilibre*, p. 217.

they joined the Belgian provinces which had hitherto formed part of the Austrian dominions to Holland. This union was subsequently confirmed in 1815 by the Congress of Vienna, and the newly-established kingdom of the United Netherlands was declared neutral by the Powers party to that Treaty. This arrangement, which neglected all the sentiments of language and religion and the traditional hostility of the Belgians and Dutch, was destined to fail, as all artificial attempts to work out a mathematical balance of forces among the nations must, and in 1830 a revolution broke out in Belgium. The Dutch were expelled, the Powers which had established the new kingdom in 1815 met in conference, and, after lengthy and dangerous delays, they were able to solve in a peaceful way, under circumstances peculiarly difficult, a singularly complicated problem. The kingdom of Belgium was established, it was to form an independent and perpetually neutral state, it was bound to observe such neutrality towards all other states (Art. 7). This was provided by the Treaty of London of 1831, and finally ratified by the Treaty of London of 1839, to which Great Britain, France, Austria, Prussia, and Russia were parties. The object of the Powers first in creating the United Netherlands, then in creating the kingdom of Belgium, and again, in 1867, in neutralizing the Grand Duchy of Luxemburg, was to provide for the continued existence of these small states as buffers between adjacent Great Powers which, apart from such guarantee, might be tempted to acts of aggression against them to the detriment of the peace of Europe. The neutralization of Belgium was undoubtedly inspired by the fear which Europe had of seeing Belgium united with France, to the detriment of the balance of power.

There is, I venture to think, considerable misunderstanding of the meaning of this expression, and it is associated in some minds with "an accompanying dis-regard of all moral obligations," and characterized as bringing "disgrace upon international politics."[1] The significance attached to a balance of power has varied from time to time, but in one form or another it is as old as the beginnings of international politics. It took the form at one time of an insistence on the maintenance of the condition of the map of Europe as prepared by some international congress, first the Peace of West-phalia, later the Treaty of Utrecht of 1713, in which the expression is used for the first time—and many wars were waged with the avowed object of preventing any change. It has played a part in our own legislation; for the Army Act in its preamble states that among the reasons for the maintenance of a standing army in time of peace is the balance of power. The doctrine in its form of the maintenance of the *status quo* has been strongly opposed by many statesmen and writers, who have laid stress on the manifold abuses to which the application of the theory has led, for it has undoubtedly been used in the past to hinder the legitimate progress and increase of states. It was an application of one view of this doctrine that led to the iniquitous de-struction, by a combination of the more powerful, of smaller states which were even subdivided and split up at congresses of the Great Powers, so as to be thrown into the balance of the European equilibrium. It was seen at its worst in the policy of Napoleon III, and his demands for compensation when any of his neighbours received any accession of strength. Such a theory of the balance of power is I think worthy of condemna-tion. But the doctrine in the form in which it is supported by statesmen and publicists to-day has a meaning which is vital to the existence of the Family of

[1] Letter of the Bishop of Hereford in *The Times*, August 12, 1914.

Nations, and is intimately bound up with the principle of self-preservation and independence. It was the application of this principle which in our own history was responsible for the alliance of Queen Elizabeth with our rivals the Dutch against Philip II of Spain; it was in furtherance of its maintenance that we fought Louis XIV, that Wellington fought in the Peninsula, and Nelson at Trafalgar, and that the allies triumphed at Waterloo. It was definitely stated in the preamble to the Treaty of March 12th, 1854, between France and England, that it was to maintain the balance of power that the allies in the Crimean War sought to check the aggrandizement of Russia. The reason why some form of the balance of power, as I understand it, must lie at the root of the modern Law of Nations arises from the fact that it comes into play when one of the members of the great international society so far forgets its social obligations as to engage in a course of action endangering the vital interests of the whole society. Dr Lawrence puts the position in words with which I agree, when he says:

If, therefore, a powerful state frequently endeavours to impose its will on others, and becomes an arrogant dictator when it ought to be content with a fair share of influence and leadership, those who find their remonstrances disregarded and their rights ignored perform a valuable service to the whole community when they resort to force in order to reduce the aggressor to its proper position. As the duty of self-preservation justifies intervention to ward off imminent danger to national life or honour, so the duty of preserving international society justifies intervention to bring to an end conduct that imperils the existence or healthful order of that society....The balance of power, understood in the sense just indicated, ought to be maintained not in Europe only, but in all quarters of the globe.[1]

This, it may be said, is putting the case from the point of view of an English writer, but appeal for support can

[1] *International Law*, p. 133.

successfully be made to French and other continental writers.[1]

Geffcken's note to his edition of Heffter's *Europäisches Völkerrecht*, a German work of deservedly high repute, emphasizes the fact that there is no possible security for the international life when one state has over the others so great a preponderance as to allow it to threaten their liberty of action, their interests, and their integrity. The desire even to obtain such a predominating position is, he holds, itself to be condemned; the fear alone of a common resistance by the other nations ought to be sufficiently strong to hold such aspirations in check. Dealing in this connection with the position of the smaller states of the world, Geffcken points out that it is essentially one of the tasks of the balance of power rightly understood to watch over the preservation of the small states, provided they are able to fulfil the conditions bound up with independence; for the more the small states are absorbed by the great, the more frequent will collisions between the latter occur. As for the idea put forward by Lasson that the small states are a perpetual danger to peace, the apple of discord between the Powers, and the natural causes and certain theatres of war, he pertinently asks when have Holland, Belgium, or Switzerland ever fomented discord among neighbouring states. All their interests are bound up with the maintenance of peace.[2] We may go further, for the small states, and especially the neutralized states of Belgium and Switzerland, have played, during the nineteenth century, an invaluable part in the life of the Family of Nations, and have done much for the advancement of International Law. We recall that the capital of Holland has been the scene of the Hague Conferences, and is the seat of the International Court of Arbitration, that Brussels and Berne are the centres

[1] See Despagnet's *Droit International*, § 180.   [2] *Op. cit.* § 5.

of nearly all the international organizations which
the increasing economic complexities of modern life
have brought into being. We remember that various
international conferences have met in the capitals of
these states, that the conventions for the care of the
sick and wounded of the armies in the field were signed
at Geneva, and that they owe their initiative to
Switzerland.

We are apt to lose sight of the fact that the immediate
cause of this great European War lies in the extraordinary demands made by Austria-Hungary on Serbia.
The ostensible reasons for Austria's ultimatum were
the circumstances surrounding the assassination of
the Archduke Francis Ferdinand and his consort at
Sarajevo in June of the present year. The Serbian
Government was charged with being cognizant of the
conspiracy and the plot which resulted in the assassination of the Austrian heir apparent. But so far the
allegation has not been proved, and we have had evidence—as in the Friedjung trial—of the capacity of
Austrian officials to forge such documents as may be
necessary to sustain a serious political charge. Be that
as it may, the answer of Serbia accepted the demands
of Austria with some qualification in all but two points,
and these she was prepared to leave to the arbitrament
of the Hague Arbitration Tribunal. Serbia, again, is an
example of a small state standing in the way of the ambitions of a Great Power, and making a valiant defence
of her liberties. She bars the advance of Austria to the
Aegean, she blocks the way of the Austro-German movement to control the Balkans, she impedes the desires of
the Germanic world for an expansion which would
include the control of the Dardanelles, Asia Minor, the
Euphrates valley, and the sea routes to Egypt and
India. Just as England could not be a passive spectator
of the overthrow of Belgium, so Russia, for equally

powerful reasons, could not silently witness the subjugation and annihilation of a small adjacent Slav Power by her ambitious Teutonic neighbours. In the latter case, especially, the strong sentiment of nationality, which has been the chief mainspring of the political movements in Europe during the nineteenth century, operated as forcibly as any desire for the maintenance of the European equilibrium. But though the immediate cause of the present war may be put down to Austria's menaces to Serbia, every day that elapses, every new diplomatic disclosure that is made, points to a deeper and more widely rooted cause—namely the increasing domination of Europe by the German Empire. I have already referred to the stages in her movement towards the assertion of a predominance in Europe. Even had Germany left intact the territory of Belgium and Holland, and begun war by an invasion of France, England would, in my opinion, have been bound in the interest of self-preservation to have stepped in and supported France. "When a state remains a passive spectator of the complete overthrow of the balance of power which it could have prevented, it loses not only its political prestige, but it has to suffer the disastrous consequences of such non-intervention." This is the opinion of Professor Geffcken on the abstract question;[1] it is the opinion of Admiral Mahan in relation to the attitude of Great Britain in the present war.[2]

The policy of non-intervention is, as a general rule, sound, and should be the normal guide for pacific statesmen, but it is apt at times to be very shortsighted. When a state from motives of selfishness, merely because it does not appear at the time that it is in any danger itself from the aggression of one state

[1] Note to Heffter, § 5.
[2] See *The Times*, August 5th, 1914.

against another, allows the weaker state to be crippled or crushed, the consequence of such a policy is apt to weigh heavily on it: it has to pay in the long run a heavy price for assuming a position of splendid isolation. Prussia, in 1805, stood aside and allowed Napoleon to overthrow Austria, but her own turn came next year in the crushing defeat at Jena and the humiliating terms of the Treaty of Tilsit. France, again, in 1866, stood aside and witnessed the overthrow of Austria, thereby allowing Germany to complete the preparations which led to her defeat in 1870. The victory of Germany, as consecrated by the terms of the Treaty of Frankfort, with the annexation of Alsace-Lorraine against the passionate protests of the inhabitants, involved the whole of Europe in constantly growing expenditure for the maintenance of huge armaments, which have been an incalculable drain on the wealth of the world and a standing menace to its peace.

The maintenance of the balance of power, as I understand it, and as I have endeavoured to describe it, as a corollary of the doctrine of self-preservation of states, thus becomes in my opinion essential to liberty— liberty of states to live their own lives, to develop themselves on their own lines; liberty for every state to pursue its own ideals of excellence without rivalry or contempt for others. This freedom is threatened with overthrow and annihilation when any one state presumes to act as the arrogant dictator of other members of the Family of Nations, and seeks to impose by force of arms its ideals of culture and civilization on all and sundry, to the detriment of their personalities and self-development. We have lived through an era of nearly half a century of aggressive militarism; we have as a result witnessed a growing disregard for the sanctity of international obligations, and even for the decencies of international comity. "Shining armour," "mailed fists," and swords rattling in their scabbards have appeared to support breaches of international obligations, and demands for economic compensation from pacific nations. The Concert of Europe broke down at the critical moment. A crisis has been reached in the development of the civilization of Europe, and on its solution depends the advance or retrogression of all the ideals which free and self-governing peoples hold most dear, both in their own internal organization and in their future international relations. Liberty and freedom of action can only come to individuals in the truest sense when these are governed and regulated by law; and the Law of Nations, self-imposed and lacking in a central executive and administrative authority, must increasingly provide and safeguard the means of self-realization and equality of opportunity of its members. States must always remain unequal in size, power, and influence; but the maintenance of the doctrine that all the members of the international society are nevertheless entitled to equal mutual consideration, has largely contributed in the past to the happiness of mankind, "though it is constantly threatened by the tendencies of each successive age."[1] The doctrine of equality witnesses to the influence of idealism in the development of the Law of Nations, but that law is still far from being in a position to give full effect to the principle. What will be the changes, if any, in the organization and rules for intercourse of the Family of Nations at the close of the present war is a matter for speculation by theorists, and will be one for practical solution by statesmen and diplomatists. That the present will be the last war in the history of the world no one who takes a wide view of history will be likely to affirm; that it should make wars increasingly difficult and rare in the future is an aspiration with

[1] H. S. Maine, *Ancient Law*, p. 101.

which all will concur. "Until there is established some form of international police power, competent and willing to prevent violence as between nations," breaches of the Law of Nations will have to be put down by force by individual states or combinations of states; and an era of disarmament is not, in my opinion, yet in sight, though the burden may, I hope, be lightened. After each great upheaval of the nations such as we are witnessing to-day, such as was witnessed in the ages of the Wars of the Reformation, of Louis XIV and of Napoleon, proposals for an era of perpetual peace have always been put forward: the projects of Henry IV and Sully, of Saint-Pierre, Rousseau, Bentham, and Sieyès bear witness to the ardent desires of statesmen and philanthropists for a speedy realization of the time when the Millennium shall be reached. Unfortunately, they also bear witness to the futility of man's endeavour to hasten the slow grinding of the wheels of God.

We all of us chafe at times at the want of progress which society seems to be making by the ordinary means of development, and long for some stupendous *coup* by which the wrongs of men may be righted and injustice be for ever prevented. The infallible lesson which the history of the past centuries teaches us is the certain though sometimes slow punishment which awaits the persistent wrong-doer, the inevitable retribution which falls upon the breaker of the laws of God and nations. The criminal state is arraigned at the bar of humanity, and history records its sentence.

We do well to cherish high ideals for the future of international relations, but it is necessary that these ideals should be those not of one state only but of all the members of the international society. The Law of Nations can only progress and develop as the ethical standard of each state is steadily elevated. The death-blow must be given everywhere to the anarchical doctrine that might is right, that war is a necessity to political idealism and politics *par excellence*, instead of being the evidence of the failure of diplomacy and the last resort in case of the clash of irreconcilable national ideals. If the present war results in the firmer acceptance of the sanctity of treaties, the complete destruction of the German doctrine of necessity justifying any and every breach of the laws of war, guarantees the safety of small states and provides means for a more general acceptance in international disputes of the Law of Nations, applied by an international body in lieu of the arbitrament of the sword, it will not have been in vain, and it will form a notable epoch in the development of the Law of Nations and of the civilization of the world.

Thirteen years have passed since the foregoing pages were written,[1] and during that time masses of material have been published relating to the diplomacy of the belligerent states in the years preceding the war, as well as to the conduct of the war itself. The "pleadings" of the belligerent states referred to above (p. 130) are now shown to have been very incomplete, and it is now recognized that none of the European nations had been free from political and economic aspirations which made the maintenance of peace increasingly difficult. Invaluable assistance to the students of the World War and its cause has been afforded by Dr G. P. Gooch who has provided a summary of the numerous publications on this subject.[2] Though "complete agreement as to the manifold causes of the conflagration will never be reached," I see no reason to change the opinion that I expressed in October, 1914, that Great Britain could not honourably have taken any other course than that which she pursued at this crisis. In view, however, of the further information which is now available, some additional observations appear to be necessary.

i. The occasions for wars and their causes are by no means

[1] With some slight omissions and modifications due to fuller knowledge they are printed as originally published.

[2] *Recent Revelations of European Diplomacy* (1927).

identical, and, as the occasion for the outbreak of war in 1914 was the Austro-Hungarian Ultimatum to Serbia, a summary of the events leading up to it may be useful.

In 1908 Austria annexed Bosnia and Herzegovina, two provinces of the Ottoman Empire which she had been "occupying and administering" under the Treaty of Berlin, 1878. For some years the condition of the Serbs and Croats under Austrian and Hungarian rule had been one of constant agitation for fuller rights, which the annexation of the two provinces did nothing to allay; it continued to exist. The agitation among these peoples in Croatia, Dalmatia and Bosnia also continued, and a corresponding agitation existed in Serbia against Austria: the two were, in fact, inseparable. Relations between the two Powers were generally tense, and the situation was rendered worse by Berchtold's rejection of the advances of the Serbian Prime Minister, M. Pashitch, in 1912. In that year local government was suppressed in Bosnia and Dalmatia, and the Constitution of Croatia was suspended, martial law being imposed on these provinces. The forces of disruption were at work everywhere; the Roumanians in Transylvania, the Italians on the Adriatic seaboard, Slovenes, Czechs and Slovaks were in a condition of ferment, the Serbian Government was suspected, possibly with some reason, of being privy to much of the agitation. The Government of Austria-Hungary had determined that it must stop, and that an attack on Serbia was the only way to put an end to it. The assassination of the Archduke Francis Ferdinand provided the occasion. The Ultimatum was presented and it was clearly never intended to be accepted, for the Austro-Hungarian Minister left Belgrade without waiting for an answer. Before despatching it the Ballplatz had received a report in which the complicity of the Serbian Government in the assassination was said to be in no way proved and to be definitely improbable. The responsibility for the delivery of the Ultimatum becomes the more grave, especially as it appears that Germany was deceived as to the facts of the case. Behind these facts there was in the minds of the Governments of both countries the feeling expressed by Conrad von Hötzendorff, Chief of the Austro-Hungarian General Staff, that every year put Austria in a less favourable position for destroying Serbian irredentism, while Moltke, the Chief of the German General Staff, emphasized that delay diminished the chances of the two Empires, since Russia was increasing in strength.

ii. In considering the part played by Germany in world politics before the war several different factors must be noted. The diplomatic records and memoirs published since 1914 afford material on which to form an opinion of the character of the Kaiser and his relations to his ministers and to the military party. They also trace the changes in policy of the Government from its abandonment of the Bismarckian standpoint to its economic and political expansion in Turkey and the Near East and the growth of German navalism and anti-British feeling, evidenced by the rejection of British overtures. Apart from the evidence of state papers and diplomatic memoirs there is also evidence of another kind which there is a tendency since the war to overlook or minimize. This is provided by the writings of professors and publicists, and indicates the wide-spread belief in the superiority of German efficiency and *Kultur*, and of their ultimate triumph in the world. The diplomacy of Germany was clumsy and rough, and characterized by a lamentable incapacity to understand that the extension of German commerce and of their ideals of *Kultur* did not necessarily involve the use of force or political control.

The Kaiser was undoubtedly a disturbing factor in international affairs; his hand was too often on his sword which he rattled from time to time, though he appeared to be fearful of withdrawing it from its scabbard. His appearances in "shining armour" were of a disquieting nature. However, it would seem that the Tangier and Agadir incidents were the work of his ministers and not due to his personal intervention. But Germany was a militarist state, a standing danger to herself and to the world. From the lowest to the highest units in the nation discipline was enforced, and military ideals pervaded every nook and cranny of the political structure.

The identification of the views of the German General Staff and the militarist party with the policy of the Government may possibly have been pressed too far in the preceding pages, but that the Government was out of sympathy with any movement for the reduction of armaments and for the organization of machinery for the pacific settlement of international disputes appears from the following considerations.

One of the objects for which the Peace Conference was held at The Hague in 1899[1] "was a possible reduction of excessive armaments." The Russian Plenipotentiary spoke strongly in

[1] See my *Hague Peace Conferences*, p. 75.

THE WAR OF 1914   151

favour of such a reduction, but he met with opposition both from
the French and the German delegates. The Conference finally
resolved that "the restriction of military charges which are at
present a heavy burden on the world is extremely desirable for
the increase of the material and moral welfare of mankind."
Nothing resulted from this, armaments everywhere increased,
and the subject of their limitation did not appear on the programme of the Second Hague Conference in 1907; Germany had
clearly intimated that she was not prepared to assist in any
proposal leading to disarmament. The British Government,
however, reserved the right to bring the matter before the Conference and this was done in a powerful speech by Sir Edward Fry.
The French delegate supported the views of the British delegate,
but the discussion was felt to be academic and the Conference
passed the colourless resolution "that it is eminently desirable
that Governments should resume the serious examination of the
question." The passing of this Resolution was hailed by the
German delegate, Baron Marschall, as the "interment" of the
movement for the limitation of armaments, and he attended its
obsequies in a joyful spirit, while the German Cabinet breathed
again on hearing the result of the discussion.[1]

Another evidence of the spirit of the German Government is
afforded by its attitude towards arbitration as a means of settling
international disputes. The German Government accepted the
Convention for the establishment of the Hague Tribunal in 1899
only after Austria-Hungary had intimated her intention of signing
it. This spirit was still more noticeable in 1907 when Germany
strenuously and successfully opposed all attempts even to formulate
a Convention for compulsory arbitration of a very limited character,
though both Austria and Italy did all in their power to provide
a compromise.[2]

The growth of the German fleet, which has already been referred
to, is of importance in the consideration of Germany's pre-war
policy. In this matter all attempts made by Great Britain to reach
agreement on their partial limitation by means of a naval holiday
failed. Speeches of the Kaiser and the unconcealed desire of those
in the naval circle for the approach of "Der Tag" left no doubt as
to the Power against whom the fleet might eventually be used.

[1] B. Schwertfeger, *Die Diplomatischen Akten des Auswärtigen
Amtes*, 4 Theil, 2 Hälfte, pp. 79–81.
[2] See my *Hague Peace Conferences*, pp. 82–4.

Austria-Hungary's extremity was Germany's opportunity. Germany made no serious attempt to restrain her ally in the Serbian crisis, in regard to which the evidence is that she was deceived as to the complicity of the Serbian Government. The circumstances for war, however, appeared to be propitious, and, in the past, Germany had been careful to select a favourable moment for making war. The Kiel Canal permitting German battleships to pass from the North Sea to the Baltic was just completed; Russia's strategic railways were unfinished and would not be ready before 1917: she was, moreover, hampered by internal dissensions; France's army reforms were incomplete and she was in a condition of political chaos; England was apparently on the verge of a civil war over the Irish question. The military party triumphed, and the signal was given for the great military machine to be put in motion according to the plans of the German General Staff, with the consequent violation of the neutrality of Belgium and the application of the doctrines of *Schrecklichkeit*.

iii. A further observation may be made supplementing and modifying what is said on p. 138 on the subject of the abrogation of treaties and the balance of power. The conditions of international life have been changed since the establishment of the League of Nations, but, although Article 19 of the Covenant contains a provision for the reconsideration of treaties which have become "inapplicable" (a word of ambiguous meaning), and the consideration of international conditions whose continuance might endanger the peace of the world, there is no provision for any systematic revision of treaties. This Article must, however, be read in conjunction with Article 11 which declares it to be the friendly right of each member of the League to bring to the attention of the Assembly or of the Council any circumstance whatever affecting international relations which threatens to disturb international peace or the good understanding between nations upon which peace depends.

The balance of power has been displaced by the Concert of Powers, for it is on this basis that the League of Nations is founded. Such a concert of all the Powers should prove to be the most effective way of checking the inordinate aspirations of every one of them, and the future well-being of the League is dependent on its adherence to the principles laid down in the preamble to the Covenant.

IX

ENEMY SHIPS IN PORT AT THE OUTBREAK OF WAR[1]

I

THE judgment of the Judicial Committee of the Privy Council in the cases of *The Blonde, Prosper* and *Hercules*[2] delivered by Lord Sumner on February 16th, 1922, determined, so far as Great Britain is concerned, questions which had, since the outbreak of the war in August, 1914, remained in suspense. The points were whether the Sixth Hague Convention, 1907, relative to the status of enemy ships in port at the outbreak of war, was binding on this country, and, if so, what were the meaning and effect of the first two Articles of that Convention. There were other points in the case relative to the interpretation of certain Articles in the Treaty of Versailles with which this paper is not concerned.

Before discussing this judgment it is proposed to deal shortly with the position of enemy ships in port at the outbreak of war apart from the Hague Convention, and also to consider the question of the Convention as regards other belligerents in the war of 1914–18.

Down to the middle of the nineteenth century enemy ships in port at the outbreak of war, enemy ships entering port after the outbreak of war and enemy ships met at sea in ignorance of the outbreak of war were all liable to capture and condemnation.[3] It was formerly the practice not only to seize enemy vessels in

[1] Published in the *British Year Book of International Law*, 1922.
[2] 3 *Brit. and Colonial Prize Cases*, 1031.
[3] Bonfils-Fauchille, *Droit International public*, § 1399; *Lindo* v. *Rodney*, 2 Doug. 613 n.

port at the outbreak of war, but also to lay an embargo
upon them in expectation of war, so that if war should
come they might be confiscated.[1] The commencement
of the modern practice whereby enemy ships in port were
exempt from capture and were given "days of grace"
wherein to depart was inaugurated by Turkey, whose
government on declaring war against Russia announced
on October 4th, 1853, that it was not deemed just to
place an embargo on Russian merchant vessels, and
that they would be warned to go within a period to be
fixed to the Black Sea or to the Mediterranean as they
chose. Russia made a similar concession to Turkish
vessels. Great Britain and France in 1854 gave days
of grace to Russian vessels. A similar practice was
followed in 1859, 1870, 1877, 1897, 1898 and 1904. The
Italian Code for the Mercantile Marine, 1877, recognized the granting of days of grace (Article 243)
and the United States Naval War Code of 1900, which
was withdrawn in 1904, proposed a delay of thirty days.
In the Turco-Italian War, 1911, neither Power being
a party to the Sixth Hague Convention, 1907 (to be
subsequently dealt with), Turkey gave no days of
grace to Italian ships and condemned those found in
her ports. Italy by way of retorsion sequestrated some
Turkish ships but subsequently allowed them to leave.[2]
In the war between Turkey and the Balkan States,
Bulgaria, Serbia, Montenegro and Greece, 1912–13,
no days of grace were given.[3]

All the foregoing cases of grants of delay were, however, recognized as mitigations of the belligerent right
of capture and condemnation; they were given as of

[1] J. B. Moore, *International Law*, Digest VII, p. 453; *The Santa Cruz*, 1 C. Rob, 563; *The Boedes Lust*, 5 C. Rob, 245.
[2] A. Rispardi-Mirabelli, "La guerre italo-turque," *Revue de Droit international* (2nd series), vol. xv, p. 578.
[3] G. Schramm, *Das Prisenrecht in seiner neuesten Gestalt*, p. 139.

grace; but they pointed towards a growing practice of making concession of varying periods of delay. The granting of forty-eight hours' grace to Japanese ships by Russia in 1904 was merely a formal acknowledgment of the existence of the practice.[1]

II

Such was the position in law when the Second Peace Conference met at the Hague in 1907. The Programme for the Conference proposed by the Russian Government in the circular of April 3rd, 1906, under the third heading was as follows: "Elaboration of a convention regarding the laws and usages of naval warfare concerning... the days of grace accorded to merchant-vessels for leaving neutral or enemy ports after the commencement of hostilities,"[2] etc., and this was one of the questions referred by the Conference to the Fourth Commission, the Rapporteur of which was M. Henri Fromageot.[3] The result of their deliberations was the Sixth Convention relative to the status of enemy merchant ships at the outbreak of hostilities. The Convention dealt with two cases in which since 1854 relaxation of the old rule of capture had been made, namely enemy merchant ships in an adversary's port at the outbreak of war, and enemy merchant ships entering an adversary's port after, but in ignorance of the outbreak of war. It also dealt with a third case, in regard to which practice had not hitherto so generally provided a restriction on belligerent rights, namely

[1] A. Pearce Higgins, *Hague Peace Conferences*, p. 301. See also the judgment of Sir Henry Duke, in *The Marie Leonhardt*, 3 B. and C.P.C. at p. 768.
[2] A. Pearce Higgins, *op. cit.* p. 54.
[3] For the *Rapport* see *Deuxième Conférence internationale de la Paix, La Haye*, 15 juin–18 oct. 1907, *Actes et documents*, vol. i, p. 250; *The Reports of the Hague Conference*, ed. J. B. Scott (1917), p. 582; A. Pearce Higgins, *op. cit.* pp. 300–7.

enemy merchant ships met at sea (*en mer*) by an adversary's warship, in ignorance of the outbreak of war.

The Report of the Commission states that the reason for the relaxations of the rules of capture which had been made before 1907 in the first two cases—at present entirely optional—was "to conciliate the interests of commerce with the necessities of war" and even after the outbreak of hostilities "to protect, as widely as possible, operations entered into in good faith and in the course of execution before the war." These words are taken verbatim from the Report to the Emperor of the French on the decree of March 27th, 1854, which gave days of grace to Russian ships in French ports at the outbreak of the Crimean War, and to those which left Russian ports before the outbreak of war and subsequently entered French ports.[1] The corresponding British Order in Council of March 29th, 1854, announced a mitigation of belligerent rights in all the three cases before mentioned, and the reason given is simply that "Her Majesty, being compelled to declare war against his Imperial Majesty the Emperor of all the Russias, and *being desirous to lessen as much as possible the evils thereof*, is pleased" to make the concession therein set forth.[2]

The motives which actuated the High Contracting Powers in concluding the Convention under consideration are stated in the Preamble to be that they were anxious to ensure the security of international commerce against the surprises of war, and wished, in accordance with modern practice, to protect, as far as possible, operations undertaken in good faith and in process of being carried out before the outbreak of hostilities. The Preamble has been referred to as giving

[1] Pistoye et Duverdy, *Traité des Prises Maritimes*, vol. II, p. 467.
[2] For text of Order in Council see *English Prize Cases* (Roscoe), vol. II, p. 239 n.

a clue to the interpretation of the Convention in several of the cases which have come before British and other Prize Courts.[1]

The following is the text in English of the operative clauses of the Convention.

Art. 1. When a merchant ship belonging to one of the belligerent powers is at the commencement of hostilities in an enemy port, it is desirable that it should be allowed to depart freely, either immediately, or after a reasonable number of days of grace, and to proceed, after being furnished with a pass, direct to its port of destination or to any other port indicated.

The same rule applies in the case of a ship which has left its last port of departure before the commencement of the war and enters an enemy port in ignorance of the war.

Art. 2. A merchant ship, which owing to circumstances of "force majeure" may have been unable to leave the enemy port during the period contemplated in the preceding article, or which was not allowed to leave, cannot be confiscated.

The belligerent may only detain it under the obligation of restoring it after the war, without indemnity, or he may requisition it on condition of paying an indemnity.

Art. 3. Enemy merchant ships which left their last port of departure before the commencement of the war, and are encountered at sea while ignorant of the hostilities cannot be confiscated. They are only liable to be detained under an obligation to restore them after the war without indemnity, or to be requisitioned or even destroyed with indemnity and under the obligation of providing for the safety of the persons as well as the preservation of the papers on board.

After touching at a port of their own country or at a neutral port, these ships are subject to the laws and customs of naval war.

Art. 4. Enemy cargo on board the vessels referred to in Articles 1 and 2 is likewise liable to be detained and restored after the war without indemnity, or to be requisitioned on payment of indemnity with the ship or separately.

The same rule applies in the case of cargo on board the vessels referred to in Article 3.

---

[1] *The Prinz Adalbert* and *The Kronprinzessin Cecilie*, 2 B. and C.P.C. 70; *The Germania*, 1 *ibid.* 527, 2 *ibid.* 365; *The Samsen* (Siam), see *infra*, p. 161; Chinese Prize Court, see *infra*, p. 162.

Art. 5. The present convention does not affect merchant ships whose build shows that they are intended to be converted into ships of war.

Art. 6. The provisions of the present convention are only applicable between the contracting powers, and only if all the belligerents are parties to the convention.[1]

III

Of the belligerents in the war of 1914–18 the following either did not sign or did not ratify or accede to the Convention: Bulgaria, Greece, Italy, Montenegro, Serbia, Turkey and the United States. Germany and Russia in ratifying did so under reservation of Article 3, and Article 4, paragraph 2.[2]

Great Britain by Orders in Council of August 4th, 1914,[3] and August 12th, 1914,[4] announced the intention of giving ten days of grace to German and Austrian merchant vessels in British ports or entering them after the outbreak of war in ignorance of hostilities, other than cable ships, sea-going ships designed to carry oil fuel, and ships whose tonnage exceeded 5000 tons gross or whose speed was 14 knots or over, on intimation being received within three days that not less favourable treatment would be accorded to British vessels in German and Austrian ports respectively. The information was forthcoming in the case of Austrian ships, but not in the case of the German ships. The Order in Council took effect as regards Austrian vessels, but not as regards German.[5]

Germany, on August 3rd, 1914, when declaring war on France, stated that she would retain French mer-

---

[1] The translation does not purport to follow the official translation in the British Parliamentary Papers.

[2] W. E. Hall, *International Law* (7th ed.), Appendix II.

[3] *Manual of Emergency Legislation*, p. 138.   [4] *Ibid.* p. 98.

[5] *Ibid.* p. 142. For further discussion of this question see *infra*, p. 171.

chant ships in her ports, but would release them if reciprocity were assured within forty-eight hours. A similar intimation was made to Great Britain, Russia and Belgium.[1]

France gave seven days of grace to German ships save those intended for conversion into ships of war and those which were destined for the public service, and the same period was given to Austrian ships.[2] Belgium gave three days of grace to German ships but they did not avail themselves of the delay. Japan gave them fourteen days.[3]

Italy was not a party to the Convention, but her Mercantile Marine Code (Article 243) provided for the giving of days of grace; she, however, suspended the operation of the Article and announced by Decree of May 30th, 1915, that she would observe the Sixth Hague Convention as regards Austrian ships so far as the laws, etc., permit, but that all enemy ships in port would be sequestrated. By a Decree of June, 1915, confiscation by way of reprisals for unlawful acts of war was threatened.[4] On March 11th, 1916, another Decree was issued requisitioning all merchant ships in port; this was, in fact, directed against German shipping.[5] Italy declared war on Germany on August 28th, 1916, and on October 1st, 1916, a Decree announced the conversion into an Italian warship of the German yacht *Königin*. The Austrian and German crews on board were repatriated.[6] A Decree of Sep-

[1] P. Fauchille, *Droit International public*, vol. II, p. 555; *Manual of Emergency Legislation*, p. 141.
[2] P. Fauchille, *loc. cit.*
[3] *Ibid.*
[4] *Parl. Papers*, Misc. No. 18 (1915).
[5] As to the rights of neutrals to requisition foreign shipping see J. W. Garner, *International Law and the World War*, vol. I, p. 176; C. Ll. Bullock, *British Year Book of International Law*, 1922, p. 124.
[6] *Revue générale de Droit international*, vol. XXIV, pp. 337–62.

tember 3rd, 1916, specified the procedure to be taken
by Italians who had suffered in consequence of unlawful acts of war by the enemy. The Italian Decree of
June 24th, 1915, did not remain ineffective; the violations of the Law of Nations by the Germans and Austrians
whereby injury was inflicted on Italian citizens were
made the subject of an enquiry by a Commission appointed by Decree of November 15th, 1918, and on
April 15th, 1919, the *Sigmaringen*,[1] a German vessel
sequestrated under Article 1 of the Decree of May 30th,
1915, was condemned and also the other German and
Austrian ships and cargoes found in Italian ports at the
outbreak of war.[2] The sums realized by the sale of the
ships and merchandise, and the sums due for insurance
and requisition of ships sunk were used to augment the
fund for the payment of indemnities due under Article 1
of the Decree of June 24th, 1915, to those who suffered
damage by hostile acts of the enemy contrary to the
laws of war.

Brazil broke off relations with Germany on April
11th, 1917, and shortly afterwards and before declaring war on October 26th, 1917, seized forty-four
German ships which were sheltering in her harbours.
The crews were subsequently interned and a large
number of the ships were placed at the disposal of
France.[3] These vessels were subsequently appro-
priated by the Brazilian Government by legislative
measures.

The action of Portugal on February 23rd, 1916, in
requisitioning German ships which had taken refuge
in her ports was followed by a protest and an ultimatum from Germany which on March 9th ended in a

---

[1] *Gazzetta ufficiale*, April 29th, 1919.
[2] E.g. *The Lily, Gazzetta ufficiale*, September 9th, 1919.
[3] Mérignhac and Lémonon, *Le Droit des gens et la guerre de
1914–18*, vol. II, p. 84; J. W. Garner, *op. cit.* vol. I, p. 178.

state of war.[1] On December 28th, 1916, a Portuguese Prize Court condemned the *Ingraben* as being a German ship "suitable" for conversion into a warship, and subsequently proceeded to condemn the other German vessels in port at the outbreak of war.

Siam declared war on Germany and Austria on July 22nd, 1917, and no days of grace were given. On September 21st, 1917, a Siamese Prize Court condemned the *Samsen*, a German ship, which had taken refuge in a Siamese port since August 3rd, 1914, on the ground that the Hague Convention did not protect vessels not set apart for commercial purposes, and it was also added that German violations of the laws of war did not entitle her to claim the benefit of the Convention; and in condemning *Five steam lighters* on October 18th, 1917, the Court held that Siam was not bound by the Sixth Hague Convention, as all the belligerents were not parties to it: Germany having by official intimation to Siam taken the same stand in regard to the Eleventh Hague Convention.[2]

The United States, who are not parties to the Sixth Hague Convention, declared war on Germany on April 6th, 1917, and on Austria on December 9th, 1917; no days of grace were given to either German or Austrian vessels in American ports. On May 12th, 1917, a joint Resolution of the Senate and House of Representatives authorized the President to take over the possession and title of any enemy vessel within their jurisdiction, and through the Shipping Board or any Government department to operate any of the vessels. On June 30th, 1917, the President exercised the authority given and enumerated a list of eighty-seven vessels, including

[1] J. Basdevant, "La Réquisition des navires allemands en Portugal," *Revue générale de Droit international*, vol. XXIII, p. 268.

[2] Clunet, *Journal de Droit international*, vol. XLV, p. 1316; *ibid.* vol. XLVI, p. 420.

two lighters, of which it was ordered that the possession and title were to be taken over through the U.S. Shipping Board.[1]

Cuba declared war on Germany on April 7th, 1917, and gave no days of grace to enemy ships in port; and on August 21st, 1917, the President signed a decree transferring to the United States four German steamships which were seized in Cuban ports on the declaration of war.[2]

Turkey and Bulgaria were not parties to the Hague Convention and no days of grace were offered by Great Britain. British Prize Courts condemned Turkish ships and goods in British ports on the outbreak of war.[3]

China declared war on Germany and Austria on August 14th, 1917, and at once seized all enemy ships in port and condemned the ships on the ground that they were not in port for the purpose of *bona-fide* trade, and therefore were not within the intention of the Sixth Hague Convention.[4]

IV

We now turn to the position in Great Britain. The first case to come before the Court was the *Chile*,[5] a German sailing ship which arrived at Cardiff on August 4th, 1914, in ballast. The Crown in this case asked only for an order for detention, and the Court

[1] *American Journal of International Law*, Suppl. October, 1917 (vol. XI), p. 199; C. C. Hyde, *International Law chiefly as interpreted and applied by the United States*, vol. II, p. 523.

[2] *American Journal of International Law*, vol. XI, p. 865.

[3] *The Eden Hall*, 2 B. and C.P.C. 84; *The Asturian*, 2 *ibid.* 208; *The Futih-jy*, unreported.

[4] *Judgments of the High Prize Court of the Republic of China*, translated by F. T. Chang.

[5] 1 B. and C.P.C. 1.

did not enter into the question whether the Sixth Hague Convention was applicable, nor as to the construction of the first two Articles. The order made in this case, and hereafter referred to as "the Chile Order," was that—

the President pronounced the said sailing ship *Chile* to have belonged at the time of seizure thereof to enemies of the Crown, and as such to have been lawfully seized by the officers of H.M. Customs at the Port of Cardiff as good and lawful prize and droits and perquisites of H.M. in his office of Admiralty; and thereupon on the application of the Attorney-General for the Crown ordered the said ship to be detained by the Marshal until a further order is issued by the Court. All question of costs reserved; liberty to apply.

This Order does not in all respects follow that prescribed in the Prize Court Rules, 1914 (O. xxviii, Form 53, ii and iv), as it omits the words "seized under such circumstances as to be entitled to detention in lieu of confiscation,"[1] which are contained therein. The propriety of the Order was, however, affirmed by the Privy Council in the *Gutenfels*.[2] The Chile Order was made by British Prize Courts throughout the Empire and by the Courts of Alexandria and Zanzibar in the case of all German and Austrian ships to which no days of grace were allowed. In Egypt, where days of grace were accorded to enemy ships, and passes offered, vessels which refused to take advantage thereof were condemned.[3] In the course of the argument in the *Gutenfels* it was submitted by the Crown that Article 2 of the Convention was not obligatory if the days of grace which Article 1 recognizes as "desirable" are not given; but on this point, as well as on the question whether the Convention applied to German ships which had taken refuge in a British port to avoid

---

[1] *Manual of Emergency Legislation*, p. 331.
[2] 2 B. and C.P.C. 36.   [3] *The Achaia*, 2 B. and C.P.C. 45.

capture by French warships, the Privy Council declined to pass judgment, and in the latter case reversed the judgment of Sir Samuel Evans condemning two German vessels, and made the Chile Order, further application to be made to it.[1] In the *Gutenfels* Lord Wrenbury said:

> The question is one of law, arising out of an international document involving a reciprocal obligation performable only at the end of the war. If this Board was now to determine this question of construction, Germany might hereafter take a different view, and the performance of the obligation, as a reciprocal obligation, might become impossible.[2]

So also as to the question whether the Convention was operative and binding on Great Britain, Lord Wrenbury said:

> The respondents (i.e. the ship-owners) say that it was. The Law Officers of the Crown have stated in the plainest terms that the British Government abide by the Hague Convention and look to Germany to do the same. The British Government, by the Order in Council of August 4th, 1914, presently mentioned, acted under the Hague Convention. It is unnecessary to determine whether the Hague Convention applies or not. Their Lordships will assume in favour of the respondents that it does.[3]

Similar statements were made by Sir Samuel Evans, leaving the question of the applicability of the Conventions open in regard to the Sixth, Tenth and Eleventh Hague Conventions, though he also raised the further question whether the German Empire or its citizens were precluded in the circumstances of the war from invoking the aid of any of the Hague Conventions.[4]

On some few points, however, the British Prize Courts did pass a definite judgment. The term "navire de commerce" in Article 1, was held not to be ap-

[1] *The Prinz Adalbert and The Kronprinzessin Cecilie*, 2 B. and C.P.C. 70.
[2] 2 B. and C.P.C. 41.   [3] *Ibid.*
[4] *The Berlin*, 1 B. and C.P.C. 36; *The Möwe*, 1 ibid. 60; *The Ophelia*, 1 ibid. 210.

plicable to a pleasure yacht, as such craft did not come within the intention of the Convention as indicated in the Preamble, not being in port for purposes of a commercial nature.[1] The Privy Council and the Jamaica Prize Court held that the Convention only applied to sea-going craft carrying merchandize from port to port, and finding themselves in an enemy port at the outbreak of war; it therefore had no application to tugs and lighters used in connection with a coaling depôt when the craft had their home in the port in which they were seized.[2] Germany on ratifying the Convention reserved Article 3, which exempts from confiscation merchant ships which left their last port of departure before the commencement of war and are met at sea in ignorance of hostilities, and the Order in Council of August 4th, 1914, had not granted immunity to such vessels. The inapplicability of this Article to German ships was affirmed in several cases,[3] and similar decisions were given in the French Prize Courts,[4] and the ships were condemned.

The British Prize Court was further called on to decide the meaning of the words "at sea" (*en mer*) in this Article, and also of the words "in an enemy port" (*dans un port ennemi*) in Article 1, and it was held that "port" did not mean fiscal port, but only a port in the ordinary mercantile sense, as a place where ships are in the habit of coming for the purpose of trading or unloading, embarking or disembarking.[5] Similar

[1] *The Germania*, 1 B. and C.P.C. 527; 2 *ibid.* 365.
[2] *The Atlas and Lighters*, 2 B. and C.P.C. 470; *The Deutsches Kohlen Depot Gesellschaft* (1919), A.C. 291.
[3] *The Marie Glaeser*, 1 B. and C.P.C. 38; *The Perkeo*, 1 *ibid.* 136.
[4] *The Porto*, *Revue générale de Droit international*, vol. XXII, p. 1, j; *Frieda Mahn*, *ibid.* 5, j; *Czar Nicolai II*, *ibid.* 9, j.
[5] *The Möwe*, 1 B. and C.P.C. 60, captured in the Firth of Forth; *The Belgia*, 1 *ibid.* 303; 2 *ibid.* 32, captured in the Bristol Channel between Newport and the Somerset coast.

decisions were given in the Prize Court of Western Australia,[1] and of Malta,[2] and also in the German Supreme Prize Court, where the English decisions were cited in the judgment.[3]

In order to obtain the benefit of Article 1, where a ship has left her last port of departure before the commencement of war and enters an enemy port after it has begun, the entry must be in ignorance of the hostilities. So also under Article 3, ignorance of the existence of war is necessary to entitle a ship met at sea to exemption from capture. No case involving the question of knowledge has come before the English Prize Court, but the Natal[4] and the Alexandria Prize Courts[5] had to consider whether a ship fitted with wireless telegraphic apparatus within reasonable distance of communication with the land or with other vessels can be presumed to possess knowledge of current events of international importance. The question was answered in the affirmative, but it was held that the presumption may be, and, in the two cases referred to was, rebutted by evidence showing that the wireless apparatus was in a defective condition.

Where days of grace have been granted a vessel may be prevented by *force majeure* from taking advantage of them. The Privy Council held that the inability of the master to procure the necessary funds for his voyage was not a case of *force majeure*,[6] and the Belgian Prize Court held that the departure of the officers and crews of German ships in Antwerp, and the consequent absence of the necessary crews was not *force majeure*

---

[1] *The Neuminster.*   [2] *The Erymanthos*, 1 B. and C.P.C. 329.
[3] *The Fenix, American Journal of International Law* (1916), vol. x, p. 909.
[4] *The Birkenfels*, November 23rd, 1914.
[5] *The Gutenfels* (No. 2), 2 B. and C.P.C. 136.
[6] *The Concadoro*, 2 B. and C.P.C. 64.

preventing those ships from departing. But where an Hungarian vessel, to which days of grace had been accorded in a New South Wales port, was deprived of her charts, and a watchman put on board, and no special intimation was made to the master that a pass would be given him, the Privy Council affirmed the decision of the Prize Court of Sydney that he had been prevented from departing by *force majeure*. It was further laid down that when days of grace are accorded, the period ought to be explicit and unambiguous with reference to the party whose opportunity of availing himself of the benefits of the Convention is to be affected by the operation of the Proclamation upon the particular case.[1]

What meaning should be attached to the words of Article 5 which provides that the Convention "does not affect merchant ships whose construction indicates that they are intended to be converted into ships of war" was a point on which, before the war, it was thought there would be considerable difficulty.[2] Very few questions, in fact, arose on this point. Two vessels were condemned by the Alexandria Prize Court under this Article, after expert evidence had been given which showed that the vessels were specially constructed for the purpose of conversion into armed cruisers, and this evidence was not contested.[3] The decision of the Portuguese Prize Court previously referred to, that vessels "suitable" for conversion were not within the operation of the Convention, appears to be an unwarranted extension of the Article.

[1] *The Turul*, 3 B. and C.P.C. 356.
[2] H. Wehberg, *Capture in War on land and sea*, p. 60; A. Pearce Higgins, *op. cit.* pp. 305, 306; Pitt Cobbett, *Leading Cases*, vol. II, p. 169.
[3] *The Lützow* (January 21st, 1915); *The Derfflinger*, affirmed by the Privy Council, 2 B. and C.P.C. 43.

V

Under Article 30 of the Armistice of November 11th, 1918, between the Allied and Associated Powers and Germany, it was agreed that—

All merchant ships now in German hands belonging to the Allied and Associated Powers shall be restored, without reciprocity, in ports specified by the Allies and the United States.

Article 9 of the Armistice of November 3rd, 1918, with Austria-Hungary is somewhat similar:

All merchant vessels held by Austria-Hungary belonging to the Allied and Associated Powers to be returned.

The British ships in German and Austrian hands, including those which were detained in German ports at the outbreak of war, except a small number which had been requisitioned and sunk to block a channel, were restored under these terms of the Armistice. Nowhere, in either the Armistice or the Peace Treaties, is any mention made of the Hague Convention. It was not until some months after the Treaty of Versailles had been ratified that the British Prize Court was called upon to decide the final fate of the detained German vessels. On October 19th, 1920, Sir Henry Duke, President of the Prize Court, delivered a reserved judgment in *The Marie Leonhardt*,[1] in which the Crown asked for condemnation of a detained German ship in respect of which the Chile Order had been made, and in the course of the arguments certain correspondence which took place between the British and German Governments after the outbreak of the war was referred to. It has already been stated that in consequence of the non-receipt from Germany of intimation that not less favourable treatment would be accorded to British ships in German ports than that offered by the Order

[1] 3 B. and C.P.C. 761.

in Council of August 4th, 1914, days of grace were not accorded to German ships, and the Chile Order was made. From the correspondence referred to it appeared that the British offer, owing to difficulties of communication between England and Germany on the outbreak of war, had not been received in Berlin in time to enable a reply to be made within the time allowed by it. It was contended by the Crown that this correspondence relating to the application of the Sixth Hague Convention was not conclusive as showing Germany's intention to abide by the Convention, and therefore that the Convention did not come into operation. Furthermore, that Germany, in consequence of her flagrant violations not only of the various Hague Conventions but of other rules of international law, was not entitled to claim the benefit of the Convention, and that Great Britain was entitled by way of retaliation to treat it as not being binding. Counsel for the ship asserted no rights under the Hague Convention or on the diplomatic correspondence; he contended that on August 4th, 1914, all enemy ships in port at the outbreak of war had acquired a right by the customary Law of Nations to receive days of grace during which they were free to depart. Sir Henry Duke found that apart from international convention no such change in the law as that contended for by Counsel for the ship had been made, that the rule stated in *Lindo* v. *Rodney*[1] that "upon the declaration of war or hostilities, all the ships of the enemy are detained in our ports, to be confiscated as the property of the enemy, if no reciprocal agreement is made," still held good, and that the correspondence between Great Britain and Germany during the months of August, September and October, 1914, as to the terms on which ships and goods should mutually be released, did not show that a "reciprocal

[1] 2 Doug. at p. 614 *a*.

agreement" had been concluded. The point as to retaliation therefore did not arise. He condemned the ship. Though notice of appeal was given, it was abandoned.

Meantime a large number of other German vessels were condemned, in many cases without argument, but in the cases of *The Blonde*, *The Hercules* and *The Prosper*,[1] vessels owned by citizens of Dantzig who lost their German nationality immediately the Treaty of Versailles came into operation, and who therefore claimed to be in a better position than if they had remained German subjects, the question of the correspondence between Great Britain and Germany, which had been of secondary importance in *The Marie Leonhardt*, was dealt with in argument: the applicability and meaning of the Hague Convention was not argued. *The Blonde* and *The Hercules* had been requisitioned by the Crown, and lost while under requisition—*The Blonde* by grounding off Flamborough Head, and *The Hercules* through being sunk by an enemy torpedo. The owners claimed the appraised values of these ships on requisition for the Admiralty and the delivery of *The Prosper* under the terms of Article 2 of the Convention. Sir Henry Duke rejected the claims of the citizens of Dantzig to any favoured position over that of other German citizens whose ships had been detained and requisitioned, and reaffirmed his judgment in *The Marie Leonhardt*. From this judgment the owners appealed to the Privy Council, and the decision of this Court, consisting of Lord Sumner, Lord Parmoor and Sir Arthur Channell, was delivered by Lord Sumner on February 10th, 1922. The Court affirmed the judgment of the President on the position of the citizens of Dantzig. Lord Sumner then dealt with the principal point, namely the claim of the appellants to the benefit of

[1] 3 B. and C.P.C. 875.

the Sixth Hague Convention, which was fully argued on the appeal, or in the alternative, of a supposed agreement to the like effect, arrived at *ad hoc* by Great Britain and Germany in the early months of the war. The Crown denied the applicability of the Convention, firstly for want of ratification by all the belligerents, and secondly because Article 2 would only apply if Great Britain had put Article 1 in force, which was never done. As to the supposed agreement *ad hoc*, the Crown argued that the negotiations were entered into for other purposes, and further that they broke down without any conclusion.

It is not proposed to analyze in detail the whole of this remarkable judgment, particularly those portions which deal with reparations and other provisions of the Treaty of Versailles; but with the subject of the Hague Convention it will be necessary to deal in detail, as well as with the retaliatory argument which, it will have been seen, was a factor which weighed with some of the other Prize Courts whose decisions have already been cited.

(*a*) As regards the correspondence between Great Britain and Germany, Lord Sumner pointed out that logically the first question to be considered was whether it was entered upon or was pursued as a negotiation intended to lead to a new international agreement at all. In their Lordships' opinion, the sole object of the two Powers was to ascertain whether, and in what way, effect would be given to the old agreement, namely, the Sixth Hague Convention, and was not to enter into a new agreement, dealing with the same subject and tending to the same effect.

(*b*) As to the results of the correspondence, it was held that the British Government was satisfied that there existed such an intention on the part of the German Government to observe the Convention reciprocally as justified them in proceeding publicly to observe it, and hence the orders of the Prize Court were made at the instance of the Crown, which were always regarded as being framed to carry out the obligations of the Convention. It was further added that the German Government had strong material interest in continuing to execute the Convention, and was unlikely to intend to abandon or to desire to forfeit the ultimate advantage which its observance would assure.

(c) In what did the obligations of the Convention consist according to its terms? The first point discussed was Article 6,

the provisions of the present Convention do not apply except between the contracting Powers, and then only if all the belligerents are parties to the Convention.

Referring to the French text for the last part of the sentence, "et seulement si les belligérants sont tous parties à la Convention," it was suggested by Lord Sumner that there may be significance in the different position in the sentence occupied by the respective words "all" and "tous," and the question was raised whether, as Germany had not declared war on Serbia, who was not a party to the Convention, at the time the ships were detained, and Serbia had not then formally become an ally of Great Britain, Serbia was a belligerent in such a sense that her failure to ratify the Convention prevented its being applicable as between Great Britain and Germany in the matter of the ships in question. Several other points under this head were raised, but their Lordships did not find it necessary to answer the questions, because whether the objection was one which could be successfully raised or not, it was held that it was one which could be, and in fact was, waived by the British Government, and days of grace were in fact allowed to Austrian ships, Austria being at war with Serbia.

The Chile Order was wholly inept if the Convention had and could have no application, and the Crown should have applied to the Court not for leave to requisition, but for a decree of condemnation.

The acquiescence of the Crown in numerous orders in that form, the statements of the Attorney-General in *The Gutenfels*[1] and *Deutsches Kohlen Depot Gesellschaft*,[2] and the fact that whilst hostilities lasted condemnation was not asked for the detained ships, were conclusive to show that any right to rely on Article 6 had been waived.

(*d*) What is the meaning of Articles 1 and 2 of the Convention? Before answering this question, Lord Sumner laid down certain broad canons for the interpretation of international instruments, in which he referred to the conditions of those negotiations which necessarily involved compromises which were embodied in them, so that it would be unreasonable in the circumstances to expect to find in them "nicety of scholarship or exactitude of literary idiom." Where broad principles are laid down and the Powers have to take the measures for their execution, great precision is not to be expected, and even incomplete provisions expressed without much detail or sometimes only in outline are not to be rejected. It is necessary to discover and give effect to "all the beneficent intentions embodied in such instruments which their general tenour indicates," and it is not to be supposed that any Power—

will seek to escape its obligations by a quibbling interpretation, by a merely pedantic adherence to particular words, or by emphasising the absence of express words, where the sense to be implied from the purport of the Convention is reasonably plain. Least of all can it be supposed that His Majesty's Government could have become parties to such an instrument in any narrow sense, such as would reserve for them future loopholes of escape from its general scope.

[1] (1916), 2 A.C. at p. 115. [2] (1919), A.C. p. 291.

With these observations may be compared the similar views expounded by Dr Lushington in several of the judgments in the Crimean War, where the British Order in Council already referred to was pleaded by owners of captured Russian vessels. In the case of *The Fenix* or *Phoenix*[1] he said that wherever a Government, by a public document, relaxes the severity of belligerent rights, it ought to be taken in favour of the party for whom it is intended, and that a liberal construction should be put upon it. If the words of the document are capable of two constructions, the one most favourable to the belligerent party in whose favour the document is issued ought to be adopted. Again, in *The Argo*[2] he laid it down that all relaxation of belligerent rights emanating from the Government of a country should receive as liberal a construction as the terms of those documents would admit of. The Supreme Court of the United States cited these two cases when dealing with the Proclamation of President McKinley of April 26th, 1898, announcing relaxations of belligerent rights in regard to Spanish merchant vessels in American ports at the outbreak of war, and accepted the doctrine laid down as being the proper and correct principles to be applied in interpreting such a document.[3]

Returning now to Lord Sumner's judgment, he proceeded to apply the principles laid down to Articles 1 and 2 of the Convention. The contention advanced by the Crown that Article 2 had no operation unless and until the days of grace which Article 1 recognizes as "desirable" were granted, was rejected.

---

[1] Spinks Rep. 1; *English Prize Cases*, vol. II, p. 230.

[2] Spinks 52; *English Prize Cases*, vol. II, p. 294.

[3] *The Buena Ventura*, 175 U.S. Rep. 384, Judgment of Peckham, J. Cp. also the dissenting judgment of White, J. in *The Pedro*, 175 U.S. Rep. 354.

To say that the compact expressed in Article 2 has been provi-
dently entered into in case two belligerents should reciprocally
grant days of grace under Article 1, but that until that event
happens it is a mere foretaste of things to come, is to attenuate
this Convention to the very verge of annulling it. It is all the more
unworthy of such an occasion to place so narrow a meaning on
the Article, because the length and character of the opportunity
for departing in peace rests entirely with the grantor of it.

Furthermore, Articles 3 and 4 placed the matter beyond doubt, and the fact of the reservation by Germany
of Article 3 was quite consistent with the adoption of
the rest of the Convention.

Their Lordships, therefore, think it clear that in effect this Convention says: "Ships which find themselves at the outbreak of
war in an enemy port, shall in no case be condemned, if they are
not allowed to leave or if they unavoidably overstay their days
of grace; but it would be better that they should always be allowed
to leave, with or without days of grace." In effect, while Article 1
is only optional, Article 2 is obligatory. They reject the construction, which makes the prohibition upon confiscation depend on
a prior election to do what Article 1 desiderates, but does not
require.

It is believed that this view represents the practically
unanimous opinion of writers on international law as
to the meaning of these Articles.[1]

(e) But the further question remained. Assuming
that the Hague Convention was binding in the early
stages of the war, it was argued that Germany had by
her conduct given this country the right to refuse to be
bound any further by its terms so far as German ships
were concerned. It appears that the German Government in 1915, instructed its diplomatic officials in

[1] J. Westlake, *International Law, War*, p. 44; L. Oppenheim,
International Law (3rd ed.), vol. II, § 102; T. J. Lawrence, *International Law*, p. 338; C. Dupuis, *Droit de la Guerre maritime* (1911),
pp. 167–9; A. Pearce Higgins, *op. cit.* pp. 303–7; P. Fauchille,
op. cit. vol. II, § 1400; F. Despagnet, *Droit International public* (4th
ed.), p. 955; G. Schramm, *op. cit.* p. 134.

Spain to inform the owners of detained ships of their arrival in Spanish ports when navigating under requisition. The object seems to have been to give the owners the opportunity of taking proceedings in Spanish Courts for recovering possession, but there was no evidence that any proceedings were taken. Again, the Circular to the King of Siam before referred to was cited as evidence of the want of binding-force of the Convention by reason of its non-ratification by all the belligerents. Neither of these points was held by the Court to be of weight. Great stress was, however, laid by the Crown on the—

many outrageous and indefensible measures adopted by Germany during the war, especially her defiance of the provisions of the Hague Conventions applicable, which, it was urged, amounted to an intimation that she intended to repudiate all obligations, and especially all conventional ones, as to the conduct of the war, and thus gave to Great Britain the right to treat herself as released from her correlative obligations under the Sixth Hague Convention.

Lord Sumner considered that there were two flaws in this argument: (1) Because Germany had flagrantly disregarded a convention to her disadvantage, it did not follow that she intended to repudiate one on the observance of which she stood to gain in the long run, and as a fact she had remained in a position to carry out the terms of the Convention down to the Armistice. On this it may be observed that it certainly seems paradoxical that the breach of nearly all the provisions of the other Hague Conventions except the Sixth by the Germans could not be taken into account in regard to their observance of the terms of the only one which it was to their advantage to observe. Each Convention is, however, separate and distinct from the other, and no two Conventions have been ratified by the same states. The Final Act of the Conference of 1907, after enumerating the Conventions and Declaration annexed to it, says: "These Conventions and this Declaration shall form as many separate Acts." (2) Great Britain had not accepted the repudiation, and had not given notice that she regarded the Convention as no longer binding. This was certainly a very narrow and municipal way of looking at the question, and the Court preferred to rely on a wider ground, namely, that it was not the function of a Prize Court as such—

to be a censor of the general conduct of a belligerent, apart from his dealings in the particular matters which come before the Court, or to sanction disregard of solemn obligations by one belligerent, because it reprehends the whole behaviour of the other. Reprisals afford a legitimate mode of challenging and restraining misconduct, to which, when confined within recognised limits and embodied in due form, a Court of Prize is bound to give effect.

In taking their stand on these principles the Privy Council has the support of Chief Justice Marshall, who in *The Nereide*[1] declared that—

reciprocating to the subjects of a nation, or retaliating on them its unjust proceedings towards our citizens, is a political not a legal measure....If it be the will of the Government to apply to Spain any rule respecting captures which Spain is supposed to apply to us, the Government will manifest that will by passing an act for the purpose. Till such an act be passed, the Court is bound by the law of nations, which is part of the law of the land.

The Privy Council in its judgments in *The Zamora*[2], *The Stigstad*[3] and *The Leonora*[4] has elucidated the whole subject of retaliation in naval warfare in a more thorough manner than it had ever before been done. The wrongful acts of the Germans might well have been a valid ground for Great Britain refusing to be bound by the Sixth Hague Convention, but though Orders in Council had been made, and retaliatory measures enforced and upheld by the Privy Council as being in

[1] 9 Cranch, 388.　　　　　　[2] 2 B. and C.P.C. 1.
[3] 3 B. and C.P.C. 347.　　　[4] 3 B. and C.P.C. 385.

accordance with the Law of Nations, the Executive had taken no such steps to denounce this Convention. This might have been done by the Treaty of Versailles, but there are no provisions therein which expressly deal with the detained ships. It is believed that attempts were made to obtain the insertion of Clauses expressly dealing with them, and refusing any claims either to restitution or compensation, but the fact remained that neither by Order in Council nor by Treaty had the application of the Sixth Hague Convention been denied.

(ƒ) The Convention having been held to be binding, and the meaning of Articles 1 and 2 explained, there remained the question of its application to the three ships. The second Article, giving the belligerent the right to detain "under an obligation of restoring it after the war without compensation" proceeds, "or he may requisition it on condition of paying compensation." If the ship is detained, the Convention imposes no duty on the belligerent to provide for her safety or to effect repairs; that was the view of the Court. The vessel has been detained at her owner's risk. There is nothing stipulated as to payment of freight or of compensation for the use of the ship while under requisition. Two of the ships had been lost; one by an illegitimate act of war on the part of the Germans, and yet, "paradoxically," as Lord Sumner said, the British Government was liable for the appraised value on their requisition. This is a very strict and literal interpretation of the Article in question, and if the Crown was accused by the Court of a pedantic interpretation of the Convention, the Court appeared to lay itself open to a similar charge. Would their Lordships hold that a belligerent Government was under no liability in respect of payment for the loss of neutral cargo on an enemy vessel which had been "illegally" sunk, as were hundreds of vessels during the late war by German submarines? The condition as to paying compensation would be frustrated, said Lord Sumner, "if, though the obligations of the Convention had not been terminated, neither ship nor compensation were forthcoming." But where the illegal act of one contracting party frustrates the performance of the Convention by the other, is not the latter discharged from the performance on his side?

(g) There was a further point with which the Court dealt, namely, the meaning of the term "requisition." It had been suggested that if the requisitioning took place, other than a "temporary" requisition under Rule 6 of Order XXIX of the Prize Rules, the substitution of the appraised value was definitive, and no order could be made to take the vessel out of the possession of the Admiralty.[1] The Privy Council did not accept this view of the meaning of requisitioning, which in their opinion meant requisition for the use of His Majesty (including consumption in the case of goods whose normal use consists in using them up), and to determine otherwise would be to "confound a thing requisitioned for use with a thing acquired for the purpose of sale." If, therefore, the thing requisitioned under the terms of the Convention is in existence at the end of the war, it is to be returned to the claimant. This interpretation of the use of the term appears to be in harmony with the intention of the draftsmen of the Convention, as evidenced by the Report of M. Fromageot.

[1] In *The Germania*, No. 2 (3 B. and C.P.C. 130), the Privy Council affirmed the decision of Cullen, C.J. of the Supreme Court of New South Wales, that when an enemy ship has been requisitioned, the date of the delivery of the ship by the Marshal of the Court is the proper date for determining the value of the ship under Order xxix.

VI

With the subsequent portion of the judgment, and the relation of the terms of the Treaty of Versailles to enemy merchant ships, it is not proposed to deal; but a general summary of the position of vessels in enemy ports at the outbreak of war (1) apart from, and (2) under the Sixth Hague Convention, may now be attempted.

(1) Where the Hague Convention is not binding on the belligerents, either under Article 6 or where neither of two belligerents has ratified the Convention, the former rules of confiscation of enemy vessels in the ports of an adversary at the outbreak of war, of such ships entering such ports after the outbreak of war, and of those met at sea in ignorance of the outbreak of war, still hold good. There is no rule of international law, apart from the Convention, requiring the giving of "days of grace" to enemy vessels in port or entering port after the outbreak of war. The United States refused to sign or to ratify the Sixth Hague Convention, on the ground that the Convention questioned a custom which seemed generally established, and that its adoption would seem to sanction less liberal and enlightened practice.[1] The American delegation to the Second Hague Conference, in its report to the President, based its recommendation against accepting the Convention on the decision of the Supreme Court in the case of *The Buena Ventura*,[2] which it cited in support of the view that the privilege enjoyed by enemy merchant vessels in port at the outbreak of war "had acquired such international force as to place it in the category of obligations." It would seem that it attached to this decision a significance to which it was hardly entitled.[3]

---

[1] J. B. Scott, *American Journal of International Law*, vol. II, p. 270.
[2] 175 U.S. Rep. 384. [3] C. C. Hyde, *International Law*, II, p. 517 n.

The Government of the United States, however, instead of leaving the question of condemnation of the enemy vessels in port to the decision of the Prize Courts, took the somewhat unusual method of appropriating them by legislative enactment.[1] The constitutionality of the joint resolution and the action of the President was upheld by the Supreme Court of the United States in the case of *Littlejohn & Co.* v. *The United States*[2] decided on March 1st, 1926. The Court held that this action was no violation of a rule of International Law and thought it unnecessary to consider the question of how far the ancient rule concerning the confiscation of enemy property had been modified by recent practice. It was further stated that even if the joint resolution were in contravention of a rule of International Law the Court would be bound to follow it, because the "duly expressed will of Congress when proceeding within its powers is the supreme law of the land."

(2) The meaning of Articles 1 and 2 of the Sixth Hague Convention regarding "days of grace" and the immunity from condemnation of enemy ships in port at the outbreak of war, or entering port after the outbreak of war, but in ignorance of hostilities, as expressed by Lord Sumner, is believed to be the true and correct view;[3] it is the view which is generally taken by all writers on the subject. Where days of grace are given to ships in an enemy port, and an effective pass is offered, and for reasons other than *force majeure* the masters do not avail themselves of the permission to leave, it seems clear that the old rule of condemnation can be properly enforced. The Convention introduces an important restriction on the right of belligerent capture, but it leaves to the state in whose ports enemy

[1] Cf. the judgment of Lord Stowell in *The Victoria*, Edwards, p. 97.
[2] 270 U.S. Rep. p. 215.
[3] *Supra*, p. 175.

vessels are found, the right of refusing to grant them leave to depart, or of restricting the permission to such vessels as it may seem good to it, as was done by the British Orders in Council of August 4th and 12th, 1914. If enemy ships are not allowed to depart, they may be detained without any compensation for their deterioration, and they lie at the owner's risk for the period of the war; or they may be requisitioned for use on condition of paying an indemnity if they are not in existence at the end of the war. There is no question of indemnity by reason of the immobilization of the vessels if they are not requisitioned. In permitting the requisition of the vessels, the Convention recognizes the impossibility of prescribing for belligerents an abstention which is not imposed on them in land warfare as regards property susceptible of employment in war. The French delegation at the Hague Conference proposed to specify that the indemnity should be due in case of requisition, in accordance with the territorial laws in force. The owners of enemy ships would then have been indemnified in the same measure as the owners of national ships. Such assimilation, as Professor Charles Dupuis points out, would be excessive; the local law takes into account, in fixing the indemnity due to nationals, the loss that may result to them from the deprivation of the use of the requisitioned ship, but there is no occasion to consider this in relation to enemy owners of ships, since, by virtue of the state of war, the belligerent has the right to prevent them from sailing the seas. The measure of the indemnity is not fixed by the Convention, but the Report of the Commission states that it must cover the loss proved by the claimant to have been caused by the requisition. This does not include loss of freight.[1] The provisions relating to requisition would be improved if fuller ex-

[1] Ch. Dupuis, *Le Droit de la Guerre maritime* (1911), p. 169.

planation were afforded of the meaning of the term, and as to the nature and method of calculation of the indemnity to be accorded where return of the detained and requisitioned ship is impossible at the end of hostilities; the unqualified undertaking to return the ship or pay the indemnity should also be modified in the sense previously suggested.

British and foreign Prize Courts do not always appear to have complied with the canons of construction laid down by the Privy Council in applying them to the Sixth Hague Convention. It is believed that the treatment of pleasure yachts as being of a class other than "navires de commerce" is a restriction on the intention of the framers of the Convention, and that the term was used in the Convention as opposed to "bâtiments de guerre" in Article 5. Though the preamble of the Convention declares that it is entered into in order to ensure the freedom of international commerce, "commerce" does not necessarily mean trade, any more than "trading" with the enemy signifies buying or selling. The Report of M. Fromageot appears to bear out this construction, for he says "it has appeared preferable not to specify that the delay shall be granted to allow the loading or unloading, in order not to limit its enjoyment to these commercial operations alone."[1]

The restriction of the Convention to vessels engaged on a port to port voyage, appears, however, to be in accord with the principles of the Convention, and the meaning of the term "port" as given in the British and German decisions previously cited is in accord with the rule *verbis plane expressis omnino standum est*.[2] The condemnation of vessels which took refuge in a neutral

[1] *Parl. Papers*, Misc. No. 4 (1908), p. 191. The German Prize Court in *The Primavera* held that yachts came within the term *navires de commerce*. *Journ. de Droit inter.* (1917), vol. XLIV, p. 2834.

[2] *The Fenix*, English Prize Cases, vol. II, p. 244.

port, and subsequently found the port to be an enemy one, though intelligible in the circumstances of the war,[1] was a narrow construction and was not adopted by the British Prize Courts.[2] A more safe, though technical, ground for their condemnation by many of the states which adopted this course would have been reliance on Article 6, that the Convention was not binding on them. The position taken by Italy seems to have been logical, and valid in accordance with the views as to retaliation enunciated by the British Prize Court.

As regards the granting of days of grace in the future, the conduct of the late war showed the immense value to a belligerent of a fleet of merchant vessels which could be used not only for the purpose of trade and the maintenance of import of commodities of all kinds, but also for use as auxiliaries to the fighting fleet; the granting or withholding of "days of grace" will, therefore, remain in the future, as it was in the past, a matter in which each belligerent will be guided by the supreme need of safeguarding national interests.

VII

The British Government on November 14th, 1925, gave notice of denunciation of the Sixth Hague Convention, 1907. In a dispatch of Sir Austen Chamberlain to His Majesty's Representatives abroad notifying the denunciation, reasons for this action are given and it is pointed out that in consequence of the decision in *The Blonde* if circumstances should again arise in which the Convention would be applicable, the interpretation which His Majesty's Government would be bound to place upon it would differ fundamentally from that adopted by the majority of the other parties to the

[1] P. Fauchille, *op. cit.* ii. p. 556.
[2] *The Prinz Adalbert*, 2 B. and C.P.C. 70.

Convention and would place them in a position less favourable than that enjoyed by other countries. The Circular concludes with the statement which is fully borne out by the examination already made of the operation of the Convention in the preceding pages: "The Convention appears therefore to have wholly failed in its original purpose. It has secured neither uniformity of practice nor liberal treatment in favour of enemy vessels."[1]

Under the terms of Article 10 of the Convention the denunciation became operative on the expiration of one year after the notification of the Netherlands Government. So far, therefore, as the British Government is concerned, enemy ships in port at the outbreak of war, enemy ships entering port after the outbreak of war and enemy ships met at sea in ignorance of the outbreak of war are all liable to seizure and condemnation. But the Government can in the future, as it has done in the past, provide for such mitigation of the operation of these rules by agreement with the enemy as may seem desirable under the circumstances.

[1] *Parl. Papers*, Misc. No. 19 (1925) [Cd. 2564].

X

SUBMARINE CABLES IN TIME OF WAR[1]

I

THE British public early grasped the importance of submarine cable telegraphs as a means of linking up its world-wide Empire, and of furthering its commerce, and in 1897, when British Companies controlled 190,000 miles of cables, France had only 19,000, Germany 2000, and Japan 1250 miles of cables.[2] It was about this time that Germany began to plan a cable policy, and to dispute the British hegemony in every part of the world where her interests were involved. Not only were cables to be used as a part of German machinery for acquiring a widespread empire, but as an aid to obtaining a position of economic and political influence in quarters where the acquisition of territorial possessions was for the time being impossible.

The encouragement by Germany of the formation of private companies for works of public utility was, to a great extent, a means of concealing the true inwardness of this imperialist policy, and this concealment was further assisted by the association of foreigners in the enterprises, as was done in the case of the foundation of the Deutsch-Niederländische Telegraphengesellschaft. There were other undertakings of a similar character. The companies were in form international but were in fact controlled by Germans in the interest of the national policy. In February, 1899, was founded the Deutsch-Atlantische Telegraphengesellschaft for

[1] Based on an Article which appeared in *The British Year Book of International Law*, 1921.
[2] *Annuaire de l'Institut*, XIX, p. 313.

the laying of the North Atlantic cable, and, in May of
the same year, the firm of Felten and Guilleaume
(which since 1853 had made telegraph cables), with the
assistance of the Deutsch-Atlantische A.G., founded
the Norddeutsche Seekabelwerke A.G. for the making
and laying of submarine cables; this company played
a great part in the execution of the German cable
policy. The Deutsch-Südamerikanische Telegraphengesellschaft was founded in 1908, for the laying of the
South American cables. In 1901, the Deutsch-Niederländische Telegraphengesellschaft was founded for the
purpose of laying the cables with Yap as a centre. The
Osteuropäische Telegraphengesellschaft, a company
subsidized by Germany and Roumania, was founded
in 1899, for the laying of the Constanza-Constantinople
cable. The firm of Felten and Guilleaume, the Norddeutsche Seekabelwerke A.G., and the four cable
companies above named were all closely interrelated,
several of the directors being on the management of all
of them, while they were also equally closely related to a
banking house in Cologne, which city was the head-
quarters of all these undertakings.[1]

When the war broke out in 1914, these cables were
all in the hands of Germans working in the interest of
their state, and their value for strategic and propaganda
purposes cannot be over-estimated. Direct communication between Germany and her overseas possessions
was severed at the beginning of the war by the cutting
of the cables by the Allies, and portions were relaid
under conditions of extraordinary difficulty. The
Emden-Teneriffe cable was partially diverted into St
Nazaire, the rest of the cable being used to connect
Brest with Casablanca, and the Teneriffe-Monrovia

---

[1] See Charles Lesage, *Les cables sous-marins allemands* (Paris,
1915).

cable was diverted so as to connect Morocco with Senegal. Something like 1200 miles of cable were lifted in very deep water, and relaid by one English Company.[1]

II

When the question of the disposal of these cables came up for discussion at the Peace Conference in Paris in 1919 difficult questions were involved. In the course of the discussions the question as to the liability to capture and condemnation of enemy-owned cables was submitted to a Committee of five international lawyers. The majority agreed that on the general principles of the law relating to the capture of enemy property at sea, they were liable to capture and confiscation; the minority considered that such cables could not be assimilated to property liable to capture

[1] An interesting account of the diversion of these cables was given by Major L. Darwin at a meeting of "The India Rubber, Gutta Percha and Telegraph Works, Ltd.," in *The Times* (Company Meetings), December 19th, 1919. The following extract shows the difficulties of the work:

"Imagine fishing for a cable in pitch darkness—not that any light at the bottom could have made matters easier—the cable lying about as far below the ship as is the Tower of London from Buckingham Palace; imagine trying to cut the cable in these circumstances in the hope of being able to haul up one of the two ends thus set free to the surface; imagine pulling it up vertically through these nearly three miles of water, then steaming away whilst continuing to drag up the cable from the bottom, coiling it up on board without any kinks or unperceived injuries, and finally relaying it exactly where required; imagine all this, and I think scepticism as to the possibility of success becomes more than excusable. If our information is correct, this remarkable performance is absolutely unique in the history of submarine cable enterprise, and this whether we look to the length of the cable lifted, 1200 miles, or to the average depth of the water in which it lay."

at sea.[1] The solution ultimately reached, though not without considerable difficulty, is set forth below, but it cannot be regarded as a decisive precedent for the future.

Two different sets of cables were dealt with in the Treaty of Versailles, (a) those connected with Shantung, and (b) other cables in which Germany had interests in various parts of the world.

(a) As regards the first, by Article 156 Germany renounced in favour of Japan, all her rights, title and privileges—particularly those concerning the territory of Kiaochow, railways, mines and submarine cables—which she acquired by virtue of the Treaty concluded by her with China on March 6th, 1898, and of all other arrangements relative to the Province of Shantung.

The German state submarine cables from Tsingtao to Shanghai and from Tsingtao to Chefoo, with all the rights, privileges and properties attaching thereto, were similarly acquired by Japan, free and clear of all charges and encumbrances.

These cables were owned by the German state, they were national property and no question of private ownership was therefore involved.

It will be remembered that China was so dissatisfied with the arrangements relating to Shantung that she declined to ratify this Treaty. As a result of the Washington Conference, 1921–2, a treaty was negotiated between Japan and China which was signed at Washington on February 4th, 1922 and ratified on June 2nd, 1922, whereby it was agreed that "Japan shall restore to China the former German leased terri-

[1] The late Professor Oppenheim stated that he had no doubt that cables belonging to an enemy company or an enemy state were subject to capture (*International Law* (1921) 3rd ed. § 214). Latifi (*Effects of War on Property*, p. 114) and Scholz (*Krieg und Seekabel*) are of the contrary opinion.

tory of Kiaochow" (Art. 1).[1] A joint Commission was appointed to make and carry out detailed arrangements for the transfer of the administration and for the transfer of public properties in the territories and to settle other matters requiring adjustment. The submarine cables are dealt with in a separate Article (26).

> The Government of Japan declares that all the rights, titles and privileges concerning the former German submarine cables between Tsingtao and Chefoo and between Tsingtao and Shanghai are vested in China, with the exception of those portions of the said cables which have been utilized by the Government of Japan for the laying of a cable between Tsingtao and Sasebo; it being understood that the question relating to the landing and operation at Tsingtao of the said Tsingtao-Sasebo cable shall be adjusted by the Joint Commission provided for in Article 2 of the present Treaty, subject to the terms of the existing contracts to which China is a party.

These purely state-owned cables were, therefore, confiscated by the Peace Treaty.

(b) As regards the other cables, the Treaty of Versailles by Article 244 (Part viii, Reparations) provided: "The transfer of the German submarine cables which do not form the subject of particular provisions of the present Treaty is regulated by Annex vii hereto." Annex vii is as follows:

> Germany renounces on her own behalf, and on behalf of her nationals in favour of the Principal Allied and Associated Powers all rights, titles or privileges of whatever nature, in the submarine cables set out below or any part thereof. (Here follows a list of the cables with their description which may shortly be summarized as follows: Emden-Vigo, Emden-Brest, Emden-Teneriffe, Emden-Azores, Emden-New York, Teneriffe-Monrovia, Monrovia-Lome, Lome-Duala, Monrovia-Pernambuco, Constantinople-Constanza, Yap-Shanghai, Yap-Guam, Yap-Menado.)

[1] For text of treaty see *Amer. Journ. of International Law*, xvi (1922), *Official Documents*, p. 84.

The values of the above mentioned cables or portions thereof in so far as they are privately owned, calculated on the base of the original cost, less a suitable allowance for depreciation, shall be credited to Germany in the reparation account.

These cables, therefore, so far as they were state-owned, are confiscated to the Principal Allied and Associated Powers, namely: the British Empire, the United States, France, Italy and Japan; but in so far as they were privately owned, the value forms part of the reparation for which Germany is to receive credit from these Powers.

The only set of cables to which attention may be specially directed is that centred at the Island of Yap, which is one of the Caroline Islands situated in the Pacific Ocean belonging to the group sold by Spain to Germany by Treaty of February 12th, 1899, which took effect on October 6th of the same year. It is a small island with an area of 79 square miles and a population of about 7000, but its importance is due to the fact that it is the centre of cable communication in the Pacific. Cables connecting it with Shanghai, Guam (a possession of the United States from whence a cable connects it with San Francisco) and Menado in Celebes (a Dutch possession), all pass through this island. The British Empire, France, Italy and Japan having agreed to confer on Japan a Mandate to administer the groups of the former German Islands lying north of the Equator, the United States protested against such an arrangement unless her interests were duly protected. Following the Washington Conference a Treaty was entered into between the United States and Japan on February 11th, 1922,[1] and ratified by the Senate on March 1st, whereby the United States consented to the administration of the said Islands by

[1] For text see *Amer. Journ. of International Law*, XVI (1922), *Official Documents*, p. 94; also Editorial Comment, p. 248.

Japan but subject to certain conditions. As regards cable rights Article 3 is as follows:

The United States and its nationals shall have free access to the Island of Yap on a footing of entire equality with Japan or any other nation and their respective nationals in all that relates to the landing and operation of the existing Yap-Guam cable or of any cable which may hereafter be laid or operated by the United States or by its nationals connecting the Island of Yap.

The rights and privileges embraced by the preceding paragraph shall also be accorded to the Government of the United States and its nationals with respect to radiotelegraphic communication; provided, however, that so long as the Government of Japan shall maintain on the Island of Yap an adequate radiotelegraphic station, co-operating effectively with the cables and with other radio stations on ships or on shore, without discriminating exactions or preferences, the exercise of the right to establish radiotelegraphic stations on the Island by the United States or its nationals shall be suspended.

Further privileges are conferred on the United States and its nationals so far as they relate to electrical communications with Yap, such as the right to acquire and hold land; no obligation to obtain permits or licences to be entitled to land and operate cables or to establish radiotelegraphic services; no censorship or supervision to be exercised over cable or radio messages or operations; no taxes, port, harbour or landing charges or exactions to be levied with respect to the operation of cables or radio stations, or with respect to property, persons or vessels; the Government of Japan to exercise, if necessary, its power of expropriation to secure to the United States or its nationals property and facilities needed for the purpose of electrical communications.

It will appear that the United States has acquired far-reaching and important rights in the Island of Yap for electrical communications, and a troublesome question was thus settled greatly to the advantage of the United States and in furtherance of the cable policy which she is actively pursuing.

III

When we turn to the question of what are the rules of International Law dealing with the treatment of cables in time of war, we are met with the difficulty that there do not appear to be any which are very clearly ascertainable.

The only international convention relating to the treatment of cables in war, as between belligerents, is Article 54 of the Regulations attached to the Fourth Hague Convention, 1907, which states that

Submarine cables connecting an occupied territory with a neutral one shall not be seized or destroyed except in case of absolute necessity; they must also be restored and the indemnities regulated at the peace.

This applies only to the case of land warfare where one belligerent occupies the territory of his adversary, and seizes or destroys the landing ends of the cables connecting the territory with a neutral state. The International Convention for the protection of Submarine Telegraph Cables of 1884 expressly states that freedom of action is reserved to belligerents (Art. 15).

The Institute of International Law has discussed the subject on two occasions and formulated proposals for their treatment, but the discussions revealed considerable differences of opinion.[1] This was only to be expected, as the rights of belligerents and the interests of neutrals are in conflict in these matters. At the meeting of the Institute at Brussels in 1879, it was agreed that "Submarine cables uniting two neutral territories are inviolable." It was also agreed that it was desirable, where telegraphic communications had to cease by reason of war, that the cessation should be limited strictly to the prevention of the user of the cable, and that this should be stopped as soon as the cessation of

[1] *Annuaire de l'Institut*, III, pp. 351–94; XIX, pp. 301–32.

hostilities allowed. The subject was again discussed at Brussels in 1902 and a more elaborate set of resolutions was adopted:

Art. 1. A submarine cable connecting two neutral territories is inviolable.

Art. 2. A cable connecting the territories of two belligerents, or two parts of the territory of one of the belligerents may be cut anywhere, except in the territorial sea and in the neutralized waters belonging to a neutral territory.

Art. 3. A cable connecting a neutral territory with the territory of one of the belligerents may not be cut in the territorial sea or in the neutralized waters appertaining to a neutral territory. On the high seas such a cable can be cut only if there is an effective blockade, and within the limits of the line of blockade, subject to the repair of the cable as soon as possible; such a cable can always be cut in the territory and in the territorial sea belonging to enemy territory up to the distance of three marine miles from low water mark.

There was a difference of opinion as to restricting the cutting of this class of cable to the limits of a blockade. Dr Perels took his stand on the exigencies of war; he admitted the desirability of the maintenance of free communication between neutrals and belligerents, but urged that it was impossible to sacrifice the interests of belligerents. Professor Westlake supported the view taken by the majority of the members of the Institute. The views held by all naval authorities to-day on the subject of blockade render such a limitation as that proposed impracticable. The Institute further laid down the principle that the liberty of a neutral state to send dispatches does not imply the power of using the cable or of permitting it to be used to render aid to one of the belligerents (Art. 4). In the application of the foregoing rules it was also stated that no difference was to be made between state cables and cables owned by individuals, nor between cables which are enemy owned and those which are neutral property.

Judging some of these rules by the stern demands of
war, the truth of Dr Perels' observation that the members of the Institute can propose what they like, but
the question is what governments can adopt becomes
evident.

The topic has also been discussed on several occasions
by a body in close touch with the realities of war, the
United States Naval War College; Articles on the matter
were contained in the U.S. Naval War Code of 1900
and Professor George Grafton Wilson delivered lectures
at the College in 1901,[1] while the College discussed the
subject in 1902 and 1903.[2] The views of the Institute
of International Law were not wholly acceptable to
the War College. Under the provisions of Article 5 of the
U.S. Naval War Code, cables connecting different
parts of the enemy territory were to be dealt with as
warlike necessities required, but cables connecting
neutral and belligerent territory were held to be liable
to interruption "within the territorial jurisdiction of
the enemy." The provisions of this Code were fully
discussed by the U.S. Naval War College in 1903, and
it was recommended that in the case of all cables,
irrespective of their ownership, satisfactory censorship
should be provided, except where they were otherwise
exempt; the treatment of cables between parts of the
enemy state, or connecting the belligerent states, laid
down in the Code was approved; interruption of
cables between an enemy state and a neutral state was
approved "outside of neutral jurisdiction" (i.e. on the
high seas or in belligerent territorial waters) "if the
necessities of war require"; but cables between two
neutral states were to be inviolable, and free from interruption. It was also recommended that the whole

[1] *Submarine Telegraphic Cables in their international relations*
(Washington, 1901).
[2] *International Law Situations*, 1902, p. 7; 1903, p. 27.

question of the treatment of cables in time of war should be referred to an international conference for settlement. The Code was withdrawn in 1904, but the changes proposed by the War College are set forth in Article 40 of the Instructions for the Navy of the United States governing maritime warfare issued on June 30th, 1917.

Professor Wilson in the Lectures referred to, dealing with "Cables as affected by Law and Policy," says:

> The laws under which cables are operated help in determining their status in time of war. If France and Germany do as they propose in establishing cable service with their dependencies with the distinct purpose of securing more fully their military defence, it will be very difficult to convince Great Britain or any other Power that in the time of war so effective means of defence are entitled to special exemption. Similarly, cables subsidized by the policy of a given state cannot expect to be free from a taint of participation in public service if the enemy wishes to maintain such a charge....It must be observed, therefore, that the attitude of belligerents towards cables in the time of war will probably be influenced by the relations of the cables to the governments of the territories which they touch. It would be as absurd to exempt a subsidized cable from the consequences of hostilities as it would to exempt an auxiliary cruiser from such consequences. Probably the cable would be the greater service. There are those who claim that the state controlling the "cables and the coal" controls the world.[1]

Rear-Admiral C. H. Stockton, U.S.N., writing on the same subject, and dealing with the use to which cables would be put by belligerents, and the consequences, said:

> It is generally recognized, certainly by the United States, that under certain circumstances and conditions, materials for the construction of telegraphs are contraband of war. Submarine cables, if found ashore in belligerent territory or afloat, bound for a belligerent destination, as an enemy's port or fleet, would certainly be liable to seizure as material for the construction of

[1] *Op. cit.* pp. 28–30.

telegraphic communication, and hence contraband of war. If it then can be considered contraband of war on its way to a hostile destination on the high seas as material or a component part of a working telegraph, how much more does such a cable become contraband of war when it is in working order, actually conveying aid, information, and possibly money to a belligerent or belligerent country in time of war.[1]

That a cable between a belligerent and a neutral is almost certain to be used for the purposes of war, even with a strict censorship established by the neutral state, renders it probable that the other belligerent will take no risks. The *Times* Correspondent in Washington, in a dispatch dated December 17th, 1920, reported that there was a strong feeling in the United States that political considerations should have led the Allies to refrain from interfering with the German cables during the war, and that an international convention should be entered into exempting cables from war-time inter-ference; the chief reason advanced being that cables should be regarded as international utility agencies, because their linking up with land telegraphs gives them an infinite radius of action. This was undoubtedly one of the chief causes why the Germans desired to have their own system, and it must have been a potent reason for their enemies cutting the cables and breaking the link. Cables which afford communications between different countries are no more international agencies than ships trading with or carrying mails to different countries.

The cutting of a cable between two neutral countries must require a strong justification, such as its forming part of a larger system, one terminus of which is in a belligerent country; and when the whole is enemy owned, and there is not an efficient censorship, the risk of its being used for unneutral service is so great

[1] *Proceedings of U.S. Nav. Inst.* vol. XXIV, p. 453.

that a belligerent is not likely to allow it to exist; but he will cut it at his peril. There are the elements of unneutral service in a case where the cable is being used for hostile purposes and in Professor Wilson's opinion "they would render any other agency liable to seizure and probable confiscation on general principles."[1]

Two theories have been advanced as to the nature of the submarine cable so as to provide analogies from other branches of law. One is that cables must be assimilated in their treatment to ships, and since it is not lawful to sink a mail steamer because circumstances prevent a verification of her contents, therefore it is not lawful to cut a cable because it cannot be ascertained what messages are being sent by it. According to another view cables are in the nature of bridges connecting two territories; they are therefore liable to be damaged or destroyed in circumstances analogous to those permitting the exercise of the rights of war on land.[2] But there appears to be no need for "bridge" or "ship" theories; cables are a means which a belligerent has of keeping open his communications with the world; the great object of naval warfare is to stop the circulation of enemy commerce and to cut his means of communication whether for the carriage of troops, property or intelligence, and cables are of the utmost importance for the last purpose.

A point on which there is no authority is whether a cable which has been cut may be the subject of proceedings in a Prize Court. The general principles relating to the capture of enemy property at sea as well as those which have been advanced by both Professor Wilson and Rear-Admiral Stockton as to the contraband nature of the material and its use for unneutral

[1] *Op. cit.* p. 34.
[2] A. Latifi, *op. cit.* p. 114.

service, lead me to conclude that there is a *prima facie* case for the condemnation of such cables in prize, when enemy owned, or used for hostile purposes. The Treaty of Versailles confiscates the enemy cables only so far as they are state owned, but compensation is awarded to the private owners. Possibly in some future war, unless meantime a comprehensive agreement is reached by the Powers, the question may be tested in a Prize Court.

IV

Turning from theory to practice it may be said that cable cutting is by no means always an easy procedure;[1] but, in the past, belligerents have resorted to it whenever they felt that it was essential to their belligerent operations. As regards cables connecting different parts of the territories of a belligerent, cables were cut in the Franco-German War, 1870, and in the Spanish-American War, 1898. Cables connecting the territories of the belligerents with each other were cut in the Russo-Turkish War, and Chile cut the cable connecting with Peru in 1882, but in 1898 neither the United States nor Spain severed the cables connecting their territories or in communication with their enemies, but a severe censorship was established at both ends. Cables connecting a belligerent state with neutral states were cut by the United States in the case of those connecting Santiago de Cuba with Jamaica and Hayti, and those connecting Manila with Hong Kong. The Chile-Peru cable was British owned and Chile paid compensation to the British company: the United States refused to make compensation to the British Cable Company whose cables from Manila and Cuba were cut. The cutting of the Manila-Hong Kong cable put out of action an instrument of especial

[1] Cf. *antea*, p. 188.

meteorological value for commercial interests in the Orient.

The refusal of the United States to make any compensation for the cutting of cables between Manila and Hong Kong, between Manila and Capiz and between Havana, Santiago de Cuba, Cienfuegos and other places in the island of Cuba formed the subject of claims before the British and American Claims Arbitration Tribunal in 1923.[1] Claims were put forward by the British Government on behalf of the Eastern Extension, Australasia and China Telegraph Company, Limited, in regard to the cutting of the Manila cables, and on behalf of the Cuba Submarine Telegraph Company, Limited, on behalf of the Cuba cables. In both cases the claims were limited to the amounts which the respective companies had spent on the repairs of their cables which had been cut during the war. In each case the Tribunal disallowed the claims, and said that it is difficult to contend that a belligerent is justified by international law in depriving the enemy of the benefit of the freedom of the high seas, but is not justified in depriving him of the use of the seas by means of telegraphic cables. Not only was the cutting of cables not to be prohibited by the rules of International Law applicable to sea warfare, but such action may be said to be implicitly justified by that right of legitimate defence which forms the basis of the rights of any belligerent nation. The owner of the cable cut has no absolute right to compensation and in both cases the cables were, in effect, under the terms of the concessions under which they were laid, Spanish works of public utility and if, as ordinary private property, they were subject to destruction without compensation in case of necessity of war, *à fortiori* they were so as an enemy public utility

[1] For texts of the Awards see *Amer. Journ. of International Law*, xviii (1924), pp. 835, 842.

undertaking. On the facts in each case the Award appears to be in accordance with the principles of International Law.[1]

In the case of a neutral-owned cable if it is not cut but operated by a belligerent occupying enemy territory, it would appear on the principle of Art. 54 of the Hague Regulations for land warfare, 1907, compensation would be due to the neutral cable company. The widely extended use of wireless telegraphy has by no means rendered submarine cables of secondary importance. Wireless stations in enemy territory have been and will be the objects of attack from the air; their destruction is possible and lawful. Both methods of communi-cation are of the greatest importance in time of peace; but in time of war a cable is a thing *sui generis*. Belli-gerents formerly sent their secret messages and dis-patches by ships which were liable to visit, search and capture; they now have cables for this purpose. Cables cannot be visited and searched and, therefore, as the late M. Renault said, "Belligerents must find in the new situation an equivalent for the protection which they have lost."[2] A cable dispatch may be of more im-portance to a belligerent than a cargo of contraband or a blockade-runner. Control of communications is vital in war, and should any international agreement be reached on the subject of submarine cables, it is almost certain to contain the formula "So far as military necessities allow," or some equivalent.

[1] See also E. J. Benton, *International Law of the Spanish-American War*, p. 212 (Baltimore, 1908). For other examples of cable cutting, see P. Fauchille, *Traité de Droit International public*, vol. II, § 1321 (Paris, 1921).
[2] *Annuaire de l'Institut*, XIX, p. 314.

XI

SHIPS OF WAR AS PRIZE[1]

I

IT is stated by the late Professor Pitt Cobbett in his *Leading Cases in International Law*, that enemy warships become at once the property of the Crown on capture, and are not treated as Prize, nor is their capture subject to adjudication by the Prize Courts.[2] The late Professor Oppenheim, after asserting the necessity for condemnation by a Prize Court to pass the property in captured enemy private property to the captor, says: "On the other hand, the effect of seizure of public enemy vessels is their immediate and final appropriation."[3] Sir Samuel Evans, in delivering judgment on September 16th, 1916, in the case of *The Baden* and *The Santa Isabel* (unreported), two German colliers attached to Admiral von Spee's fleet, and sunk in the Battle of the Falkland Islands, also appeared to be under the impression that since public enemy vessels passed at once to the captor, they were not the proper subject of prize proceedings. He said:

It is quite clear that both these vessels were enemy vessels. They were also apparently in attendance upon the vessels of the German Government. But they are here treated not as part of the fleet, but as enemy vessels which could be properly treated as Prize.

It should be added that no grant of prize had been made by the Crown at this date. At subsequent stages of the war other enemy warships were condemned as prize, e.g. *The Emden* and *The Königsberg*.[4]

[1] Published in *The British Year Book of International Law*, 1925.
[2] Vol. II, pp. 275, 311.
[3] *International Law*, vol. II, sec. 185.
[4] 2 Lloyd's List Law Reports, p. 7.

These views, so far as they state that, on the capture of an enemy public ship, the property passes at once to the state, undoubtedly represent the generally accepted rule of International Law, but in so far as they suggest that public enemy ships are not treated as prize in British Prize Courts, they do not accord with the practice of the Courts. There is, however, an approach to uniformity of practice in foreign Prize Courts in this matter, as will be seen from the following evidence:

The United States. It has been held in the United States that the property in a vessel which had been fitted out as a gunboat by the Confederate states passed immediately on capture to the state without the necessity of Prize proceedings.[1] And the United States Attorney-General in 1900, gave it as his opinion that Spanish vessels wrecked in battle by the naval vessels of the United States during the war with Spain, and lying along the coast of Cuba, were the property of the United States.[2] Article 99 of the Instructions for the Navy of the United States governing naval warfare (June 30th, 1917), is to the same effect:

By the fact of capture a public vessel in the military service of the enemy passes into the possession of the captor's Government, in which title immediately vests. The vessel, therefore, becomes a public vessel belonging to the captor's Government, and subject to its disposal. It is unnecessary to send a captured public vessel into port for adjudication. The vessel may be immediately converted to the use of the captor, and sent to any port at his convenience, as a public vessel of the United States.

France. The French *Instructions sur l'application du Droit International en cas de guerre* (June 30th, 1916), after describing the procedure to be observed after the capture of a merchant ship, or a privateer furnished

[1] *Oakes* v. *U.S.*, 30 Ct. Cl. 378.
[2] J. B. Moore, *Dig. Int. Law*, vol. vii, p. 563.

with Letters of Marque by a Power not a party to the
Declaration of Paris, 1856, states in Section 118:

> Dans le cas de capture d'un bâtiment de guerre, vous vous
> bornerez à le constater sur votre journal et vous pourvoirez à la
> conduite de la manière la plus conforme à la sécurité des équipages
> auxquels vous la confierez.

In the case of the German converted cruiser *Seeadler*,
formerly an American merchant ship, the French Prize
Court decided that in conformity to the traditional
principle of French Law jurisdiction in prize was only
applicable to merchant ships and the *Seeadler* was left
to be disposed of by the Ministry of Marine.[1]

Italy. By Article 227 of the Italian Code for the
Mercantile Marine, 1877, it is provided that captured
warships pass to the Italian Ministry of Marine. A case
illustrating this is *The Kaiserrie*, a Turkish vessel which
was captured by an Italian warship during the Turco-
Italian War, on December 18th, 1911. *The Kaiserrie* was
proceeded against in the Italian Prize Court, and condemnation was resisted on the ground that she was a
hospital ship and therefore not liable to capture under
the Third Hague Convention, 1899. The Court held
that she was in fact a Turkish warship which had been
used as a transport, and accordingly ordered her to
be placed at the disposal of the Ministry of Marine.

In 1917 the Italian Government issued "Norme per
l'esercizio del diritto di preda" in which the term warship was extended to all public vessels of the enemy.[2]

Germany. The German Prize Court Regulations of
April 15th, 1911, provide as follows (Sec. 2):

> Prizes within the meaning of this Ordinance are enemy or
> neutral merchant vessels, i.e. all vessels not being the property
> of the state, as well as all enemy or neutral goods, &c.

---

[1] *Rev. gén. de Droit international* (1921), Jurisprudence, p. 1;
J. H. W. Verzijl, *Le Droit des Prises*, p. 319; C. J. Colombos, *The
Law of Prize*, p. 40.   [2] Verzijl, *op. cit.* p. 321.

Public vessels are thus expressly excluded from the definition of prize, and in various cases during the late war, German Prize Courts refused to exercise jurisdiction over captured or destroyed enemy public ships.[1]

Russia. The Russian Prize Regulations of July 14th, 1895, provide as follows (Art. 10):

"Ships of war and merchant vessels of the enemy are subject to condemnation as prizes, as well as articles on board" with certain exceptions.

This is qualified by Article 27 which states that the confiscation of captured warships and their cargoes is effected by order of the competent naval authority.[2] It thus appears that, except by British practice, it is the general rule that ships of war captured from the enemy are not condemned by the Prize Court, but pass at once to the state.

II

The treatment of ships of war as prize by British Prize Courts is governed by Statutes, Royal Proclamations, and Orders in Council, and the matter is closely connected with the grants of prize to captors.[3]

Under the Commonwealth, an Ordinance of 1649 directed

that in all prizes taken from the enemies of the Commonwealth, a moiety should be given to the captors, and that the other moiety

---

[1] Verzijl, *op. cit.* p. 314; for similar decisions in the Austrian Prize Courts see *idem*, p. 315.

[2] *Idem*, p. 323.

[3] The history of prize has been carefully studied by Mr R. G. Marsden in three articles in the *English Historical Review* in 1909, 1910, and 1911; he has also edited for the Navy Records Society two volumes on *The Law and Custom of the Sea*, where much valuable information is to be found. Sir Christopher Robinson in his *Collectanea Maritima* brought together a number of public instruments illustrative of the history and practice of Prize Law to which he added some valuable notes. See also E. S. Roscoe, *A History of the English Prize Court* (1924).

should be disposed in the name of the Treasurer of the Admiralty, to raise a fund for charitable purposes, rewards, &c. For all enemy's ships of war, burnt, sunk, or destroyed, was to be paid, for an Admiral's ship £20 per gun; for a Rear-Admiral's £16 per gun; for other ships of war, £10 per gun.[1]

An Act of 1661, passed for the better regulation and discipline of the Navy, only incidentally mentions the interest of captors in prizes, directing

that nothing shall be taken out of a prize ship, till condemned; that an account shall be given of the whole without fraud, on pain of such punishment as the Court Martial or Admiralty Court shall inflict except everything above the gun deck; but arms, ammunition, tackle, furniture or stores, which are not to be touched.

This practice of allowing pillage was an ancient one, but does not appear in the later Statute of 4 and 5 Will. and Mary, c. 25, which makes provision for the division of the proceeds of the prize, giving one-fifth to their Majesties in case of captures by privateers, and one-third in cases of captures by ships of the Royal Navy. It reappears again in a Prize Proclamation of 1702 which orders prizes to be condemned and sold openly "by inch of candle to the best advantage" and one-half of the net proceeds to be paid to the captors,

but all such ships of war of France or Spain, or privateers of either of those nations which may be fit for H.M.'s service are not to be disposed of till such time as H.M. shall have the refusal thereof. And in case H.M. shall take any such ship into her service, the captors shall have £10 per ton for the ships of war, and the whole of such privateers taken as aforesaid, according to appraisement, except one-tenth part to the Lord High Admiral.

The provisions as to pillage give officers and crews of H.M. ships all goods and merchandises as may be found on any ship they shall take in fight upon or above the gun-deck. The gun-money provisions of the Proclama-

[1] Scobell's *Acts*, April, 1649; C. Robinson, *op. cit.* 193; R. G. Marsden, *Eng. Hist. Rev.* 1911, p. 37.

tions give to any of H.M. ships of war as should take in fight, or sink, fire or destroy any enemy ship of war, as a reward for each piece of ordnance whether iron or brass in any ship of war, etc., so taken or destroyed, £10 to be paid out of H.M.'s share of prizes.[1]

The Prize Act of 1708, an Act for the encouragement of a particular service on the coasts of America, for the first time gave to the captors the *whole* interest in Prizes taken in America, and in the same session of Parliament a general Act was passed transferring the whole benefit from the Crown to the captors. The Act was limited to the then-existing war, but corresponding provisions were inserted in Acts passed at the beginning of subsequent wars. The provisions regarding the allocation of the values of condemned enemy warships and privateers to the captors are explicit, but there is a provision for the appraisement of ships taken into the Queen's service, by persons appointed by H.M. or the Admiralty and an equal number appointed by the captors.

"Gun-money" was changed to "Head-money"; Sec. 8 gave £5 for every man living on board any enemy ship of war or privateer at the beginning of the engagement. "Head-money" became permanent, but it is now, by the Naval Prize Act, 1864, called "Prize Bounty."

Prize Acts subsequent to the Act of 1708 were framed on similar lines, though many of them were of greater length and dealt more fully with questions of prize law. Grants of Prize to the captors were made by Royal Proclamation, confirmed by Prize Acts passed at the beginning of all subsequent wars down to 1914, except in the case of a war with Turkey in 1807. In the course of this war various captures were made, and taken into Malta and Gibraltar. These Vice-Admiralty Courts not having received any Commission to proceed to

[1] R. G. Marsden, *Law and Custom of the Sea*, vol. II, p. 186.

adjudication, and the captors having no authority to detain the prizes in their own names, no Prize Proclamation having been issued, such vessels and cargoes were handed over to the Receiver of Droits, and sold by him and the proceeds transmitted to England. On December 5th, 1808, nearly two years after Turkey had declared war against England, an Order in Council was issued to the Court of Admiralty, "to judicially proceed upon the said Turkish ship of war, *Badere Zaffer*, and ... upon proof that the said ship was a ship of war bearing the flag of the Ottoman Empire to adjudge and condemn the same as good and lawful prize to His Majesty." There was a direction, after condemnation, for the sale of the vessel, and for the distribution of the proceeds in accordance with the General Proclamation for the distribution of prizes. It was not till September 29th, 1812, that the Prize Court was empowered to deal with other captures taken in this war, and the proceeds of the sale of the prizes were not vested in the captors, as had been the case in former wars, but in His Majesty.[1]

III

The Naval Prize Act, 1864, together with amending Acts and Orders in Council, is the basis of the modern law relating to prize procedure. Section 55 expressly states that nothing in the Act shall give to the officers and crews of H.M. ships of war any right or claim in or to any ship or goods taken as prize or the proceeds thereof; it being the intent of the Act that officers and crews should continue to take only such interest (if any) in the proceeds of prize as may from time to time be granted by the Crown. No grant of prize was made to the officers and crews of H.M. Navy at the beginning of the war in 1914. In 1918 a Naval Prize Act was

[1] H. C. Rothery, *Prize Droits*, p. 95.

passed (8 and 9 Geo. V, c. 30) under the authority of which a Royal Proclamation was issued creating a Naval Prize Fund composed of the net produce of all prizes captured during war as should be declared by the tribunal appointed by the Act to be Droits of the Crown, to be distributable according to the terms of that Act. Proceedings in prize still remained under the Naval Prize Act, 1864, and the amending Acts and Orders in Council.

The Naval Prize Act, 1864, and the Prize Court Rules, 1914, contain provisions for dealing with captured enemy warships. Section 16 of the principal Act orders that enemy ships taken as prize, and brought into port within the jurisdiction of a Prize Court, shall forthwith, and without bulk broken, be delivered up to the Marshal of the Court. 4 and 5 Geo. V, c. 13, section 1 repeals certain provisions of the Act of 1864, but provides that nothing in such repeal shall have the effect of extending Section 16 of that Act to ships of war taken as prize, and accordingly that section shall have effect as if the following words were inserted therein: "Nothing in this section shall apply to ships of war taken as prize." This provision was to enable proceedings to be taken against ships of war without the necessity of placing the ships under the custody of the Marshal. As we have seen, such ships were frequently purchased into the Navy before proceedings in prize were taken. There is also a further provision (Sec. 30) under which captors can include in one adjudication any number, not exceeding six, of armed ships not exceeding 100 tons each taken within three months next before institution of proceedings. Various provisions in the present Prize Court Rules also refer to prize proceedings relating to ships of war, including a form of condemnation (e.g. I, 1; X; XV, 1; XXXIII). It is, therefore, clear that the older Prize Acts as well as those at present in force make express provision for ships of war being made the subject of proceedings in prize. It is, however, to be noted that though a capture may come under the definition of prize, it does not necessarily pass to the captors, and as all prizes belong to the Crown, if no grant is made every prize captured would be adjudged to the King *jure Coronae* and would be condemned to him.[1]

IV

When we turn to the reports of Prize Cases there is singularly little information to be found regarding the proceedings against ships of war. This is as might well be expected, as in the majority of cases they would be undefended, and no point of law would arise. Sometimes, however, the interest of the alleged captor would be challenged by another ship and questions of joint capture be raised by single ships, squadrons, or fleets. The army might sometimes claim to share in the proceeds of prizes taken by a conjoint naval and military expedition. In such cases interesting and frequently difficult questions of law and fact would arise, and there are a number of cases of this type in the old prize reports.[2]

It has already been noticed that special provisions for the incorporation into the Royal Navy of suitable captured enemy vessels were made by the Statute of 1708. The subsequent Prize Acts do not appear to have contained similar provisions, but it long remained a common practice for captured enemy ships to be added to the Navy in this way. Whether they were first condemned or condemned at all, it was by no means easy

---

[1] *The ships taken at Genoa*, 4 C. Rob. 388.
[2] *The Minerva* (6 C. Rob. 396); *The L'Alerte* (6 C. Rob. 238); *The Matilda* (1 Dod. 367); *The La Bellone* (2 Dod. 343); *The L'Etoile* (2 Dod. 106). See also the American case of *The Georgia* (7 Wall. 32).

to ascertain, but a search in the Admiralty Library, and the assistance of the authorities at the Public Record Office enabled definite information to be obtained. A typical case is that of *La Hoche* and her consorts, captured off Tory Island on the coast of Ireland during the attempted descent of a French force. *La Hoche* was captured on October 12th, 1798, and appears in the Navy List as *The Donegal* on December 21st of the same year. In this case proceedings appear to have been taken in the ordinary way for the condemnation of the vessels, and *La Hoche* was condemned on February 5th, 1799. One other case will suffice, that of "the famed *Belle Poule*" referred to in the old song "The Arethusa." She was captured off the coast of France on July 14th, 1780, and appears in the Navy List on August 16th, 1780, but she was not condemned until September 20th following. In all the cases examined there is a record of condemnation.

The value of the warships awarded to the captors was that of "the hull, ordnance and ordnance stores" and notices of distribution of Prize Money in the *London Gazette* state the proportions of the hull, stores (and in some cases, head-money) arising from the capture.

But when enemy warships were destroyed, the loss of Prize Money thus occasioned was felt to be a serious matter for the Fleet, and two examples taken from the life of Nelson show how he regarded the question.

After the Battle of the Nile, Nelson appointed Alexander Davison sole agent for the captured ships. Before leaving Egypt, he ordered three of these to be burnt, owing to the difficulty and delay in fitting them for passage to Gibraltar. In regard to this action of his he wrote to the Admiralty:

I rest assured that they will be paid for, and have held out that assurance to the squadron. For if an Admiral after a victory is to look after the captured ships and not to the distressing of the

14-2

enemy, very dearly indeed must the nation pay for the prizes. I trust that £60,000 will be deemed a moderate sum for them.... An Admiral may be amply rewarded by his own feelings, and by the approbation of his superiors, but what reward have the inferior officers and men but the value of the prizes?[1]

In the Battle of Copenhagen, six battleships and eight praams were taken, but all of them except *The Holstein* (64 guns) were burnt by order of Admiral Hyde Parker, the Commander-in-Chief. Nelson took up the cause of those who had thus been deprived of Prize Money. He asked for a message from the King to the House of Commons for a gift to the Fleet; "for what," he asked, "must be the natural feelings of the officers and men belonging to it, to see their rich Commander-in-Chief burn all the fruits of their victory, which, if fitted up, and sent to England (as many of them might have been, by dismantling part of our fleet), would have sold for a good round sum."[2]

It appears to be clear that the necessity for proceeding in prize to be taken in British Prize Courts in the case of enemy warships arises from the provisions of the Royal Proclamation granting prizes to the captors which it has been the custom of the Crown to issue. The interest of the captors only becomes effective after condemnation has been decreed. If there has been no grant of prize, it does not appear that proceedings in prize are necessary, as the property would pass to the Crown when the capture is complete.

[1] Southey's *Life of Nelson*, chap. v.
[2] Southey, *op. cit.* chap. viii.

XII

RETALIATION IN NAVAL WARFARE[1]

INTERNATIONAL Law has at its disposal certain means for insuring compliance with its rules, as and when these rules are broken. Among these methods is that of reprisals or retaliation, by which one belligerent retaliates upon another by acts which are otherwise illegitimate in order to force his adversary to cease from the commission of illegitimate acts of warfare and to compel him to comply with the rules of International Law. Retaliation may be resorted to by a belligerent to compensate himself for wrongful acts done; more frequently, in order to secure a cessation of the illegitimate acts of which he complains.

All the codes of warfare published by states recognize the legitimacy of reprisals, but every attempt which has hitherto been made to regulate them by international agreement has been unsuccessful. These attempts were made at the Brussels Conference of 1874 and at The Hague Peace Conferences of 1899 and 1907 with reference to land warfare. No similar attempts have been made as regards naval warfare, but that a right of retaliation exists both in land and sea warfare is incontestable and the war of 1914–18 unfortunately afforded examples too numerous to mention in detail.

The principle of reprisals or retaliation may be established by analogy to the rules of the so-called natural law, and also to those of the common and civil law. Where there is a bilateral engagement and one of the parties refuses to fulfil his part, the other is exonerated

[1] Based on a lecture delivered at the United States Naval War College, 1927. Published in *The British Year Book of International Law*, 1927.

from his share in the undertaking. So, too, when a state is prosecuting its demand by war, it cannot in reason be expected to observe all the rules at the risk of defeat or of leaving its forces exposed to avoidable suffering, when its adversary has refused to keep those rules.

In the course of reprisals or retaliation it follows that one man is punished for the wrongful acts of another, a measure in itself clearly repugnant to all feelings of justice. It has, therefore, been universally held that belligerents are bound not to resort to such a proceeding in haste or by the exercise of excessive measures, but only under pressure of necessity when no other means appear to be capable of deterring the enemy from the commission of his offences. The method of reprisals need not be identical with the wrong done.

The subject involves fundamental ideas as to the real nature of war, whether it is the relation of state to state, and to what extent, if any, the citizens of a state other than its combatant forces are involved. It is a subject on which much has been written and we cannot now enter into the realm of philosophic theory—valuable though it may be. I prefer to accept the summary of the arguments given by Westlake, who, after examining the subject from both the inductive and deductive standpoints, lays down broadly the following positions:

1. War is undoubtedly a relation of state to state whatever else it may be as well.

2. War establishes between each of the states which are parties to it and the subjects of the enemy state a relation which entitles the former to treat them as identified with their state, in other words, as enemies so far as the necessities of war require, under the limitations which are recognized as being imposed by humanity.... The men who form a state are not allowed to disclaim their part in the offences alleged against it, whether those on account of which the war was begun or those charged as having been committed by it in the course of the war, or therefore to claim that

hostile action shall not be directed against their state through them in their respective measures. And this is just. Whatever is done or committed by a state is done or committed by the men who are grouped in it, or at least the deed or the commission is sanctioned by them. The state is not a self-acting machine. And if we look more closely at the facts, we shall probably find that in the foreign affairs of a state the rulers more often act under the impulse of a mass than by its tacit permission, and that tacit permission is seldom conceded by the mass except those who embody and represent the national character.

3. War establishes no direct relation between the members of the respective belligerent states, and in that sense it is true that war is not a relation of individual to individual. The personalities of a state and its subjects are distinct....To use the analogy of private law, a state may be described as a corporation or technical person, though not as one with limited liability. The limitation by the laws of war of the hostile action which may be taken against an individual is analogous, not to any limitation in private law of a shareholder's liability for the debts of a company in which the shares are held, but to the joint effect in private law of the principle that the incorporated company must be the primary object of attack, the shareholder's liability, even though unlimited, being only subsidiary to that of the company, and of whatever limitation the law may have imposed for the sake of humanity on the execution to be obtained against a debtor in any case.[1]

It is necessary to be clear on this relation of the state to the individuals composing it because as regards the question of retaliation it becomes of importance. This is especially true as regards naval warfare, where the capture of privately owned property is recognized as legal by the general consensus of states and has been universally practised.

War, says Dana,[2] is undertaken to cause your enemy to do the act of justice assumed to be necessary, and nations must have it in their power to coerce the body politic with which they are at war by a coercion applied to all its citizens in all their interests, and to

[1] *Collected Papers*, p. 269.
[2] Dana's note to Wheaton, p. 401.

identify the private interests of each of their subjects with the national fortunes in the war. Students of naval history who accept Mahan's views on the nature and object of naval warfare recognize the truth of his doctrine that property belonging to private individuals embodied in the process of commerce is like money in circulation. It is national in its employment and only private in its ownership. To stop such circulation is to sap national prosperity, on which war depends for its energy.

When there has been a violation of the laws of war, retaliation in naval warfare is primarily directed against the delinquent state and may take the form of denying it and its citizens certain rights and immunities to which they have become entitled either by the general rules of International Law or under special convention. The only limitation on the right is the overriding law of humanity; for instance, because state A sinks at sight the merchant ships of state B, state B does not become entitled to retaliate by doing the like. Hence it is within the competence of the offended state to declare that certain property otherwise immune from capture shall cease to enjoy the immunity, as a retaliation for illegal practices, and that trade which the belligerent subjects have hitherto carried on shall henceforth be restricted or forbidden.

It will rarely happen that illegalities committed in naval war by one belligerent will affect the other belligerent alone. Experience has shown that neutral rights, or alleged rights, will invariably be involved. Moreover, it has also been demonstrated by experience that when the injured belligerent decrees reprisals, neutral rights, or alleged rights, will likewise come into conflict with the methods of reprisals adopted. In land warfare such complications are not often likely to occur, though even here it may happen that neutral-owned property will suffer, as where devastation of a territory has been ordered by way of reprisals.

In the Napoleonic wars and again in the war of 1914–18, Great Britain resorted to reprisals at sea to meet illegal acts on the part of an adversary; and in the latter war Germany and the Central Powers resorted to acts which they also sought to justify under the name of reprisals. In 1812 the United States went to war with Great Britain on account, amongst other reasons, of the exercise of the right of retaliation against France whereby her interests as a neutral state were affected. The war of 1812–14 was inconclusive as regards the objects for which it was waged. The Treaty of Ghent is silent on the important questions which were the *casus belli*.[1] Again, in the course of the war of 1914–18, when Great Britain and France decreed reprisals against Germany and the Central Powers, protests were made by the United States and other neutral Powers. In this case, however, the United States and other neutrals took up arms in the cause of Great Britain and the Allies and proceeded to perform acts on the high seas in conjunction with the British Fleet for which, apart from the doctrine of retaliation, it may not be easy to find a safe line of legal defence. I refer here to the work done by the United States Navy in its co-operation in the establishment of the North Sea barrage in laying the mine-field between Orkney and the coast of Norway with a view to limiting the passage of German submarines and of restricting their access to the Atlantic through the southerly and more dangerous channels. On this operation Dr Charles Cheney Hyde makes the following observations:

The nature of the service in which those vessels were then engaged, and the effect of their operations (if not so thwarted) upon the duration, if not the outcome of the conflict, together

[1] H. Wheaton, *History of the Law of Nations*, p. 585.

with the insufficiency of other means of combating them, will doubtless be acknowledged to have justified recourse to this extraordinary and efficacious measure, despite the restrictions which it necessarily imposed upon neutral shipping.[1]

The history of the British and French proceedings during the Napoleonic wars would involve a study of the British Orders in Council and of the famous Berlin and Milan Decrees, which it is not my intention to pursue.[2] Suffice it to say that the Berlin Decree, issued by Napoleon on November 21st, 1806, after making charges of illegality against Great Britain, proceeded to declare that the whole of the British Islands were in a state of blockade, and prohibited all trade and intercourse with them. Neutral ships were threatened with condemnation for breach of this Decree. To this the British Order in Council retaliated by prohibiting the trade of neutrals between two ports, one of which should be in possession of France, and likewise threatened condemnation of neutral vessels violating the Order. The foundation of this Order in Council was stated to be that the attempts of the enemy illegally to prohibit the commerce of neutrals with British dominions gave an unquestionable right of retaliation and warranted Great Britain in enforcing the same prohibition upon all commerce with France. The Milan Decree, with still greater severities, followed on December 17th, 1807, and in its turn was followed by the British Order in Council of April 26th, 1809.

[1] *International Law*, vol. II, p. 422.
[2] See *Camb. Mod. Hist.* vol. IX, chap. xiii, in which Professor Holland Rose points out that the facilities granted to neutrals under the British Orders in Council were clearly of such a kind as to disprove the charge that the British Government deliberately sought to ruin neutral commerce. Though they pressed severely on all states which freely placed their resources at the disposal of Napoleon, they sought to lessen the hardships of those on which the Continental System was imposed by force (p. 367).

Many cases were heard and decided in the British Prize Courts under these Orders in Council by Sir William Scott (Lord Stowell), and many of these were affirmed by the Lords of Appeal. Of the latter decisions, some were first brought forth from the public records during the arguments in cases during the late war, though there were plenty of decisions by Sir William Scott in the Law Reports showing that retaliation was recognized by the British Prize Courts as a legal right, and that breach of the blockade of France was not the only basis of the decisions. It may be stated that apart from the question of blockade, Sir William Scott proceeded on the principle that where there is a just cause for retaliation neutrals may by the Law of Nations be required to submit to inconvenience from the act of a belligerent Power ordering retaliation greater in degree than would be justified had no cause of retaliation arisen.[1] Sir William Scott's words on this point are very explicit:

Retaliatory measures they are. I have no hesitation in saying they would cease to be just if they ceased to be retaliatory, and they would cease to be retaliatory from the moment the enemy retracts in a sincere manner from those measures of his which they are intended to retaliate. So far, this retaliatory blockade (if blockade it can be called) is coextensive with the principle that neutrals are prohibited to trade with France because they are prohibited by France from trading with England.[2]

At the time when Sir William Scott was administering the law of the Prize Court it was a recognized rule of Anglo-American Prize Law that enemy goods were liable to capture under any flag. It was an old rule dating back to the *Consolato del Mare* of the thirteenth or fourteenth century, and it is surprising to read Mahan's statement that in the Seven Years' War "it

[1] See also *The Zamora* (1916), A.C. 77, 97.
[2] *The Fox* (1807), Edwards 314–21. Cf. *The Snipe* (1812), *ibid.* 381–3.

suited England to maintain that enemy's property was liable to capture on board neutral ships, thus subjecting these nations not only to vexatious detention but to loss of valuable trade."[1] This was nothing new, but at the opening of the war in 1914 this rule had been changed as regards the signatories of the Declaration of Paris, of which the United States is not one, so that under it, enemy goods, except contraband of war, are free when under a neutral flag. This is undoubtedly a restriction on belligerent rights. Until the issue by Great Britain and France of the Retaliatory Order and Decree of March, 1915 (Portugal adopted the same rule in August, 1916), the rules of the Declaration of Paris were observed. In consequence of the German violations of the laws of war, violations against which no neutral state made an effective protest though their citizens were seriously affected thereby, the British Order in Council of March 11th, 1915, and the corresponding French Decree purported to stop all trade between Germany and the outer world. No neutral vessel was to be allowed to proceed to any German port. Goods on board were to be discharged in a British or French port and detained for the duration of the war. No vessel which sailed from a German port was to be allowed to proceed with goods laden in such port. Goods on board were to be discharged in British or French ports and detained or sold, and the proceeds held till the end of the war. Vessels carrying goods to any port other than German, but with an enemy destination, were subject to similar treatment, as were also vessels having on board goods of enemy origin or enemy ownership. Subsequently this order was extended to the other Central Powers on January 10th, 1917, and on February 16th, 1917, after the German

[1] A. T. Mahan, *Influence of Sea Power on History* (12th ed. 1896), p. 312.

War Zone decree of February 1st, 1917, which was declared to be "in flagrant contradiction with the rules of international law, the dictates of humanity, and the treaty obligations of the enemy," all vessels encountered at sea on their way to or from a port in any neutral country affording means of access to enemy territory without calling at a British or Allied port were, until the contrary was established, declared to be carrying goods with an enemy destination or of enemy origin, and were to be brought in for examination and, if necessary, for adjudication by a Prize Court. Goods found to be of enemy origin or destination and the vessels carrying them were to be liable to condemnation. It will be noticed that the complications caused by the use of the term "blockade" in the Napoleonic Orders in Council were avoided by the non-user of this term in these Orders in Council, though the effect undoubtedly was of a similar character to that obtained by blockade.

It may be well at this point to note that when the Judicial Committee of the Privy Council decided in the case of the *Zamora*[1] that the Prize Court was not bound by executive acts such as Orders in Council which violated the Law of Nations, it laid down the principle that as regards Orders in Council authorizing retaliation the facts recited as showing that a case for reprisals existed would be treated as conclusive as to the opinion of His Majesty's advisers of the best and only means of meeting the emergency, but it would not preclude the right of the Court to hold that the means taken were unlawful as entailing on neutrals a degree of inconvenience unreasonable considering all the circumstances of the case.

What then were the facts which led to the issue of these Orders in Council decreeing retaliation first

[1] (1916), 2 A.C. 77.

against Germany and then against the other Central
Powers? They are recapitulated by Sir Samuel Evans
in his judgment in the case of the *Leonora*:

In the first week of February, 1915—I think on February 4—
the German Government issued an official declaration that the
English Channel, and north and west coasts of France, and all
waters round the British Isles would be treated as a "war area,"
and that all enemy ships, whatever their character, found in that
area would be destroyed, and neutral vessels would be exposed to
danger. Even before this the enemy had shown how they were
prepared to treat vessels belonging to their adversaries, whatever
the class or mission of such vessels might be. Near the end of
October, 1914, a German torpedo had sunk a French passenger
steamer—the *Amiral Ganteaume*—with more than 2,000 unarmed
refugees on board, including a large proportion of women and
children. By good fortune a British steamship, happening to be
near, succeeded in rescuing most of the passengers, but a considerable number lost their lives.

The declaration by Germany of the "war area" already referred to was communicated by this country to all the important
neutral countries (including of course, Holland and Sweden),
in a Note dated March 1, 1915. The Note commented upon the
declaration and also foreshadowed the retaliatory measures which
would be adopted, and were afterwards incorporated in the Order
in Council of March 11, 1915.

.   .   .   .

Then followed in due course the first Order in Council as a
retaliatory order. It recited that the German Government had
issued certain Orders which in violation of the usages of war
purported to declare the waters surrounding the United Kingdom
a military area, in which all British and Allied merchant vessels
would be destroyed, irrespective of the safety of the lives of
passengers and crews, and in which neutral shipping would be
exposed to similar danger in view of the uncertainties of naval
warfare, and had warned neutrals against entrusting crews,
passengers or goods to British or Allied ships. It contained further
recitals to the effect that the enemy's conduct gave to this country
an unquestionable right to retaliation; that His Majesty had
therefore decided to adopt measures in order to prevent commodities of any kind from reaching or leaving Germany, but that such
measures would be enforced without risk to neutral ships or to

neutral non-combatant life, and in strict observance of the dictates of humanity; and that the object of such measures was to restrict the commerce of Germany.

.   .   .   .

To revert to the history of the enemy's conduct at sea after the declaration of February, 1915, the German authorities lost no time in carrying into effect their threats. Their submarines sank British ships, and destroyed lives of innocent persons in March. In April they sank Dutch, Swedish and Portuguese ships (Portugal at that time being neutral). They also torpedoed a Belgian relief ship without warning and sank her in five minutes, causing the loss of 17 lives—although it was in the daytime and the vessel was flying the Belgian Relief Commission's flag and displaying the Commission screens on both sides, marked "Commission Belgian Relief, Rotterdam," in letters over 2 ft. high; and had actually been granted a safe conduct by the German consul at The Hague.

And it will be remembered—can it ever be forgotten?—that on May 7, the *Lusitania* was torpedoed and sunk when she was carrying nearly 2,000 persons of all classes and ages, and that in the frightful disaster 1,198 men, women and children were drowned. No more callous or cruel crime has been committed since the day of Cain....

In the beginning of 1917 the severity of the submarine atrocities was to be increased, and a formal announcement of an almost unlimited submarine warfare in European waters was made by a Memorandum of the German Government, which was expressly directed against "all sea traffic."[1]

These were the facts on which the Retaliatory Orders in Council were based which claimants were not allowed to dispute, but neutrals could plead that the measures taken in return inflicted on them an unreasonable measure of inconvenience.

The British Prize Court has, on more than one occasion, emphasized its position as a protector of neutral rights, and in the case of the *Stigstad*, in which the first of the retaliatory orders was upheld, Lord Sumner said of the court:

[1] B. and C.P.C. vol. III, p. 181.

Its function is, in protection of the rights of neutrals, to weigh on a proper occasion the measures of retaliation which had been adopted in fact, and to inquire whether they are in their nature and extent other than commensurate with the prior wrong done, and whether they inflict on neutrals, when they are looked on as a whole, inconvenience greater than is reasonable under all the circumstances.[1]

In the following passage from the same judgment the Court proceeds to explain the principles which were to guide it in estimating the reasonableness of the inconvenience to which neutrals were subjected:

In considering whether more inconvenience is inflicted upon neutrals than the circumstances involve, the frequency and the enormity of the original wrongs are alike material, for the more gross and universal those wrongs are, the more are all nations concerned in their repression, and bound for their part to submit to such sacrifices as that repression involves. It is right to recall that, as neutral commerce suffered and was doomed to suffer gross prejudice from the illegal policy proclaimed and acted on by the German Government, so it profited by, and obtained relief from retaliatory measures, if effective to restrain, to punish and to bring to an end such injurious conduct. Neutrals, whose principles or policy lead them to refrain from punitory or repressive action of their own, may well be called on to bear a passive part in the necessary suppression of courses which are fatal to the freedom of all who use the seas.

The argument principally urged at the bar ignored these considerations, and assumed an absolute right in neutral trade to proceed without interference or restriction, unless by the application of the rules heretofore established as to contraband traffic, unneutral service and blockade. The assumption was that a neutral, too pacific or too impotent to resent the aggressions and lawlessness of one belligerent, can require the other to refrain from his most effective, or his only defence against it, by the assertion of an absolute inviolability for his own neutral trade, which would thereby become engaged in a passive complicity with the original offender. For this contention no authority at all was forthcoming. Reference was made to the Orders in Council of 1806 and 1809 which were framed by way of retaliation for the

[1] L.R. (1919), A.C. 286.

Berlin and Milan decrees. There has been much discussion of these celebrated instruments on one side or the other, though singularly little in decided cases or in treatises of repute; and, according to their nationality or their partisanship, writers have denounced the one policy or the other, or have asserted their own superiority by an impartial censure of both. The present Order, however, does not involve for its justification a defence of the very terms of those Orders in Council. It must be judged on its merits and, if the principle is advanced against it that such retaliation is wrong in kind, no foundation in authority has been found on which to rest it. Nor is the principle itself sound. The seas are the highway of all, and it is incidental to the very nature of maritime war that neutrals, in using the highway, may suffer inconvenience from the exercise of their concurrent rights by those who have to wage war upon it. Of this fundamental fact the right of blockade is only an example. It is true that contraband, blockade, and unneutral service are branches of international law which have their own history, their own illustrations, and their own development. Their growth has been unsystematic, and the assertion of rights under these different heads has not been closely connected or simultaneous. Nevertheless, it would be illogical to regard them as being in themselves disconnected topics or as being the subject of rights and liabilities which have no common connexion. They may also be treated, as in fact they are, as illustrations of the broad rule that belligerency and neutrality are states so related to one another that the latter must accept some abatement of the full benefits of peace in order that the former may not be thwarted in war in the assertion and defence of what is the most precious of all the rights of nations, the right to security and independence. The categories of such cases are not closed. To deny to the belligerent under the head of retaliation any right to interfere with the trade of neutrals beyond that which, quite apart from circumstances which warrant retaliation, he enjoys already under the heads of contraband, blockade, and unneutral service, would be to take away with one hand what has formally been conceded with the other. As between belligerents, acts of retaliation are either the return of blow for blow in the course of combat, or are questions of the laws of war not immediately falling under the cognizance of a Court of Prize. Little of this subject is left to Prize Law beyond its effect on neutrals and on the rights of belligerents against neutrals, and to say that re-taliation is invalid as against neutrals, except within the old limits of blockade, contraband, and unneutral service, is to reduce retaliation to a mere simulacrum, the title of an admitted right without practical application or effect.[1]

It will be recalled that the Order in Council of March, 1915, only provided for sequestration of goods removed from vessels violating its terms. We now pass to the *Leonora*, in which the validity of the Order in Council of February 16th, 1917, which decreed condemnation of goods of enemy origin or destination and vessels carrying such goods when they failed to comply with its terms, was upheld. In delivering the judgment of the Privy Council in this case, Lord Sumner said:

Upon the validity of the Order in Council itself the appellants advanced a two-fold argument. The major proposition was that the Order purported to create an offence, namely, failure to call at a British or Allied port, which is unknown to the law of nations, and to impose punishment upon neutrals for committing it: in both respects it was said that the Order is incompetent. The minor proposition was that the belligerent's right to take measures of retaliation, such as it is, must be limited, as against neutrals, by the condition that the exercise of that right must not inflict on neutrals an undue or disproportionate degree of inconvenience. In the present case various circumstances of inconvenience were relied on, notably the perils of crossing the North Sea to a British port of call and the fact that no particular port of call in Great Britain had been appointed for the vessel to proceed to.[2]

He then stated the Court's adhesion to the principle previously laid down in the *Stigstad* dealing with the right of retaliation, and added a further pronouncement on the general position of belligerents and neutrals:

There are certain rights, which a belligerent enjoys by the law of nations in virtue of belligerency, which may be enforced even against neutral subjects and to the prejudice of their perfect freedom of action, and this because without those rights maritime war would be frustrated and the appeal to the arbitrament of arms be made of none effect. Such for example are the rights of visit and search, the right of blockade and the right of preventing traffic in contraband of war. In some cases a part of the mode in

[1] L.R. (1919), A.C. p. 287.   [2] *Ibid.* p. 983.

which the right is exercised consists of some solemn act of proclamation on the part of the belligerent, by which notice is given to all the world of the enforcement of these rights and of the limits set to their exercise. Such is the proclamation of a blockade and the notification of a list of contraband. In these cases the belligerent Sovereign does not create a new offence *motu proprio*; he does not, so to speak, legislate or create a new rule of law; he elects to exercise his legal rights and puts them into execution in accordance with the prescriptions of the existing law. Nor again in such cases does the retaliating belligerent invest a Court of Prize with a new jurisdiction or make the Court his mandatory to punish a new offence. The office of a Court of Prize is to provide a formal and regular sanction for the law of nations applicable to maritime warfare, both between belligerent and belligerent and between belligerent and neutral. Whether the law in question is brought into operation by the act of both belligerents in resorting to war, as is the case with the rules of international law as to hostilities in general, or by the assertion of a particular right arising out of a particular provocation in the course of the war on the part of one of them, it is equally the duty of a Court of Prize, by virtue of its general jurisdiction as such, to provide for the regular enforcement of that right, when lawfully asserted before it, and not to leave the enforcement to the mere jurisdiction of the sword. Disregard of a valid measure of retaliation is as against neutrals just as justiciable in a Court of Prize as is breach of blockade or the carriage of contraband of war. The jurisdiction of a Court of Prize is at least as essential in the neutral's interest as in the interest of the belligerent, and if the Court is to have power to release in the interest of the one, it must also have inherent power to condemn in justice to the other. Capture and condemnation are the prescriptive and established modes by which the law of nations as applicable to maritime warfare is enforced. Statutes and international conventions may invest the Court with other powers or prescribe other modes of enforcing the law, and the belligerent Sovereign may in the appropriate form waive part of his rights and disclaim condemnation in favour of some milder sanction, such as detention.[1]

It had been argued that the cases decided by Sir William Scott in the Napoleonic era were all cases of

[1] L.R. (1919), A.C. p. 984.

blockade, and that he had not pronounced on the legality of retaliation. To this Lord Sumner's reply is:

> In their [Lordships'] opinion Sir William Scott's doctrine consistently was that retaliation is a branch of the rights which the law of nations recognizes as belonging to belligerents, and that it is as much enforceable by Courts of Prize as is the right of blockade. They find no warrant or authority for holding that it is only enforceable by them, when it chances to be exercised under the form or the conditions of a valid blockade. When once it is established that the conduct of the enemy gave occasion for the exercise of the right of retaliation, the real question is whether the mode in which it has been exercised is such as to be invalid by reason of the burden which it imposes on neutrals, a question preeminently one of fact and of degree.[1]

But it was further argued, neutrals must be compensated for any inconvenience caused to them, and the belligerents must make it worth their while to comply with the terms of the retaliatory order. This, said the Court, is inconsistent with the whole theory on which the right of retaliation is exercised.

> The right of retaliation is a right of the belligerent, not a concession by the neutral. It is enjoyed by law and not on sufferance; and doubly so when, as in the present case, the outrageous conduct of the enemy might have been treated as acts of war by all mankind.[2]

Finally, as to the peril to which neutrals were subjected by the gravity of the offences which called forth retaliation, the Court said:

> Their Lordships recall and apply what was said in *The Stigstad*, that in estimating the burden of the retaliation account must be taken of the gravity of the original offence which provoked it, and that it is material to consider not only the burden which the neutral is called upon to bear, but the peril from which, at the price of that burden, it may be expected that belligerent retaliation will deliver him. It may be—let us pray that it may be so— that an Order of this severity may never be needed and therefore may never be justified again, for the right of retaliation is one to

[1] L.R. (1919), A.C. p. 987.   [2] *Ibid.* p. 990.

be sparingly exercised and to be strictly reviewed. Still the facts must be faced. Can there be a doubt that the original provocation here was as grave as any recorded in history; that it menaced and outraged neutrals as well as belligerents; and that neutrals had no escape from the peril, except by the successful and stringent employment of unusual measures, or by an inglorious assent to the enslavement of their trade? Their Lordships have none.[1]

I have confined myself so far to a statement of the objections raised to retaliatory measures and the reasons for the legality of retaliation as laid down by the Prize Courts of Great Britain. These objections cover in the main those raised by neutral states in diplomatic notes. Among neutral states, the most vigorous protests came from the United States, and the correspondence between the British and American Governments on the British Orders in Council was not concluded when the United States entered the war in 1917. During their belligerency no seizures were made by warships of the United States, nor did American Prize Courts sit during the war. Dr Charles Cheney Hyde, formerly Solicitor to the State Department of the United States, expresses grave doubts whether International Law, as tested by the practice of maritime states up to 1917, gave to a belligerent a right to establish hostile presumptions against neutral ships not following the course prescribed in the British Orders, and he declines to admit that general grounds for retaliation afforded the basis of a valid excuse. He says, however, "It was natural that the retaliatory plea should have found favour with the belligerent prize court. Possibly a like result might be anticipated in the United States under similar circumstances."[2] The French Prize

[1] L.R. (1919), A.C. p. 991.
[2] *International Law*, vol. II, § 831, note 2. This note contains an able, but, to me, unconvincing differentiation between the British treatment of neutral shipping under the Orders in Council which the learned author criticizes adversely, and the mining of the

Courts, so far as they were concerned with the administration of the corresponding Decree of March, 1915, were limited to questions of fact as to whether particular cargoes were or were not within the operation of the Decree. They never passed any judgment as to its conformity to the Law of Nations. That is in general accord with the position of Prize Courts both in France and most other European countries, where they have not the independence from executive control which characterizes in such a remarkable manner the position of the British Prize Courts.

Though the Italian Prize Courts were not concerned with the enforcement of the Anglo-French Orders and Decrees, still in one case before them they laid down principles very similar to those enunciated by the British Courts. In the case of the *Cervignano*[1] the Court held that it was legitimate for belligerents to take, as a basis of their action, particular measures resorted to by their enemies, provided such actions did not violate the "imperious obligations of humanity," and were capable of being included under the rules of maritime law, characterized as they were at the actual time by the supreme effort which each group of belligerents was making in order to annihilate the sea-borne commerce of the enemy and prevent him from obtaining supplies of arms and ammunition.

Orkney-Norway passage in which the United States Navy cooperated (see *antea*, p. 217). For the latter Dr Hyde considers that the plea of self-defence, and not retaliation, is the justification. Is not retaliation by way of self-defence? The inference seems to be that a belligerent may resort to acts of self-defence which may imperil neutral ships and human lives, if his warnings are not observed, but that he may not, by way of retaliation, issue orders interfering with the neutral's trade with his enemy, when the non-observance of these will involve the sequestration or condemnation of neutral ships or goods.

[1] Fauchille and Basdevant, *Jurisprudence italienne*, p. 178.

Reprisals ordered by the Anglo-French Orders and Decrees were directed against property and involved the detention and, under the Order in Council of February, 1917, the condemnation of neutral ships; but the reprisals ordered by Germany and the Central Powers were far different in their operation. The declaration of war zones around Great Britain and France and in the Mediterranean, and their enforcement by means of submarines, were stated to be by way of reprisals for British and French illegalities. In the course of the execution of their Decrees the Central Powers destroyed no less than 1716 *neutral* ships, involving a loss of over 2000 lives, of whom over 900 were Dutch sailors. As to the destruction of British and Allied vessels, and the lives lost thereby, Sir Samuel Evans dealt with them sufficiently for our purpose in the extract previously cited. These facts show the dangers to which neutrals were being subjected, and from which they would obtain relief if the retaliatory measures were successfully executed.

The validity of the German declaration of war zones and the indiscriminate sinking of vessels at sight did not come up for adjudication before the German Prize Courts. These Courts decided that all such measures were actions of the executive government relating to operations of war, and were therefore not within their competence. Their jurisdiction only applied to acts done after the seizure of ships in prize; and if the destruction took place for any other reason, and without the vessel being seized in prize, the Court was incompetent.[1] Neutral claimants were thus deprived of all means of access to the courts for the prosecution of their cases or for the examination of the legality of the acts done.

The defence of British policy, which was put forward

[1] *The Eemland, The Gaasterland.* Verzijl, *Le Droit des Prises*, pp. 18, 25, 36, 708, 1046, 1262.

in the diplomatic correspondence and was based chiefly on the ground that the means adopted were a legitimate extension of the law of blockade to meet novel conditions, has not been dealt with here.[1] The blockade argument was adverted to by Sir Samuel Evans in his judgment in the *Leonora*, but was not adopted as the basis of the decision of the Court. The position taken both by the British Government and the British Prize Courts was attacked at the time by neutral states and writers, and has since been examined by text-book writers and others who are now dealing with the history of the war. There is, I believe, a general agreement, apart from some German writers, that the methods adopted by the Central Powers, even against their enemy, were illegal.

It is an accepted principle that retaliation directed solely against an enemy who violates the laws of war is, with the restrictions imposed by the laws of humanity, permissible. There are doubts as to the extent to which such reprisals may be carried. When, however, the means taken to enforce retaliation affect not only the enemy but neutrals, either directly or indirectly, there is no agreement; and it is difficult to suggest very definite lines on which one may be based. One clear rule at least may be laid down, namely, that reprisals must not violate the imperious obligations of humanity; and to this rule Anglo-French reprisals conformed. In no single case did the application of these principles involve the loss of life to either enemy non-combatant or neutral, thus differing in a striking manner from the proceedings of their adversaries.

Neutral rights have been won by a long series of struggles, and though in principle they have now become generally recognized, their content has varied

[1] See H. W. Malkin, "Blockade in modern conditions" in *The British Year Book of International Law*, 1922–23, p. 87.

with changed conditions, as witness the difficulties regarding the rules of contraband, continuous voyage,
and blockade. The Law of Nations must from its nature
have room for expansion. But if neutrals have rights,
they also have duties which correspond to those rights;
and while they have been insistent in season and out of
season on the former, they have seldom shown the same
scrupulous care in the fulfilment of the latter. The
conduct of Great Britain during the American Civil War
may be referred to in this connection. Not only in time
of war but in time of peace it is equally necessary to lay
stress on this doctrine of state duties. States must learn
that they cannot insist on the enjoyment of the liberty
accorded to them under the Law of Nations unless and
until their own acts are in harmony with the standard
of international ethics, which is predicated by the
existence of national rights.

In war this is especially the case, and if it be admitted,
as I submit it must be, that a belligerent has a legal
right of retaliation, it must follow that this right cannot
in naval warfare be exercised without an encroachment
on certain rights which neutrals could otherwise claim.
To answer illegality by illegality is obviously a procedure which is repugnant to the fundamental principles of jurisprudence, but sometimes it is unavoidable.
The war of 1914 began with a flagrant act of illegality,
the violation of Belgian neutrality. The injured state
did all it could to resist and Great Britain and
France went to Belgium's assistance. Further illegal
acts followed, involving neutral lives and property.
Paper protests by neutral states were ineffective and
feeble. Where one belligerent violates the sovereignty
of a neutral state and the latter either cannot or will
not take the necessary steps to prevent such acts of
illegality, it cannot complain if the other belligerent
refuses to be placed at a disadvantage by his adver-

sary's action and does the like. Where one belligerent
unlawfully interferes with neutral trade with the other
belligerent, and neutral states refrain from taking the
necessary means to enforce their rights, it follows that
as neutral rights are based on a compromise, the compromise breaks down and the injured belligerent has
left to him only the means of retaliation, which may
injuriously affect neutral trade. Tacit or express
acquiescence by neutrals, in the violation of their
rights, evidenced by their refraining from action tending to terminate the continuance of illegalities, is at the
same time an abandonment of their neutral duties.

On this point reference may be made to the dispatch of Sir Edward Grey of April 24th, 1916, to the
United States in which he dealt with the point raised
by the State Department, that the Government of the
United States regarded all such measures of retaliation
in war as illegal if they should incidentally inflict injury
upon neutrals. He said:

The advantage which any such principle would give to the
determined law-breaker would be so great that His Majesty's
Government cannot conceive that it would commend itself to the
conscience of mankind. To take a simple instance, suppose that
one belligerent scatters mines on the trade routes so as to impede
or destroy the commerce of his enemy—an action which is
illegitimate and calculated to inflict injury upon neutrals as well
as upon the other belligerent—what is that belligerent to do?
Is he precluded from meeting in any way this lawless attack upon
him by his enemy? His Majesty's Government cannot think that
he is not entitled by way of retaliation to scatter mines in his turn,
even though in so doing he also interferes with neutral rights. Or
take an even more extreme case. Suppose that a neutral failed
to prevent his territory being made use of by one of the belligerents
for warlike purposes, could he object to the other belligerent
acting in the same way? It would seem that the true view must
be that each belligerent is entitled to insist on being allowed to
meet his enemy on terms of equal liberty of action. If one of them
is allowed to make an attack upon the other regardless of neutral
rights, his opponent must be allowed similar latitude in prosecuting

the struggle, nor should he in that case be limited to the adoption of measures precisely identical with those of his opponent.[1]

But, it may be said, no one state can alter the law as regards other states not parties to the war without their consent. International Law has given to neutral states certain rights of commerce with belligerent states, and these rights may not be interfered with except by methods known to International Law, such as blockade or seizure of contraband. To this the answer appears to be that given by Lord Sumner, namely, where inconvenience is caused to neutrals and their rights are limited by retaliation, in estimating the burden imposed upon them regard must be had to the original offence which provoked the means of retaliation; and the neutral must accept as the price of deliverance from his peril the burden which he may be called upon to bear.[2] The belligerent is doing something for the neutral which the neutral ought to have done for himself.

But there remains a grave difficulty—that of ascertaining who is the real offender among the belligerents —who in fact first broke the law. This is not by any means always easy to ascertain, and where reprisals are decreed which would interfere with neutrals, it is the neutral who has to decide this difficult question of fact. It is against the original wrongdoer whose violation of law has given the other belligerent a right of retaliation that the neutral must bring his complaint. The neutral is not allowed by the Prize Courts of Great Britain to dispute the facts giving rise to the right to retaliate. He is not allowed by the Prize Courts of Germany to call in question the retaliatory measures at all. He is therefore at a disadvantage. It may be

---

[1] *American Journal of International Law* (1916), Spec. Supp. vol. x, p. 137.

[2] See *antea*, p. 228.

that the employment of an international commission
of enquiry to ascertain the facts on which orders for
retaliation are based may be a part solution of the
difficulty; but on the whole subject the chief remedy
for injuries caused to neutrals by illegal acts of belligerents lies in the hands of the neutrals themselves.
They must, if they demand complete exercise of their
rights, undertake the duty of seeing that a belligerent
does not violate the laws of war to their detriment. In
the end this proved to be the real sanction for the laws
of war in 1914–18. The effect of neutral opinion is the
final determining factor in the maintenance of the
legal and ethical standards which states have accepted
for belligerent operations. Non-intercourse decreed
by a powerful neutral state with a law-breaking
belligerent may prove a very serious sanction. If this
should be insufficient there remains nothing for it but
the final arbitrament of war. A belligerent, however,
would have but a poor chance if he relied solely on
neutrals who had been affected by his adversary's
illegalities. Neutrals are slow to sacrifice the peace
which they enjoy, especially when their position is one
which is bringing them great material gains. When
they do move their first steps are invariably diplomatic,
and these are always slow. The belligerent who is the
prime sufferer from breaches of the law by his enemy
will undoubtedly claim the right to disregard the law
and will refuse to fight with his arms tied by legal
regulations. The right to retaliate has been claimed as
a legal right, and should circumstances require it in the
future it will in all probability again be so claimed.
By the British practice, at any rate, its exercise is subject to review by the Prize Courts, which are independent of executive control; but neutral states will
best consult their own interests by becoming themselves
strong and prompt defenders of International Law, and

so preventing occasions from arising when an injured belligerent finds retaliation its only weapon of defence. It is in the general interests of mankind that wars should be brought to a termination as speedily as possible. Lord Grey of Fallodon, in a recently published work, says: "One lesson from the experience of the war is that we should not bind ourselves to observe any rules of war, unless those who sign them undertake to uphold them by force, if need be, against an enemy who breaks them." He communicated these ideas to Mr Theodore Roosevelt, who, in a letter dated February 1st, 1915, expressed his concurrence.[1]

Fortunately, retaliation in naval wars has been rare. Attempts to regulate it by international agreement have never been made. After the lengthy examination of the subject which has been made, it may be expected that some suggestions for the future should be offered. I venture to submit the following bases for consideration:

1. Retaliation is a right of the belligerent which must be exercised only after the greatest provocation, and as a last resort.

2. Retaliatory measures must primarily be directed only against the enemy and need not be of an identical character with the wrong complained of.

3. In the exercise of retaliation the fundamental laws of humanity must be observed.

4. In all cases of retaliation which involve inconvenience or detriment to neutrals, Prize Courts of the belligerents should have jurisdiction both to enquire into the facts alleged as giving rise to the retaliatory measures, and also to decide whether the means adopted inflict on neutrals a degree of inconvenience in excess of that necessary to terminate the alleged illegalities.

[1] *Twenty-five Years*, vol. II, pp. 102, 143.

5. Neutrals should be allowed compensation in all cases where there is undue delay in dealing with their cases in the belligerent Prize Courts under retaliatory orders, or where ship or cargo is released in consequence of an erroneous application of the order.

6. Retaliatory orders, since they are in derogation of the general rules of law, must, in case of ambiguity of language, be construed against the states issuing them.

XIII

DEFENSIVELY ARMED MERCHANT SHIPS. I

Early in July, 1914, before the Sarajevo murder, I prepared a paper which I had undertaken to read at the meeting of the International Law Association which was to be held at The Hague in the following September. I sent the manuscript to the Honorary Secretary and a copy to Dr James Brown Scott, the Editor of *The American Journal of International Law*, and then went abroad. I was unable to return to England until the end of August, owing to the disorganization of the continental railways by the outbreak of war, and I then found that the paper was in type. As the meeting of the International Law Association had necessarily been abandoned and the subject of defensively armed merchant ships had become one of immediate importance, I arranged for its publication in pamphlet form;[1] it also appeared in the October number of *The American Journal of International Law*.[2] Early in 1916 it was published, together with other articles and extracts from works on International Law on the same subject, by the United States Government as a Senate document.[3] At the request of the Director of the Trade Division of the Admiralty, Captain Richard Webb, R.N. (now Admiral Sir Richard Webb, K.C.M.G.), I wrote a short memorandum on defensively armed merchant ships, in September, 1914. This memorandum together with a copy of the paper above mentioned were transmitted by Sir Edward Grey to Sir Alan Johnstone, British Minister at The Hague, for communication to the Netherlands Government, on June 9th, 1915, in connection with the discussion in which the British Government was engaged with the Dutch Government regarding their refusal to admit British defensively armed merchant ships to their ports.[4] In 1917 I published a further paper on "Defensively armed merchant ships and submarine warfare" in which I recapitulated the evidence

[1] Also published in the Council Reports and Hague Papers of the International Law Association for 1915.
[2] Vol. VIII, pp. 705–22.
[3] International Relations of the United States, 64th Congress, 1st Session, Document No. 332.
[4] *Parl. Papers*, Misc. No. 14 (1917), p. 3 [Cd. 8690].

and the conclusions reached in the former paper and added further evidence on the same subject, with a discussion on the unprecedented situation created by the German use of submarines against merchant shipping. Both of these papers are now out of print.

The first of the two following papers is a reprint with slight amendments of that prepared for the International Law Association with the addition only of some further historical matter obtained after the paper had been printed; the second is supplementary in character, and deals with occurrences during the war of 1914–18, and subsequent discussions of the subject.

I

So long as the rule of capture of private property at sea exists unimpaired, states with mercantile marines of any importance will find that one of the problems they have to face in war is to defend their sea-borne commerce, and to attack that of their adversary. On March 26th, 1913, Mr Winston Churchill, the First Lord of the British Admiralty, made an important statement in the House of Commons regarding the methods proposed by Great Britain for the protection of trade. As reported in *The Times*, Mr Churchill's speech was as follows:

I now turn to one aspect of trade protection which requires special reference. It was made clear at the second Hague Conference and the London Conference that certain of the Great Powers have reserved to themselves the right to convert merchant steamers into cruisers, not merely in national harbours but if necessary on the high seas. There is now good reason to believe that a considerable number of foreign merchant steamers may be rapidly converted into armed ships by the mounting of guns. The sea-borne trade of the world follows well-marked routes, upon nearly all of which the tonnage of the British Mercantile Marine largely predominates. Our food-carrying liners and vessels carrying raw material following these trade routes would, in certain contingencies, meet foreign vessels armed and equipped in the manner described. If the British ships had no armament they would be at the mercy of any foreign liners carrying one effective gun and a few rounds of ammunition. It would be obviously absurd to meet the contingency of considerable numbers of foreign armoured merchant cruisers on the high seas by building an equal number of crusiers. That would expose this country to an expenditure of money to meet a particular danger altogether disproportionate to the expense caused to any foreign Power in creating that danger. Hostile cruisers, wherever they are found, will be covered and met by British ships of war, but the proper reply to an armed merchantman is another merchantman armed in her own defence. This is the position to which the Admiralty have felt it necessary to draw the attention of leading shipowners. We have felt justified in pointing out to them the danger to life and property which would be incurred if their vessels were totally incapable of offering any defence to an attack. The shipowners have responded to the Admiralty invitation with cordiality, and substantial progress has been made in the direction of meeting it as a defensive measure by preparing to equip a number of first-class British liners to repel the attack of an armed foreign merchant cruiser. Although these vessels have, of course, a wholly different status from that of the regularly-commissioned merchant cruisers such as those we obtain under the Cunard agreement, the Admiralty have felt that the greater part of the cost of the necessary equipment should not fall upon the owners, and we have decided, therefore, to lend the necessary guns, to supply ammunition, and to provide for the training of members of the ship's company to form the guns' crews. The owners on their part are paying the cost of the necessary structural conversion, which is not great. The British mercantile marine will, of course, have the protection of the Royal Navy under all possible circumstances, but it is obviously impossible to guarantee individual vessels from attack when they are scattered on their voyages all over the world. No one can pretend to view these measures without regret or without hoping that the period of retrogression all over the world which has rendered them necessary may be succeeded by days of broader international confidence and agreement than those through which we are now passing.

On April 15th, 1914, it was stated in the *Morning Post* that a Bill for the establishment of a mail line of armed vessels to South American ports had been introduced into the United States Senate, with the approval of Mr Daniels, Secretary for the Navy. If this is passed the United States will go further even than the British Admiralty in establishing a state-owned line of armed mail steamers, and it is of interest to note that the United States' Government is also turning its attention to the South American trade routes, as it was on ships of the Royal Mail Steam Packet Company on this route that guns for defence were first placed. There are now between 40 and 50 British merchant ships carrying guns for defence and others are in process of being equipped. It has also been stated that German merchant ships are being similarly armed.[1]

The reasons for this reversion to a means of defending commerce by arming the ships engaged in trade, a development justly characterized by Mr Churchill as regrettable and retrogressive, are to be found in the methods in which states have, since the abolition of privateering, arranged to increase their fighting forces on the outbreak of war by the conversion of certain specially built merchant ships into fast cruisers, and in the fact that several important naval Powers maintain the right to convert these merchant ships into ships of war on the high seas. There are, therefore, on all the great trade routes of the world, merchant ships which may at a moment's notice, on receipt of a wireless message, change their peaceful character and from being commercial vessels become commerce destroyers.

This is not the place to deal with the arguments for and against the legality of such conversion; we can only take note of the fact that the Seventh Hague Convention of 1907, for the conversion of merchant ships into war ships, and the London Naval Conference of 1908–9 left the whole question of the place of conversion open.[2]

---

[1] See *Morning Post*, April 16th, 1914, "Merchantmen in war time," where a list of British ships already armed is given.

[2] See "The Conversion of Merchant Ships into War Ships," in the writer's *War and the Private Citizen* (1912), pp. 113–65.

The possibility of conversion on the high seas is undoubtedly a serious menace to great trading states such as Great Britain and the United States, both of whom deny the legality of such conversion. They have, however, to face the facts and take such measures in the defence of their sea-borne trade as shall best ensure its continuance in time of war. Already the naval charges of many states impose burdens on their peoples of increasing hardship, and instead of a great increase of cruisers for commerce protection, Great Britain, reverting to a practice common in the eighteenth and early nineteenth centuries, is arming her merchant ships in order that they may offer resistance to, and defend themselves against, the converted merchant cruisers of her potential adversaries. Mr Churchill expressly stated in the House of Commons in introducing the Naval Estimates in 1914 that instructions are given to the armed merchant ships to attempt no resistance to the ordinary ships of war, but only to endeavour to ward off attacks of the converted merchant cruiser. The armed merchant ship is therefore armed solely for defence, not for attack.

II

The laws of naval warfare are drawn almost entirely from the practice of states in the past. In considering the position of the defensively armed and uncommissioned merchant ship, it is the customary Law of Nations that is of chief importance. The position of these ships and their treatment in the past must, therefore, be first considered.

Three classes of armed merchant ships may be distinguished in the naval wars of the seventeenth, eighteenth and early nineteenth centuries.

(1) *Merchant ships hired or bought by the State for incorporation temporarily or permanently into the Navy.* From

time to time states made up deficiencies in their naval forces by hiring or purchasing strongly built and fast sailing merchantmen. The Dutch in 1652 made up this deficiency in their navy by hastily arming merchantmen, the French did the same in the eighteenth century, and this was also done by England. The merchant captains were frequently left in command and were often part owners, with the result that they were reluctant to risk their ships. This reluctance was in no small degree responsible for the defeat of the English fleet off Dungeness on November 30th, 1652. To remedy this, the laws of War and Ordinances of the sea published on December 25th, 1652 (the first Articles of War to which the English Navy was subjected) rendered the captains and ships' companies displaying reluctance to engage, and those guilty of slackness in defending a convoy liable to the penalty of death. It was further ordered that captains of hired ships should be "chosen and placed by the state," and other officers were "likewise to be approved of."[1] These vessels were in all respects men-of-war and call for no further consideration.

(2) *Privateers.* The terms "privateers" or "private men-of-war," and "letter-of-marque ships" were in the latter part of the eighteenth century convertible. "Privateer" does not appear in use till the time of Pepys, and in 1718 it is not used in the issue of "Instructions for such merchants and others who shall have letters of marque or Commission for Private men-of-war against the King of Spain." There was at one time in England a distinction between Privateers and Merchant vessels furnished with letters of marque, "the one being entitled to Head-money and the other not, but" said Sir W. Scott, in the case of the *Fanny* (1814), "that

[1] J. R. Tanner in *Cambridge Mod. Hist.* vol. IV, p. 474.

distinction has been entirely done away with."[1] Privateers were vessels owned and manned by private persons but granted the authority of the state to carry on hostilities. They were used to increase the naval force of a state "by causing vessels to be equipped from private cupidity, which a minister might not be able to obtain by general taxation without much difficulty."[2] In practice, any prizes they captured were adjudged to their owners. British revenue cutters, though fitted out, manned and armed at the expense of the Government, were given letters of marque and were held to be private ships of war.[3] Privateers did not confine themselves to attacks on the enemy's commerce, but in many cases they combined this with trading[4]; thus East Indiamen were usually furnished with letters of marque, not for the purpose of enabling them to defend themselves, but to ensure to the owners and crew, prize money and head-money in case they captured their assailant.

The learning on the subject of privateers, of which there is a large body, may, however, since the Declaration of Paris, 1856, by which "Privateering is and remains abolished," be considered as obsolete as between the parties to the Declaration. Their modern substitutes, the converted merchant cruisers, are of a very different character, and, as between the parties to the

[1] 1 Dod. 443. Head-money was paid to encourage ships of war and privateers to attack warships and privateers of the enemy. There was a tendency to seek out rich merchantmen on account of their value in prize money, and by the Prize Act, 1805 (sec. 5), £5 was to be paid for every man who was living on board the ship which was taken, sunk, burnt or otherwise destroyed at the beginning of the attack. Originally it was the reward of actual combat only; later, of the capture alone, whether with or without actual fighting. (*The Clorinde*, 1 Dod. 436). See *antea*, p. 206.

[2] W. O. Manning, *Law of Nations* (1875), p. 157.

[3] *The Helen*, 3 C. Rob. 224; *The Sedulous*, 1 Dod. 253.

[4] E.g. *The Fanny*, 1 Dod. 448.

Seventh Hague Convention, 1907, and so far as they conform to its terms, are on the same footing as warships and subject to the "direct authority, immediate control and responsibility of the Power whose flag they fly" (Art. 1).[1]

(3) *The defensively armed but uncommissioned merchant ship.* The practice of ships arming in self-defence is a very old one. The seas were often infested with pirates, and when later, privateering became the normal method of attacking commerce, merchant ships were forced either to sail in convoys or to arm themselves; often they did both. Ships sailing on the Indian and American voyages, and even those in the Levant trade, carried large crews, heavy guns and a complete equipment.[2]

But, in the seventeenth century, arming was made compulsory in England. A proclamation of Charles I of December 24th, 1625, forbidding ships of 60 tons and upwards to go to sea unless fully armed,[3] appears to be • one of the earliest orders issued in England, compelling merchant ships to arm in their own defence. Statutes were also passed on the subject in 1662 (13 and 14 Car. II, c. 11), 1664 (16 Car. II, c. 6) and 1670 (22 and 23 Car. II, c. 11). The most important order, and one frequently referred to on subsequent occasions during the seventeenth and eighteenth centuries, was an Order in Council of Charles II of December 4th, 1672, which was made at a meeting at which the King and 26 members were present. Its importance warrants its being set forth in full:

His Majesty having taken into his consideration of what ill consequences and loss it is, as well as to the whole kingdom, as to

[1] For commentary on the Convention see the writer's *Hague Peace Conferences*, pp. 315–21, and *War and the Private Citizen*, pp. 130–6.

[2] J. R. Tanner, *Cambridge Mod. Hist.* vol. IV, p. 467.

[3] R. G. Marsden, *Law and Custom of the Sea*, vol. I, p. 405.

the persons particularly concerned that merchant ships going out on foreign voyages in time of war are not sufficiently provided with guns, fire arms and other necessaries for their defence against the enemy, as well also that such ships are found frequently to forsake their convoys and the rest of their company, by which means they fall into the hands of the enemy—It was this day ordered by His Majesty in Council, that all masters of vessels going out on any foreign voyage, as aforesaid, shall before they be cleared at the Custom house or permitted to sail out of any port of this kingdom on their respective voyages give good security to the Commissioners and officers of His Majesty's Customs that they will not separate or depart from such men of war as shall be by His Majesty appointed for their convoy, nor from the rest of their company, but that they will keep together during such their voyage, and mutually assist and defend each other against any enemy to the utmost of their power, in case they shall happen to be attacked, and that to this end they will take care their respective ships and vessels shall be well provided with muskets, small shot, hand grenades and other sorts of ammunition and military provisions according to the proportion of the men they carry. And of this His Majesty's pleasure the Commissioners and officers of His Majesty's Customs, and all others whom it may concern are to take notice and have due regard thereto accordingly.

In the reign of William and Mary, 1694 (5 and 6 W. and M. c. 24) another statute was passed with a view of encouraging and enforcing the ordinary trading vessel to provide herself with the necessary means of defence. The practice was common, but sometimes dangerous, and an Act was passed in 1732 (5 Geo. II, c. 20) forbidding armed merchant ships lying in the Thames above Blackwall to keep their guns shotted or to fire them between sunset and sunrise. In order, however, that small ships should not take advantage of the practice of carrying guns to resist or evade revenue-cutters, Statutes were passed limiting their armament, and later forbidding it altogether, except in the case of foreign-going traders (24 Geo. III, c. 47; 34 Geo. III, c. 50), but the restrictions imposed by the

Statute of 1784 were removed on the outbreak of war in 1793 by Order in Council.

Several times during the course of the eighteenth century, merchant ships were ordered to arm in self-defence, so as to avoid the necessity of sailing with convoys. In order to ascertain that no ammunition was sold and that the ship fought only in self-defence, the master had to account for any expenditure of ammunition. Owing to the great demand for sailors to man the fleet during the Napoleonic era, a demand which was enforced by impressment, there was a lack of able-bodied seamen for ships of the British mercantile marine; compulsory arming fell into abeyance, and compulsory convoy was enforced. Nevertheless, many ships continued to carry arms for their own defence, and ships so armed were distinguished carefully by Prize Courts from those with Letters of Marque. The British Prize Court stated in one case: "They may be armed only for their own defence; as they have no commission to act offensively they cannot be considered legally as ships of war, to the effect of entitling the captors to head-money."[1]   And in 1815 Chief Justice Marshall of the United States Supreme Court said: "In point of fact, it is believed that a belligerent merchant vessel rarely sails unarmed....A belligerent has a perfect right to arm in her own defence."[2]

It is thus clear that up to the end of the Napoleonic wars merchant ships either were compelled to arm in

[1] By the Court in *Several Dutch Schuyts*, 6 C. Rob. 48. This was a claim for head-money for the capture of armed, but uncommissioned Dutch transports. See also *The Two Friends*, 1 C. Rob. 271; *The Catharina Elizabeth*, 5 C. Rob. 232.

[2] *The Nereide*, 9 Cranch, 388; *Talbot* v. *Seeman* (*The Amelia*), 1 Cranch, 1; *U.S.* v. *Quincy*, 6 Peters, 445; *Cushing* v. *U.S.* 22 Ct. Cl. 1; *Hooper* v. *U.S.* 22 Ct. Cl. 408.

self-defence or armed in order to resist capture,[1] and the right to do this was recognized by the Prize Courts of England, the United States and France.[2] Not only did the merchant ships of belligerent states carry guns for self-defence in war time, but vessels also carried arms in time of peace, and the continuity of the practice after the close of the Napoleonic wars, is to be seen in the fact that the ships of the East India Company went armed certainly down to 1834, and probably till a much later date.[3] The ships of the Dutch East India Company also carried defensive armament.

III

The situation in 1914 bears a curious resemblance to that which existed a century ago with, however, certain

[1] The evidence of the arming of merchant ships and of their defending themselves from attack is to be found in such works as R. Beatson's *Naval and Military Memoirs* and naval histories in general and in the records preserved in the British Public Record Office, Admiralty Secretary "In-letters". Vice-Admiral Sir H. W. Richmond, K.C.B., has kindly given me reference to several cases, such as the dispatch from Admiral Sir Chaloner Ogle of December 1st, 1743, the capture of the San Domingo Convoy on June 20th, 1747, the action between Commodore Barnett and three French-China merchant ships on January 25th, 1745 (see Beatson, vol. I, p. 258). In the case of the San Domingo Convoy, Beatson gives a list of the captured ships (vol. I, p. 343) but does not mention whether they were armed or not; the original papers show that with few exceptions all were armed. At the Battle of Finisterre, May 3rd, 1747, the four armed French East India merchant ships, *Philibert*, *Apollon*, *Thétis* and *Dartmouth*, sailing under convoy took part in the fight (Beatson, vol. I, p. 341).

[2] *Le Pigou*, Pistoye et Duverdy, *Prises Maritimes*, vol. II, p. 51; Ch. de Boeck, *Propriété Privée*, § 212; E. Nys, *Droit International* (1906), vol. III, p. 181; J. B. Moore, *Digest of International Law*, vol. II, p. 1070.

[3] Low, *History of the Indian Navy*, vol. I, p. 12; Hannay, *The Sea Trader, his friends and enemies*, pp. 347–58. See also *The Times*, February 2nd, 1916, "Armed Traders."

modifications resulting from the Declaration of Paris, 1856, and the Seventh Hague Convention of 1907 which may be considered as a supplementary and explanatory treaty. Private merchant ships are hired as transports, though they are not generally armed or commissioned, and therefore retain their character of merchant ships. Most states have arrangements whereby in time of war certain vessels armed by private owners, companies or individuals, are taken over by the state and equipped with arms and incorporated into the fighting forces of the state. These vessels take the place of the old letter of marque or private ships of war; they are, however, no longer fitted out by private owners for their own pecuniary profit, but rank in all respects, when conforming to the Seventh Hague Convention, as public ships of war.

And lastly there is a return to the armed and un-commissioned merchant ship, not armed compulsorily under an Order in Council but armed at the expense of the state, by the willing co-operation of the owners.

I am not concerned here with the policy, expediency, or efficacy of the method which Great Britain and possibly other states are adopting as an additional protection to their sea-borne commerce; there are, however, several points of International Law in regard to these armed merchant ships which their re-introduction makes of practical importance. Those to be dealt with in this paper are (1) The right of such vessels to arm and defend themselves—(2) The consequence of a successful resistance and capture of the assailant— (3) The liability to condemnation of neutral cargoes on board enemy merchant ships.

(1) It is of interest to note that the late Professor Freeman Snow in his *International Law*, the 2nd edition of which was published at Washington in 1888, anticipated the action of Great Britain and other

states. He said, "It may be reasonably expected in coming naval wars that steamers of the great mail lines will be armed so as to defend themselves from attack, rather than seek convoy, and the defence will be legitimately carried to the point of seizure of the attacking vessel, or a recapture if once taken. Without a proper commission, a private vessel, however, should act only directly or indirectly on the defensive, and not go out of the way to capture enemy vessels. It cannot, of course, take any belligerent action towards vessels of a neutral power" (p. 83). This statement may be taken as embodying the rule generally acknowledged by English and American judges and writers. The right of an armed, but uncommissioned, merchant ship to resist is expressly laid down by Sir William Scott in the *Catharina Elizabeth*.[1]

> If a neutral master attempts a rescue, he violates a duty which is imposed upon him by the Law of Nations, to submit to come in for enquiry as to the property of the ship or cargo, and if he violates that obligation by a recurrence to force, the consequence will undoubtedly reach the property of his owner, and it would, I think, extend also to the confiscation of the whole cargo entrusted to his care and thus fraudulently attempted to be withdrawn from the rights of war. With an enemy master the case is very different. No duty is violated by such an act on his part— *lupum auribus teneo*—and if he can withdraw himself he has a right so to do.

The following extracts from the judgment of Chief Justice Marshall in the *Nereide*[2] also show that the law of the United States was the same:

> The argument respecting resistance stands on the same ground with that which respects arming. Both are lawful. Neither of them is chargeable to the goods or their owner, where he has taken no part in it. They are incidents in the character of the vessel; and may always occur where the cruiser is belligerent....
>
> The *Nereide* was armed, governed and conducted by belligerents....It is true that on her passage she had a right to defend

[1] 5 C. Rob. 232.   [2] 9 Cranch, 388, 428, 430.

herself, did defend herself, and might have captured an assailing vessel; but to search for the enemy would have been a violation of the charter party and of her duty.

If the practice of arming merchant ships in self-defence became less common during the latter part of the nineteenth century, it did not wholly die out, and American Secretaries of State in 1877 and 1894 gave their opinion that there was no international prohibition against an American ship carrying guns and arms for self-defence in the South Sea Islands, and the laws of the United States did not forbid the carrying of guns and ammunition on a schooner which entered Haytian waters, so long as no hostilities were committed against the persons or property of foreign powers with whom the United States were at peace.[1] The question of the position of defensively armed merchant ships was incidentally discussed in the case of the *Panama*,[2] which came before the United States Supreme Court in 1899. She was a Spanish vessel which left port before the outbreak of the Spanish-American War in 1898, carrying two 9-centimetre bore guns and a Maxim, together with arms and ammunition, and, being captured in ignorance of the outbreak of war, claimed exemption from condemnation as a mail ship under the terms of the President's Proclamation of April 20th, 1898. She was, however, under contract with the Spanish Government to be taken over for war purposes, and the Court, in these circumstances, decided that she was not entitled to the exemption granted by the President's Proclamation. (The *Panama* would, since the Sixth Hague Convention, 1907, have come under the designation of a ship "whose construction indicates that she is intended to be converted into a warship.") But in the course of his judgment, Mr Justice Gray said: "It must

[1] J. B. Moore, *Digest of International Law*, vol. II, p. 1070.
[2] 176 U.S. Rep. 535; J. B. Moore, *op. cit.* vol. VII, p. 456.

be admitted that arms and ammunition are not contraband of war when taken and kept on board a merchant
vessel as part of her equipment and solely for her defence against 'enemies, pirates and assailing thieves,'
according to the ancient phrase still retained in policies
of marine insurance." He also quoted Pratt (*Contraband of War*, pp. xxii, xxv, xl), who, after speaking of the
class of articles of direct use in war, said: "But even
in the case of articles of direct use in war, an exception
is always made in favour of such a quantity of them as
may be supposed to be necessary for the use or defence
of the ship." Again speaking of "warlike stores," he
adds: "These are, from their very nature, evidently
contraband; but every vessel is, of course, allowed to
carry such a quantity as may be necessary for purposes
of defence: this provision is expressly introduced in
many treaties." In the same judgment the French case
of *Le Pégou* or *Pigou* is also cited with the following
opinion of Portalis:

> I do not think it is enough to have or to carry arms to incur the
> reproach of being armed for war. Armament for war is of a purely
> offensive nature. It is established when there is no other object in
> the armament than that of attack, or, at least, when everything
> shows that such is the principal object of the enterprise; then a
> vessel is deemed enemy or pirate, if she has no commission or papers
> sufficient to remove all suspicion. But defence is a natural right,
> and means of defence are lawful in voyages at sea, as in all other
> dangerous occupations of life. A ship which had but a small
> crew, and a considerable cargo, was evidently intended for com-
> merce and not for war. The arms found on this ship were evidently
> intended not for committing acts of rapine or hostility, but for
> preventing them; not for attack, but for self-defence. The pretext
> of being armed for war, therefore, appears to me to be un-
> founded.

This ship, it will be observed, was a neutral captured
as being an uncommissioned ship of war, but released
on the evidence showing that she was armed solely for

defence. The reasoning of Portalis, quoted by the Supreme Court of the United States without disapproval, and as a high authority, applies generally to the legitimacy of arming in self-defence as well as to the nature of the armament, which may be evidence that the ship is a warship and not a defensively armed merchant ship.

The right of resistance of merchant ships is recognized, either directly or inferentially, by the following National Codes or Naval Instructions:

The U.S. Naval War Code (1900), Article 10, para. 3: "The personnel of merchant vessels of an enemy, who, in self defence and in protection of the vessel placed in their charge, resist an attack, are entitled, if captured, to the status of prisoners of war."

The Italian Codice per la Marine Mercantile (1877), Article 209: "Merchantmen, on being attacked by other vessels, including war vessels, may defend themselves against and even seize them."

The Russian Prize Regulations (1895), Article 15: "The right to stop, examine, and seize hostile or suspected vessels and cargoes belongs to the ships of the Imperial Navy. Vessels of the mercantile navy have a right to do so only (1) when they are attacked by hostile or suspected vessels," &c.

This rule is also recognized by writers of weight and authority in Great Britain,[1] the United States,[2] France,[3] Italy,[4] Belgium[5] and Holland.[6]

Lastly, the Institute of International Law at its meeting at Oxford in 1913, by Art. 12 of the *Manuel des Lois de la Guerre maritime* which it then adopted laid down the following rule:

La course est interdite. En dehors des conditions déterminées aux articles 5 et suivants, les navires publics et les navires privés,

[1] Hall, § 182; Oppenheim, vol. II, §§ 85, 181; Phillimore, vol. III, § 339; Twiss, vol. II, § 97.
[2] Snow, pp. 83, 84; Wheaton, § 528; Stockton, p. 335.
[3] De Boeck, *De la Propriété privée ennemie*, sec. 212; C. Dupuis, *Le Droit de la Guerre maritime* (1899), p. 121.
[4] P. Fiore, §§ 1627, 1698.   [5] E. Nys, vol. III, 181 (1906).
[6] J. H. Ferguson, § 225.

ainsi que leur personnel, ne peuvent pas se livrer à des actes d'hostilité contre l'ennemi.

Il est toutefois permis aux uns et aux autres d'employer la force pour se défendre contre l'attaque d'un navire ennemi.[1]

The discussion at the Institute showed that there was some opposition to the second paragraph of the Article. Professor Triepel, of Berlin, desired to obtain its suppression, on the ground that an enemy merchant ship had no right to resist capture (as distinct from attack),[2] while Professor Niemeyer supported its suppression on the very different ground,[3] viz., that to insert such a provision was equivalent to conceding that a contrary opinion was possible! Ultimately the Article was voted by a large majority.

The view unsuccessfully put forward by Professor Triepel at Oxford has since been advanced by Dr Georg Schramm, legal adviser to the German Admiralty, in his *Das Prisenrecht in seiner neuesten Gestalt* (1913), pp. 308–10. This author attempts to prove that "from the point of view of the modern law of war" there is no legal foundation for the rule allowing a merchant ship to defend itself, and he carries on the same line of thought in regard to the treatment of the crew of such a ship when he says "it would have to be decided whether the hostilities were committed by members of the crew who are enrolled in the enemy forces or not. The former would be made prisoners of war, according to the analogous application of Art. 3 of the Regulations of the Laws and Customs of land warfare; the latter would have forfeited treatment as peaceful subjects of the hostile state, according to usages of war they would be subject to the criminal law of the captor state" (p. 357).

---

[1] *Annuaire* (1913), p. 644.
[2] *Ibid.* pp. 516, 517.   [3] *Ibid.* p. 519.

Professor L. Oppenheim has dealt faithfully with Dr Schramm's views in the *Zeitschrift für Völkerrecht* for April, 1913.[1] He has written therein what appears to me to be "*une réponse sans réplique.*" I do not propose to enter into the details of the arguments advanced, I shall content myself with a summary of what in my opinion is the present position.

The right of a merchant ship to defend herself, and to be armed for that purpose, has not, so far as I am aware, been doubted for two centuries, until the question has again become one of practical importance. The historical evidence of the practice down to the year 1815 is overwhelming. Dr Schramm in his elaborate denial of the right, fails to distinguish between the position in which a belligerent warship stands to an enemy merchant ship, and that in which it stands to a neutral merchant ship. This failure is important, and goes to the root of the matter; for whereas the visit of a belligerent warship to an enemy merchant ship is, under existing law, merely the first step to capture and is itself a hostile act, and undertaken solely in order to enable the captor to ascertain that the ship is one which is not exempt by custom, treaty, or convention from capture, the visit to a neutral ship, though justified by the fact of the existence of war, is not a hostile act. By long custom a belligerent warship has a *right* of visit and search of all neutral merchant vessels, and this right is exercised in order to ascertain whether a vessel is in fact neutral, and not engaged in any acts such as attempting to break blockade, the carriage of contraband, or the performance of any unneutral service which would justify its detention and condemnation. "It has been truly denominated a right growing out of, and ancillary to, the greater right of capture. Where

[1] *Die Stellung der feindlichen Kauffahrteischiffe im Seekrieg*, vol. VIII, pp. 154–69.

this greater right may be legally exercised without search [as in the case of enemy ships] the right of search can never arise or come into question."[1] A belligerent warship has the right to capture an enemy merchant ship, but the latter is under no duty to submit; it has a corresponding right to resist capture which is an act of violence and hostility. By resisting, the belligerent violates no duty, he is held by force and may escape if he can. But forcible resistance, as distinct from flight, on the part of a neutral merchant ship is universally admitted as a just ground for the condemnation of the ship,[2] for a neutral is under a duty to submit to belligerent visit.

(2) Another important point differentiates neutral from belligerent merchant ships, namely the position of their crews when the ships are detained. The officers and crew of an enemy merchant ship, even if they offer no resistance to capture, become prisoners of war, while the officers and crew of a neutral do not.

The United States Naval War Code in the passage already cited (Art. 10) recognizes that the personnel of merchant vessels of an enemy who, in self-defence and in protection of the vessel placed in their charge, resist an attack, are entitled, if captured, to the status of prisoners of war; and Dr F. Perels, who was formerly legal adviser to the German Admiralty, quotes this with approval.[3] But this view is based, according to Dr Schramm, on a complete misunderstanding of the

[1] Marshall, C.J. in the *Nereide*, 9 Cranch, 388, 427.
[2] See Declaration of London, Art. 63.
[3] "Gegen das Personal der Schiffsbesatzung soll im übrigen eine vorläufige Zurückhaltung an Bord soweit zulässig sein, als dessen Vernehmung für die Feststellung des Tatbestandes erforderlich erscheint, und es soll diesen Leuten eine anständige Behandlung zu teil werden. Dem entsprechen auch die folgenden Festsetzungen in den Artikeln 10 und 11 des N.W.C." (*Das Internationale Seerecht*, ed. 1903, p. 191.)

modern conception of the legal regulations of war as an armed conflict between states. Enemy merchant seamen have, however, for centuries been liable to this treatment whether they resist capture or not, in consequence of their fitness for use on ships of war,[1] and this fact has an important bearing on the question of their resistance to capture. It may, however, be truly said that by virtue of the Eleventh Hague Convention, 1907, officers and members of the crew of a captured enemy merchant ship who are subjects of the enemy state, are entitled to be released if they give a written promise not to engage, while hostilities last, in any service connected with the operations of war (Art. 6). But if they refuse to give their parole (and by the laws of some states, such as Spain, they were formerly, at any rate, forbidden to give such promises)[2] they remain prisoners of war. Therefore the crew in defending their ships are defending themselves and their liberty; for release on the terms of the Convention is but a modified liberty. The Eleventh Hague Convention recognizes that the crews of merchant ships are liable to be made prisoners of war by providing for their liberation on parole, but Article 8 states that the provisions of the preceding Articles allowing release on parole, "do not apply to ships taking part in hostilities." Crews who forcibly resist visit and capture cannot therefore claim to be released—they remain prisoners of war. If an enemy merchant ship is called on to stop, the crew can, if they wish, "submit to capture and thereby have their freedom restricted, or they may resist and as a result be overpowered. In case they choose the latter course,

---

[1] W. E. Hall, *International Law*, § 131. Hall's note on Bismarck's denial of the right to treat merchant sailors as prisoners of war is emphatic, but, in my opinion, by no means too strong. See F. Perels, *Das Internationale Seerecht*, p. 191.

[2] J. B. Moore, *Digest of International Law*, vol. VII, p. 371.

their potential membership turns into actual membership of the armed forces of their state, and if overpowered they become prisoners of war. In case they choose the former course, their merely potential membership of the armed forces of their state remains intact, and they must either give parole or become prisoners of war."[1] It would appear, however, that this Convention "is only applicable between the contracting Powers, and only if all the belligerents are parties to the Convention." (Art. 9.) Among the Great Powers, Russia has not signed, and Italy has not ratified the Convention, and many of the other Powers, e.g. Bulgaria, Greece, Montenegro and Serbia, have not ratified it. Where such a Convention is not legally applicable, any of the belligerents may, of course, mutually agree to its terms being carried into effect.

(3) The chief reason why in land warfare special requirements and organization are necessary to confer the privileges of lawful combatants on armed bodies of men, is to ensure that the peaceful artisan or agricultural labourer shall not change his character from day to day. If he is to have the immunities of a non-combatant, that character must be clear and unequivocal. But even in land warfare, Article 2 of the Regulations annexed to the Fourth Hague Convention, 1917, makes provision for the exceptional case of the spontaneous resistance of the inhabitants of a territory who rise at the approach of an invader, and grants them belligerent rights if they do not comply with all the requirements of Article 1, but only "carry arms openly and respect the laws and customs of war." The crew of a merchant ship is a body of men acting together in defence of their ship and their liberty, a body of identifiable individuals who, by the customary Law of Nations, have received combatant privileges

[1] L. Oppenheim, *op. cit.* p. 164.

when resisting capture by an enemy warship. They offer a striking analogy to the spontaneous rising of the inhabitants of an unoccupied territory, who have now received by Convention the right which merchant sailors have had for centuries.

IV

Should the resistance of the crew of a defensively armed, uncommissioned merchant ship be so successful as to enable them to effect the capture of their assailant, such captured ship is good prize as between the belligerents. But the right of the captors to Prize money in respect thereof, is a matter of municipal legislation. The general rule of English law, as stated by an Order in Council of January 4th, 1666, was that "all ships and goods casually met at sea and seized by any vessel not commissioned do belong to the Lord High Admiral." Some four years later, in order to encourage masters to fight their ships more stoutly against pirates, a statute was passed (22 and 23 Car. II, c. 9 (1)) modifying this rule and providing that "in case the company belonging unto any English merchant ship shall happen to take any ship, which ship shall first have assaulted them, the respective officers and mariners belonging to same, shall after condemnation of such ship and goods have and receive to their own proper use such part and share thereof, as is usually practised in private men of war."

The rule of law laid down by the Order in Council of 1666 has been observed in England since that date, such goods and ships taken by uncommissioned ships belonging to the Crown as Droits of Admiralty. The present law is contained in the Naval Prize Act, 1864, section 39—"Any ship or goods taken as prize by any of the officers and crew of a ship other than a ship of war of Her Majesty shall, on condemnation, belong to

Her Majesty in Her office of Admiralty." The Naval Prize Bill introduced in 1911 and rejected by the House of Lords contained a similar clause.

The law of France was formerly the same as that of England, but to-day the prize is given to the captor. A similar rule prevails in Holland.[1]

V

The re-introduction of the armed merchant ship raises another question which is of importance to neutrals, viz., how far a neutral merchant has a right to lade his goods on board an armed enemy vessel, and what will be the consequence of resistance on the part of the enemy master. This question was discussed by the Prize Courts of Great Britain and the United States during the war of 1812–14. The cases dealing with this matter are the *Fanny*[2] in England, and the *Nereide*[3] and the *Atalanta*[4] in the United States. In the *Fanny* neutral goods were laded on an armed merchant ship furnished

---

[1] "En France, sous l'ancien régime, les prises faites *en se défendant* étaient acquises à l'amiral 'dont la générosité le portait, la plupart du temps, à en faire don au capteur, en récompense de sa bravoure,' au témoignage de Valin et d'Emerigon. Aujourd'hui, aux termes de l'art. 34 de l'arrêté du 2 prairial an xi, la prise faite par un bâtiment attaqué qui parvient à s'emparer de l'agresseur est acquise au capteur; l'art. 34 a été assez fréquemment appliqué par le Conseil des Prises dans les guerres de l'Empire. La même règle est admise, notamment en Hollande." C. de Boeck, *Propriété privée*, § 212. Professor de Boeck adds the following footnote: "Quant à la prise qu'un navire non commissionné et armé pour sa défense aurait faite en attaquant, elle est bonne quant à l'ennemi, mais confisquée au profit de l'État; l'auteur pourra même être poursuivi et condamné comme pirate."

See also Abdy's edition of Kent's *International Law*, p. 246; E. Nys, *Le Droit international* (1906), vol. iii, p. 181.

[2] 1 Dod. 448.   [3] 9 Cranch, 387.

[4] 3 Wheaton Rep. 400 (see on this subject Wheaton, *Elements*, § 529 and Dana's note); R. Wildman, *Institutes of International Law*, vol. ii, p. 126.

with letters of marque, the neutral having knowledge of the facts. Sir W. Scott held that a ship furnished with a letter of marque was manifestly a ship of war, and could not be otherwise considered though she acted in a commercial capacity. The mercantile character being superadded did not predominate over or take away the other. A neutral subject was entitled to put his goods on a belligerent merchant vessel subject to the right of the enemy who might capture the vessel, but had no right, under the modern practice of civilized states, to condemn the neutral property. Neither would the goods of the neutral be subject to condemnation, although a rescue should be attempted by the crew of the captured vessel, for that was an event which the merchant could not have foreseen. But if he put his goods on board a ship of force, which he had every reason to presume would be defended against the enemy by that force, the case then became very different. It was clear, he held, that if a party acted in association with a hostile force, and relied upon that force for protection, he was *pro hac vice* to be considered as an enemy. In the American case of the *Nereide*, which was subsequently affirmed in the *Atalanta*, the Court was divided. Five judges sat, two (one of whom was Chief Justice Marshall) decided in favour of the neutral claimant, two (one of whom was Mr Justice Story) against him, and the majority was obtained by the course taken by Mr Justice Johnson, who decided for the neutral on special grounds, though in the *Atalanta* he gave his adherence to the general principle laid down by Marshall, C.J. The dissenting opinion of Story emphasized a fact on which the majority laid no stress, viz., that the vessel was sailing under enemy convoy, and that the claimant, being the charterer of the whole vessel, had bound her to sail under this convoy: that the vessel was captured with the claimant on board, while accidentally separated from the convoy and endeavouring to rejoin it. The case of the *Nereide* differs in an important point from the *Fanny*, in that the former appears to have been an uncommissioned armed belligerent merchant vessel which resisted capture: whereas the latter was a commissioned ship of war. The *Nereide*, however, was under enemy convoy, and it is submitted that the dissenting judgment of Story is on the facts of the case more in accord with the principle of unneutral conduct.

Since these cases were decided, the parties to the Declaration of Paris have agreed that neutral goods, with the exception of contraband of war, are not liable to capture under the enemy's flag (Art. 3), and that privateering is and remains abolished (Art. 1).

It does not appear that there is a definite decision on the question of the fate of neutral goods laden on a defensively armed and uncommissioned enemy merchant ship either in Great Britain or the United States. Sir W. Scott, in the *Catharina Elizabeth*, stated that in case of rescue by the captured ship, neutral goods would be free. Between such an attempt made after capture, and a resistance to capture involving an attempt to take the assailing vessel previous to capture "there does not seem to be a total dissimilitude."[1] It is submitted that in such a case the opinion of the American Court in the *Nereide* will probably be that which will be adopted, namely, that neutral goods placed on an uncommissioned armed merchant vessel belonging to a belligerent, and resisting capture, are not subject to condemnation if the armament be entirely and exclusively the act of the belligerent owner, and the resistance in no degree imputable to the neutral. The Declaration of Paris by abolishing privateering left the status of the merchant ship untouched. The right of an enemy

[1] *The Nereide*, 9 Cranch, 388.

merchant ship to defend herself was unquestioned, as was also her liability to capture. The granting of the right to neutrals to send their goods on belligerent vessels does not deprive the belligerent of his right to resist visit and capture so long as his ship remains an uncommissioned ship of war, "a ship of force," to use Lord Stowell's expression; but belligerents, by according neutrals the right, have at the same time deprived themselves of the advantage they might once have had of saying that the neutral is in fault and his goods are liable to condemnation, because the carrier being armed can the better effectuate his right to defeat search or capture. The enemy ship and cargo may still be captured as an act of war, but if the neutral shipper has done no more than send his goods in an enemy vessel, his cargo or its value should be restored.[1]

There is a great distinction between commissioned and uncommissioned armed merchant vessels; the former may, the latter may not act on the offensive, and the arguments of Sir W. Scott and Mr Justice Story in regard to the treatment of goods placed on board vessels of the former class may well be accepted, but rejected in the case of the latter which were not in question. It is submitted therefore that neutral cargoes placed on board merchant vessels converted into warships under the terms of the Seventh Hague Convention, 1907, would be liable to be condemned on the principle laid down by these two distinguished judges, while those placed on armed but uncommissioned merchant ships should, under the Declaration of Paris, be released.

[1] See Dana's note in Wheaton's *Elements*, § 529.

I

COMING events, it is said, cast their shadows before them, and it would seem that the opposition
of Dr Triepel to the rule adopted by the *Institut
de Droit International* in 1913 recognizing the lawful-
ness of the resistance of merchant ships to capture, and
the views of Dr Schramm published in the same year,
were a foreshadowing of the action of the Germans
during the war of 1914–18. One other writer, in addition to the two German Professors, adversely criticized
the policy of the British Admiralty in arming merchant
ships before the outbreak of war in 1914. Jonkheer
W. J. M. van Eysinga, Professor of Law at Leyden
University, had also prepared a paper on armed merchantmen for the meeting of the International Law
Association at The Hague in 1914 in which he approached the subject from a different point of view
from that which I had taken in my paper. He dissented
from Professor Oppenheim's reply to Dr Schramm, in
which he rebutted the view that resistance offered by a
merchantman to an enemy man-of-war constitutes an
illegal act. He contended that the British decision to
arm merchant ships was a retrograde step and likely
to have sorry consequences, as the arming of merchant
ships gives them an official character for which the
government does not assume any responsibility, "and
yet their essential character is that of warships." He
raised the question of the difficulty of neutral Powers
admitting armed merchant ships of belligerent nationality to their ports, a very significant point having
regard to the subsequent action of the Netherlands

Government. He further proposed that such ships should be regularized by giving them commissions as auxiliary men-of-war. He considered that as privateering had been abolished, and consequently the irregularities associated with it, there was no longer any reason for allowing merchant ships to be armed. In this respect Professor van Eysinga had not envisaged the irregularities which German and Austrian submarines were to commit. The arguments of the Dutch Professor are not in my opinion substantiated by the practice of states on which the rules of International Law are based, and are dealt with in other parts of these essays.

In 1915 Dr Hans Wehberg, a German International Lawyer, published a work on the law of naval warfare and his views on the subject of the legality of merchant ships carrying arms in self-defence and of their right to resist are in full accord with those already set forth. "The resistance of enemy merchant ships to capture would then only be unlawful if a rule against this found common recognition. But, in truth, no single example can be produced from international precedents in which the states have held resistance as not being lawful." He then cites Lord Stowell's decision in the *Catharina Elizabeth* and the provisions of the United States Naval War Code, 1900, and the twelfth Article of the Rules proposed by the *Institut de Droit International* in 1913, and he adds,

If it was a question of making a new rule, ships ought to be allowed to defend themselves. Should great merchant ships worth millions allow themselves to be taken by smaller vessels simply because the latter comply with the requirements of a warship?

In the early days of privateering, merchant ships bravely defended themselves against these vessels and many a privateer was sent home with a bleeding head. This condition led finally to a stronger military control over the privateers, and care was taken that more heavily armed ships were used against merchant vessels. As time went on privateers were so strongly armed that enemy merchant ships surrendered themselves willingly in ever increasing numbers. With the arrival of the modern auxiliary cruiser the possibility presents itself anew of successfully with-drawing from capture by armed resistance. Why should an act be forbidden as against auxiliary cruisers, which stand in the place of the old privateers, which was undoubtedly allowed formerly as against privateers?[1]

Dr Schramm had suggested that if the crew of an uncommissioned ship resisted capture they must be dealt with as *francs-tireurs* or unlawful combatants. This is denied by Dr Wehberg, who says:

It is unfounded to say that because in war on land armed resist-ance may not be carried out by civilians, therefore that is also the case in war at sea. It might equally well be said that on land private property is inviolable, therefore the same must apply to war at sea. But such a position is untenable....The doctrine that "armed resistance" is only allowed to organized troops is, in the general view, as false as the assertion that war is only a legal relation between States and excludes the peaceful population (p. 283). The act of resistance has no influence on the fate of the crew of an enemy merchantman (p. 286).

It may be worth while looking a little more closely at this point of the alleged similarity between the rules applicable to land and sea warfare, since one of the "Wishes" (*Vœux*) of the Hague Conference, 1907, was to the effect that the Powers should, as far as possible, apply to war by sea the principles of the Convention relative to the law and customs of war on land. This *Vœu* was passed as the result of a long and unsuccessful attempt by one of the Hague Committees to prepare a code for naval warfare on the same lines as those on which the Hague Regulations for land warfare had been drawn. The Committee found this task impossible, as there were so many points of difference between land and sea warfare as to render fundamental modi-

[1] *Das Seekriegsrecht* (1915), p. 284.

fications necessary. Wehberg truly remarks: "One can in no way draw conclusions for sea warfare from principles which have found common recognition in land warfare" (p. 284).[1]

Private property on land is not to be confiscated, but at sea, enemy merchant ships, though private property, have always been liable to capture and confiscation. The crews have always been liable to be treated as prisoners of war; they are therefore justified, if they can, in rescuing their ship from the captor if it has been captured, for their action is no more than a continuation of that resistance to the enemy's force which it is their duty to offer whenever there is a chance of success.[2]

II

We now turn to the views of the German Admiralty as shown in their Naval Prize Regulations. These Regulations, dated September 30th, 1909, together with an Appendix dated June 22nd, 1914, relating to the procedure to be adopted in regard to armed merchant ships in war, were published in Berlin on August 3rd, 1914. The Regulations in the main are unexceptionable. They are based on the Hague Conventions and the Declaration of London, but they are incomplete on many points, and received alterations after the outbreak of the war of 1914. The Appendix contains two Articles, which are as follow:

(1) The exercise of the right of visit, search and capture, as well as every attack on the part of an armed merchant ship upon a German or neutral merchant ship is considered an act of piracy. The crew is to be proceeded against in accordance with the Regulations as to extraordinary martial law procedure.

(2) If an armed merchant vessel offers armed resistance against measures taken under the law of prize, this is to be broken down

[1] See *antea*, pp. 258–260.
[2] See *The Two Friends*, 1 C. Rob. 271.

by all means possible. The enemy Government is responsible for any damage thereby caused to the ship, cargo and passengers. The crew are to be treated as prisoners of war. The passengers are to be liberated unless it is proved that they have taken part in the resistance. In the latter case they are to be proceeded against in accordance with the extraordinary martial law procedure.

On these two Articles there is little to be said. In the main they admit the validity of the argument in favour of enemy merchant ships arming themselves in self-defence and resisting by armed force the exercise of the right of visit, search and capture on the part of enemy warships, and place the burden of compensating such merchant ships for any damage done as a result on the enemy Government.

The first Article of the German Appendix is in accord with the generally accepted rules of International Law. A defensively armed merchant ship must not exercise the right of visit, search and capture, and must not make an attack on an enemy ship. A good deal will turn on the meaning of the word "attack."

The second Article of the German Appendix does not speak of defence and resistance to visit and search by an *unarmed* enemy vessel, and it was apparently because the *Brussels* was unarmed and attempted to ram a German submarine that Captain Fryatt was shot as a *franc-tireur.*[1] But the rule in the past was that

[1] Dr James Brown Scott discussing the execution of Captain Fryatt in the *American Journal of International Law*, vol. x (1916), at p. 877, speaking of Article 2 of the Appendix to the German Naval Prize Regulations, says: "It left untouched the right of belligerent merchant vessels to defend themselves against attack, whether armed or unarmed, by means of guns or by ramming the enemy vessel, if the master of the merchantman is skilful enough so to do. The Article does not state the manner in which the vessel is to be armed, and it is no strained construction to consider

any merchant vessel, armed or unarmed, might resist. Obviously, in practice it would rarely happen that an unarmed ship would venture to resist, but there is not the slightest doubt of the legality of resistance. Recapture of a vessel was also not uncommon, and the members of the crew that failed in its attempt were not treated as unlawful combatants, pirates or robbers, any more than are prisoners of war who unsuccessfully attempt to escape from confinement; clearly they ran grave risks of being killed in the proceeding.[1]

The Austro-Hungarian Prize Regulations contain no specific reference to armed merchant ships. These Regulations are merely extracts from Hague Conventions and the Declaration of London, but under the heading of "Crews of captured enemy merchant ships," Article 8 of the Eleventh Hague Convention is included, which states that the provisions relating to the release on parole of the crews of enemy merchant ships who become prisoners of war do not apply to ships taking part in hostilities.

As to the German action it is needless to speak. The submarine campaign was conducted with ruthlessness and in the great majority of cases vessels were sunk without warning and often under conditions rendering it impossible to ascertain whether the ship was enemy or neutral, armed or unarmed.

the merchantman in its entirety as an arm so far as the submarine is concerned." The conclusion which Dr Scott reaches as to the execution of Captain Fryatt is that if the views he has expressed are correct, "the execution of Captain Fryatt appears to have been without warrant in international law and illegal, whatever it may have been according to the municipal ordinances of Germany."

[1] As to rescue by neutrals, see Dana's note in Wheaton, *Elements of International Law*, p. 475.

III

It may be advisable to say a few words on the subject of the nature of the armament of defensively armed ships. Several of the Statutes already referred to provide for merchant ships carrying from 16 to 30 guns, and many of the East Indiamen carried as many as 38 guns; none of the latter armed ships appeared to have carried less than 10.[1] There was not, nor is there to-day, any ground for suggesting that while one or two guns placed in the stern of a ship determine her character as a merchant ship, the possession of more guns placed in other parts of the vessel would convert her into a warship. The possession of armament no more converts a merchant ship into a warship than the cowl makes the monk. There are, however, very practical considerations which must limit the number of guns placed on merchant ships. They are chiefly these: the capacity of the vessel to carry the guns and their mountings, and the number of guns and mountings that are available. International Law places no restriction on the armament of merchant vessels. It is, however, certain that occurrences during the progress of a war may lend support to a belligerent's determination to increase the defensive armament of his merchant ships beyond that which was deemed necessary in its earlier stages.

There is sometimes apparent a confusion of thought in respect of the term "defensive" armament. There is, in fact, no difference between offensive and defensive armament; a four-inch gun can be used for either purpose; but a four-inch gun is placed on a merchant ship in order to enable her to defend herself from capture. "It is not the nature of the armament, but the use

[1] See a list given in Steel's *Navy List* for 1815.

which is made of it, that makes it offensive."[1] A warship is entitled to act on the offensive, to visit, search and capture enemy or neutral ships; the armed merchantman must do none of these things, except when capture follows on a successful resistance to attack by an enemy warship.

The unarmed merchant ship, by heading for a submarine is as much defending herself as the armed merchant ship is by firing her gun. The action has not infrequently proved effective, as it causes the submarine to submerge, its power of vision is lost, and the merchant ship also presents the smallest possible target for attack. The merchant ship thus obtains an opportunity of escape. It is unnecessary to labour this point; it would have been unnecessary even to refer to it but for the judicial murder by the Germans of Captain Fryatt for having taken this action to defend his ship.

It was suggested by Professor van Eysinga, and by others during the war of 1914–18 that all British armed merchant vessels should be commissioned as warships and their officers given commissions in the Royal Naval Reserve. There are three main reasons for not granting commissions to defensively armed merchant ships. First, to adopt the suggestion would be a complete surrender of the position for which Great Britain has contended, on the basis of a continuous practice for more than a century, that merchant vessels, as such, have, and always have had, a right to defend themselves and to carry armament for the purpose. Secondly, the conditions on which neutral states permit belligerent warships to make use of their ports are such as would effectually prevent a commissioned merchant ship from loading or unloading cargoes and from carrying on commercial intercourse with them. A third reason is, that if armed merchant ships were com-

[1] Dr Ellery Stowell in *The New York American*, March 7th, 1916.

missioned as ships of war, the enemy would at once have the undoubted right of attacking and sinking without warning. Further, the suggestion which has been made that the possession by a captain of a commission in the Royal Naval Reserve would in any way increase his legal powers of self-defence is equally inadmissible, and betrays the confusion of thought which fails to distinguish between the rules of land and sea warfare.

IV

The old law of resistance by merchant ships was developed in relation to warfare which was conducted by non-submersible vessels. The master of a belligerent merchant ship, seeing on the horizon a suspicious vessel, either determined to attempt to escape by flight, or, realizing the impossibility of this procedure, had two courses open to him—either to continue his voyage and wait till summoned to surrender by the enemy cruiser, and then to haul down his flag; or to resist. His decision would largely depend on the type of ship whose approach he was awaiting. If she were a heavily-armed warship, he would generally decide to avoid useless waste of life, but if she were a privateer or a small and lightly-armed cruiser, he would, and in practice often did, defend his ship.

Assuming that he decided to adopt the latter course, the cruiser overhauled the merchant ship, and when within gunshot hailed her, but the latter was under no obligation to wait till summoned to surrender before opening fire. The evidence of offensive action on the part of the enemy was and is sufficient.

The right to resist capture includes the right to resist visit and search, and the latter includes the right to resist approach. As soon as the belligerent merchant ship is aware that an enemy warship shows an intention to effect its capture, that is the moment for the defensive-offensive to commence. Dr Wehberg is clear on this point: "The enemy merchant ship has then the right of defence against an enemy attack, *and this right he can exercise against visitation, for this is indeed the first act of capture.*"[1] The possibility that a merchant ship might carry guns and resist visit and capture was always present to the minds of the captains of warships and privateers, but it was never suggested that they were entitled, without warning, to open fire with heavy guns or torpedoes on enemy merchant ships at a distance merely because of the possibility that if they went closer it might be found that the merchant vessel carried guns and would defend herself. "The presumption was conclusive that the war vessel would be sufficiently strong to overcome and render useless any defence. If not, so much the worse for the attacking party. He was not permitted to make the merchantman's possible strength the excuse for a surprise attack."[2] Dr Ellery Stowell expresses the same view when he says: "If a belligerent wishes to prey upon his enemy's commerce he must be in sufficient strength to overcome the armament which will be opposed against him by the merchantman."[3]

v

During the war of 1914–18 neutral states almost unanimously recognized the legality of the arming of merchant ships, by admitting them to their ports on the usual terms of ordinary merchant vessels. Some states, in order the more surely to enforce respect for their neutrality, made special rules on the subject of the evidence necessary to be produced in order to

[1] *Das Seekriegsrecht*, p. 285.
[2] Professor Raleigh C. Minor in *Proceedings of the American Society of International Law*, April, 1916, p. 53.
[3] *The New York American*, March 7th, 1916.

convince the port authorities that the merchant ships
would not undertake offensive operations.

United States. The first Memorandum on the Status
of Armed Merchant Vessels issued by the United States
on September 19th, 1914, placed an undue burden
on defensively armed ships. It commenced by giving
full recognition to the arming of merchant ships in
self-defence, in these words: "A merchant vessel of
belligerent nationality may carry an armament and
ammunition for the sole purpose of defence without
acquiring the character of a ship of war," but the
Memorandum then proceeded on the basis that the
presence of armament and ammunition on board a
merchant vessel created a presumption that the armament was for offensive purposes, which presumption
the owners had to overcome by evidence. Amongst the
various indications that the armament would not be
used offensively was the fact that the calibre of the guns
did not exceed 6 inches: that they were few in number
and not carried on the forward part of the ship; that
the vessel was manned by its usual crew, the officers
being the same as those on board before the war; that
the vessel carried passengers, particularly women and
children, and that the speed of the ship was slow.

Many of these indications appear to be oppressive
and unnecessary. The old defensively-armed ships were
not limited as to the number of guns carried, their
position, or their calibre. If they were not commissioned
ships of war they were merchant ships, and enjoyed all
the privileges of hospitality accorded to merchant ships.
However, the Memorandum just referred to was
followed by another issued on March 25th, 1916,[1]
which contains an admirable statement of the position

[1] Both of these Memoranda are printed as Appendices to this
chapter, as is also the British Admiralty's Instruction to Captains
of Defensively Armed Merchant Ships. See *postea*, pp. 296–304.

of armed merchant ships from the two points of view—
(1) of a neutral, when the armed vessel enters its ports,
(2) of an enemy, when the armed vessel is on the high
seas; this is followed by a consideration of the rights and
duties of neutrals and belligerents as affected by the
status of armed merchant vessels in neutral ports and
on the high seas. One important paragraph dealing
with the position of an armed merchant ship on the
high seas may be quoted: "(7) When a belligerent
warship meets a merchantman on the high seas which
is known to be enemy-owned, and attempts to capture
the vessel, the latter may exercise its right of self-protection either by flight or by resistance. The right to
capture and the right to prevent capture are recognized as equally justifiable."

No other states are known to have issued so full a
statement on the subject as the United States. Some
few others issued regulations for the admission of armed
merchantmen to their ports.

Brazil. Defensively armed merchant ships were
allowed to enter Brazilian ports on a written guarantee
being given by the Legation concerned that their armament had not been and would not be used for offensive
purposes.[1]

China. Any belligerent merchant ship armed for the
purpose of self-defence was permitted to enter and
depart from Chinese ports, but regulations were issued
to ensure that the armament was carried solely for
defensive purposes.[2]

Chile. The Chilean Government, in a letter of July
7th, 1915, to the British Minister at Santiago, stated that
Chilean ports would receive merchant vessels armed
for defence if previous notification was made, but that

---

[1] *British Year Book of International Law*, 1920–1, p. 131.
[2] *U.S. Naval War College, International Law Documents*, 1918,
p. 38.

any armed merchant vessel arriving without notification would be considered suspicious.[1]

Cuba. The Cuban Government reproduced the United States Memorandum of September 19th, 1914.

Argentine. Foreign merchant ships carrying cannon for their defence were forbidden to use them in waters under the control of the Argentinian Government, but were not considered as having the legal status of warships.[2]

Uruguay. On September 8th, 1914, Uruguay issued Regulations, in the first of which it was provided that ships which arrived at Uruguayan ports, although carrying arms, but carrying passengers and cargoes in the ordinary operations of navigation, would be considered as devoted to commerce, while if armed merchant ships carried neither passengers nor cargo they would likewise be considered as merchant ships if the Legation of the country to which they belonged made a declaration in writing to the Foreign Minister that they were in fact solely intended for commerce.[3]

Spain. Spain required the captain, owner or agent of a defensively armed merchant vessel, on visiting a Spanish port, to make a written declaration within twenty-four hours after arrival (through the intervention of the consul, if there were one at the port), that the vessel was destined exclusively for commerce; that it would not be transformed into a ship of war or auxiliary cruiser before returning to its own country; and that the armament on board would only be used for the defence of the vessel in case of attack.

[1] *U.S. Naval War College, Neutrality Proclamations,* 1916, p. 30; A. Alvarez, *La Grande Guerre Européenne et la Neutralité du Chili,* p. 259.
[2] *U.S. Naval War College, International War Documents,* 1917, p. 23.
[3] *Rev. Gén. de Droit International public,* vol. xxii, Doc. 193.

Holland. Only one state, so far as is known, refused to admit defensively armed merchant ships into its ports on the footing of ordinary merchant ships. The Dutch Government considered that as such ships are in case of necessity to commit acts of war they are assimilated to warships, and by Article 4 of the Declaration of Neutrality issued by it, the presence of no belligerent ship of war or ship assimilated thereto was allowed within the jurisdiction of the state, except on account of distress or of weather. The Dutch Government admitted, in correspondence with the British Government, that the Law of Nations authorized ships to defend themselves, but contended that it did not follow that neutrals were bound to admit ships armed for the purpose of war into their ports; the right of self-defence was a matter falling within the laws of war, but the admission of defensively armed ships into neutral ports was a question falling within the law of neutrality. The Dutch Government contended that the view it adopted was supported by the great majority of writers on International Law.[1]

In view of the uniform practice of all other states as to the admission of such defensively armed merchant vessels into their ports, the attitude of the Dutch Government appears to have been unjustifiable. The general rules of neutrality afford every protection to a state whose hospitality may be abused by a defensively armed belligerent merchant vessel. Every vessel armed or unarmed is entitled to defend itself, and so, in case of necessity, to commit acts of war, and the *Brussels*, after having successfully driven off a German submarine, continued for many months to enter Dutch ports. The explanation, if any, of the Dutch attitude in thus refusing admission of armed merchant ships into its ports

[1] Dutch Orange Book (French translation), September, 1916, p. 163; *Parl. Papers*, Misc. No. 14 (1917), [Cd. 8690].

and waters must, it would seem, be found in policy and expediency, and not in law.

It is probable that other neutral states made regulations for the admission of armed merchant ships to their ports which have not come under my notice. It is also understood that many such states freely admitted armed merchant ships without having issued any formal regulations, relying on the general principles of the Law of Nations that if it should be proved that they had misused the hospitality of such ports their states would be liable to make reparation for the violation of the neutrality of such state. No such occurrence is known to have taken place.

VI

The legality of arming merchant ships came under the consideration of the Mixed Claims Commission of the United States and Germany established under the Treaty of Berlin, 1921.[1] The Commission had first to consider the meaning of the expression "naval and military works or materials" in the following paragraph 9 to Annex i of Article 232 of the Treaty of Versailles under which Germany undertook to make compensation for: "Damage in respect of all property wherever situate belonging to any of the Allied or Associated States or their nationals, *with the exception of naval and military works or material*, which has been carried off, seized, injured or destroyed by the acts of Germany or her allies on land or sea or from the air, or damage directly in consequence of hostilities or of any operations of war." It took as the test: "Was the ship when destroyed being operated by the United States for purposes directly in furtherance of a military operation

[1] For text of the Awards see *U.S. Naval War College, International Law Decisions and Notes*, 1923, pp. 189–206.

against Germany or her allies? If it was so operated, then it is embraced within the excepted class and Germany is not obligated to pay the loss."[1] The Award was delivered on March 25th, 1924, in the cases of the *Rockingham, Motano, Rochester, Moreni, Alamance Tyler*, and *Santa Maria*, all of which were armed with guns, in some cases 4-inch, in others 3-inch, and carried gun crews. All of these ships were sunk by German submarines, generally without fighting or warning, though in the case of the *Moreni* a long running fight took place. In all these cases the Commission, composed of Mr E. B. Parker (Umpire), Herr W. Kiesselbach (German Commissioner) and Mr Chandler P. Anderson (American Commissioner), unanimously held that the vessels were being operated as merchant ships, and that the possession of defensive armament did not deprive them of their status as private peaceful trading ships and bring them within the excepted class as being "naval and military...materials"; Germany was, therefore, held liable to make compensation for their destruction.

In the case of the *Rockingham* in which the fullest Award was made, the Commissioners said:

The arming for defensive purposes of a merchantman and the manning of such armament by a naval gun crew, coupled with the routing of such ship by the Navy Department of the United States for the purpose of avoiding the danger of submarines, and the following by the civilian master of the ship of instructions given by the Navy Department for the defence of the ship when in danger of attack by submarines, certainly do not change the juridical status of the ship or convert it from a merchant ship to a warship or make of it naval material.[2]

The case of the *Motano* differed from the others in that she was sunk while being convoyed with other vessels from Plymouth to Portsmouth by British destroyers The Commissioners said in this case:

[1] *Op. cit.* p. 193.　　　　[2] *Op. cit.* p. 201.

We have no quarrel with the contention that a vessel, whether neutral or belligerent, forming part of a convoy under belligerent escort may, through the methods prescribed by international law, be lawfully condemned and destroyed as a belligerent. But that is not the question before this Commission. If we assume that the *Motano*—a belligerent merchantman—was lawfully destroyed this does not affect the result....The control exercised by the British Government over the *Motano* was not such as to affect its status.[1]

It should be added that the Commissioners in the general part of their Award covering all these cases and others of a different type were careful to say:

The Commission is not here concerned with the quality of the act causing the damage. The terms of the treaty fix and limit Germany's obligation to pay, and the Commission is not concerned with inquiring whether the act for which she has accepted responsibility was legal or illegal as measured by rules of international law.[2]

It follows from the foregoing that the arming of merchant ships in self-defence was recognized by this Arbitral Commission as legitimate and did not deprive them of their normal character of merchant ships.

VII

Of the writers on International Law who have discussed the subject of defensively armed merchant ships since 1919 it may be said that when they do not tend to reflect the views of the state to which they belong, they are concerned with the future policy as much as, possibly in some cases more than, with the legality of action in the past. The lengthy and able article on this subject by Dr Grau in Strupp's *Wörterbuch des Völkerrechts und der Diplomatie* (1924)[3] is a defence of the German action in treating armed merchant ships as

[1] *Op. cit.* p. 203.   [2] *Op. cit.* p. 191.
[3] Sub nom. *Handelsschiffe im Kriege*, vol. I, pp. 503–19.

warships and therefore liable to be sunk at sight, and contains an argumentative discussion on the illegality of the resistance to capture by enemy merchant ships. It calls for no special examination as Dr Grau's points have, it is thought, been met already in the foregoing pages. Dr Strupp adopts the same point of view.[1]

M. Fauchille, while admitting that the view he puts forward is against that generally received, is of opinion that an enemy merchant ship is not justified in resisting *lawful* operations of an enemy cruiser, that an enemy merchant ship is justified in using force by way of resistance only as an answer to an irregular visit or capture.[2] He cites the German annex of June, 1914, already referred to, and says his thesis resembles that of the Germans. It appears that this is to misapprehend its meaning, since the statement that if an armed merchant vessel offers armed resistance to an enemy cruiser it is the duty of the cruiser to overcome it, and that any damage or loss of life occasioned thereby is the penalty the ship incurs, is not in contradiction to the old practice. The regulation adds that the crew are to be treated as prisoners of war, thus acknowledging that they had the right of lawful combatants. M. Fauchille's view is that the belligerent warship has the right to visit enemy merchant ships, which is undoubted, but the merchant ship has hitherto been recognized as having a right to resist such visit. Resistance is certainly at the peril of the merchant ship. However, under the conditions of the German submarine warfare M. Fauchille considers that the action of the Allied armed merchant ships was lawful.

Dr Charles Cheney Hyde, in by far the ablest work on International Law which has appeared in America

[1] *Éléments du Droit International public*, 1927 (a French translation of *Theorie und Praxis des Völkerrechts*), p. 376.

[2] *Droit International public*, § 1313.

in recent years,[1] discusses the subject of armed merchant ships at some length. He admits the legality of resistance to capture by enemy merchant ships, and of their carrying arms for this purpose. He considers, however, that as privateering has been abolished, one reason for the maintenance of defensive armament has become weaker and that, owing to the great increase in power of modern warships, another reason for the continuance of defensive armament has been removed, because an encounter between ships of the two types means the destruction of the private vessel. This fact, he urges, has an important bearing on the claim that unarmed belligerent merchant ships should enjoy immunity from attack at sight. He also appears to consider that armament should only be carried in case a merchant ship has reason to expect illegitimate treatment at the hands of her enemy; for that reason, arming of merchant ships against the German submarine peril was lawful. A merchant ship when carrying guns of great force and range becomes a weapon of offence, and the master is encouraged to engage enemy warships of inferior strength, irrespectively whether the latter initiates hostilities. He criticizes adversely the Memorandum issued by the United States Department of State in March, 1916, on the subject, and claims that the immunity of merchant ships from attack at sight grew out of their impotency to endanger the safety of warships of the enemy; that the retention by an armed merchant ship of its status as a private ship is not decisive as to the treatment to which it may be subjected by the enemy, as its potentiality for hostile operations should allow of its being lawfully attacked at sight; that to test the propriety of an attack at sight by the existence of conclusive proof of the aggressive

[1] *International Law chiefly as interpreted and applied by the United States* (1922), vol. II, secs. 709, 742.

purpose of the merchant ship places an unreasonable burden on a vessel of war of an unprotected type. His conclusion is that the equipment of a belligerent merchant marine for hostile service, even though designed to be defensive rather than offensive serves, on principle, to deprive the armed vessels of the right to claim immunity from attack without warning. In the main Dr Hyde supports the views put forth by Mr Lansing in January, 1916, as against the Memorandum issued by the same Department of the United States in March of the same year.

Many of the arguments of Dr Hyde have already been dealt with, and both on historical and legal grounds, it is believed that the Memorandum of March, 1916, is more accurate than the views of Mr Lansing which Dr Hyde supports. The claim that the comparatively fragile character of submarines renders the exercise of the right of visit and search or of the summons to surrender dangerous, and is a reason for their non-compliance with this requirement, is contrary to the hitherto accepted principles of war. If a belligerent uses force against his adversary's commerce, it is his duty to see that it is strong enough for the purpose, and capable of conforming to the humane rules adopted in naval warfare; it is not for him to complain if the weapon he employs turns out to be too feeble for the purpose for which it was employed. The suggestion that because an armed merchant ship may turn the tables on its opponent, the warship is justified in refraining from visiting or attempting to visit her before proceeding to forcible measures, is an endeavour to evade the consequence of naval weakness. War is not conducted on the analogy of race meetings. Rules developed and observed for over a century are not to be swept away because of the invention of a new instrument incapable of complying with them. In the wars of the eighteenth century a commissioned ship when approaching a merchant ship with a view to visit, often found herself in the presence of an armed ship of equal, and sometimes of greater strength than herself. A warship cannot tell whether a merchant ship is armed or unarmed until the latter is summoned to lie to.

The immunity of merchant ships from attack at sight did not grow out of their impotency to endanger the safety of the visiting warship. The rules relating to visit and search, and the principle that merchant ships must not be attacked at sight were enforced during the period when the arming of merchant ships was most common. The fact that the arming of ships had fallen into desuetude during the period that elapsed since the close of the Napoleonic wars was due to the disuse of privateers, and also to the fact that there were no wars in the period, with the exception of the American Civil War, in which naval operations against commerce played a serious part. The uncertainties relating to the conversion of merchant ships into warships, and later, the operations of submarines against merchant ships, were valid reasons for the revival of a practice which, as has already been shown, had never completely died out. Piracy of the old type had ceased, but acts to which the name was frequently applied in a loose and improper manner were met by the same means as the old peril had been combated.

There appears in the arguments advanced both by Mr Lansing, Dr Hyde and others, a tendency to confuse the position of enemy and neutral merchant ships as regards their right to resist visit and search. Both must be summoned to submit to this operation before force is applied, but while the latter may not, the former is entitled by long custom to resist, though such resistance is at its peril. The first of the Root Resolutions adopted at the Washington Conference in 1922, which states that

it is an established rule of International Law that a
merchant vessel must be ordered to submit to visit and
search to determine its character before it can be seized,
and that a merchant vessel must not be attacked unless
it refuses to submit to visit and search after warning or
to proceed after seizure as directed, is thoroughly sound
in principle. The only criticism of this rule, which was
unanimously adopted by all the members of the Conference, (though the Convention embodying the rules
has failed to receive the ratification of all the signatory
Powers,) was made by one of the Italian delegates, who
suggested that as a limitation had been imposed on
the armament of light cruisers by the Conference,
a similar limitation should be applied to merchant
ships.[1]

Professor George Grafton Wilson of Harvard University, who has for many years been lecturer at the
United States Naval War College, discusses the subject
in the recently published edition of his "International
Law."[2] He refers to the first Memorandum issued by
the United States regulating the admission of defensively armed merchant ships to their ports, which
has already been mentioned, and which proceeded on
the basis that the presence of arms and ammunition on
board a merchant ship raised a presumption that they
were there for offensive purposes. He further quotes
a confidential letter of January 18th, 1916, from the
State Department to American diplomatic representatives in the Allied belligerent states in which it was
said that the Government of the United States was

impressed with the reasonableness of the argument that a vessel
carrying an armament of any sort, in view of the character of
submarine warfare and the defensive weakness of undersea craft,
should be held to be an auxiliary cruiser and so treated by a

[1] *U.S. Naval War College, International Documents*, 1921, p. 170.
[2] *Handbook of International Law* (2nd ed. 1927), pp. 303–6.

neutral as well as by a belligerent government, and is seriously considering instructing its officials accordingly.

It is remarkable, however, that Professor Wilson does not even mention the Memorandum issued by the United States on March 25th, 1916, which took the place of the one from which he quotes. The second Memorandum takes a very different standpoint from that indicated in the letter of the State Department of January 18th in the same year, and states that

a presumption based solely on the presence of an armament on a merchant vessel of an enemy is not a sufficient reason for a belligerent to declare it to be a warship and proceed to attack it without regard to the rights of the persons on board. Conclusive evidence of a purpose to use the armament for aggression is essential.

As regards the entry of armed merchant vessels into neutral ports, it is stated in this Memorandum that "Merchantmen of belligerent nationality, armed only for the purposes of protection against the enemy, are entitled to enter and leave neutral ports without hindrance in the course of legitimate trade." While Professor Wilson notes the refusal of the Dutch Government to allow defensively armed merchant ships to enter their ports, he does not mention the fact that its action in this respect stood almost, if not entirely, alone as an exception to the general rule of admission. Furthermore, we must entirely dissent from his statement that "the revival of the use of armed merchant vessels was due to the introduction of the submarine as an instrument of war and its use in an unlawful manner." This assertion is, in fact, contradicted a little later by the statement that "arming might be to meet a merchant vessel of the enemy similarly armed, as was the British contention just before and in the early part of the World War." Mr Winston Churchill in his speech on March 26th, 1913, gave very clear and cogent reasons why the British Government made arrangements for arming merchant ships, and submarines were not mentioned. The statement also that armed merchant ships in common with German submarines misused their rights under the claim of retaliatory measures, is very misleading. If there were any cases of the misuse by defensively armed merchant ships of their rights of defence, and, having regard to the methods adopted by the German submarines of sinking at sight not only enemy but neutral merchant ships, it is difficult to conceive that there were, to class them together as on an equality of guilt is surely not what Professor Wilson intended to do. The master of an armed merchant ship undoubtedly did "use his arms against what he might consider an inferior vessel," but this was in self-defence, and in so doing he was carrying on the tradition of merchant vessels for centuries, and he was no more guilty of a violation of the rules of naval warfare than the defensively armed East Indiamen who in the Napoleonic wars frequently put up successful fights against cruisers which were more weakly armed than themselves. No master of a defensively armed merchant ship fights for the mere joy of fighting. He will do everything possible to avoid it, because he has his crew and cargo, and often passengers, as his first charge, and he will do all in his power to avoid endangering them.

VIII

This study would be incomplete if reference to the position of neutral merchant ships in the matter of defensive armament were omitted. It is a recognized rule of International Law that neutral merchant ships must submit to visit and search by belligerent warships. If such vessels are convoyed by warships of their own flag, most states admit that the word of the officer of the convoying warship is sufficient, though if the visiting belligerent officer can show that the confidence of the neutral officer has been misplaced as regards any vessel in the convoy, the protection of his ship will be withdrawn. Great Britain, however, does not admit the right of Convoy, and in the English leading case of *The Maria*,[1] Sir William Scott (Lord Stowell) condemned neutral vessels under convoy for resisting visit and search. In that case Sir William Scott was considering the position of a neutral merchant ship where "the utmost injury threatened is being carried into the nearest port, subject to a full responsibility in costs and damages if this is done vexatiously and without just cause." The master of a neutral merchant ship had no right to say "I will submit to no such inquiry, but I will take the law into my own hands by force."

In the past, when neutral states considered that a belligerent was acting in a way injurious to their subjects, they have either, individually or collectively, taken steps to protect them. It is not necessary to refer in detail to the Armed Neutrality Leagues of 1780 and 1800, though it is not unimportant to remember that both were formed against Great Britain for the enforcement of rules which the latter Power declined to recognize as part of the Law of Nations. The Northern Powers banded themselves together to resist visit and search of their vessels under the convoy of their warships.

In the *Maria*, from which the preceding quotations on resistance by neutrals are taken, Lord Stowell made a decree of condemnation. Resistance, however, continued for a while, and the Second Armed Neutrality added to the principles of the First, the doctrine that belligerents should not have the right to visit and

[1] 1 C. Rob. p. 363.

search in case the commanding officer of the convoying vessel should declare that no contraband was on board the convoyed vessels. A temporary compromise was reached, but the question remained unsettled.

The action of the United States to protect neutral rights was more striking, and forms a more important precedent for neutral states in the face of gross illegalities committed by a belligerent. France was in close relationship with the United States, treaties of amity, commerce and alliance having been entered into between these Powers in 1778. But France was bitterly chagrined that the United States had granted rights to Great Britain similar to those which she enjoyed under the Treaty of Commerce of 1778, and acts of aggression commenced on American commerce in 1796 of a similar character to those complained of by the Northern Powers. The proceedings of the French privateers and Prize Courts, particularly of the latter sitting in the West Indies, at length caused the President to withdraw the *exequaturs* of the French Consuls, and Congress proceeded to pass an Act on June 25th, 1798, which permitted the arming of American merchant vessels for the purpose of defence against capture, as well as to "subdue and capture" any armed French vessel. There was, however, a reservation that the President might thereafter instruct the armed merchantmen to submit to search, when French armed vessels should observe the Law of Nations. A subsequent Act of July 7th, 1798, abrogated treaties between France and the United States, and another of July 9th, 1798, gave the President power to instruct commanders of public armed vessels to capture any French armed vessel, and to issue Letters of Marque to privateers. The nature of the relationship brought about between the United States and France by these proceedings is a matter on which American lawyers and politicians do not agree. The position was considered by the Supreme Court of the United States in *Bas* v. *Tingy*.[1] Several of the judges considered the position of the two Powers to be one of war. Chase, J., called it "limited, partial war," but it was also "a public war." Patterson, J., said the two countries were "in a qualified state of hostility." It was war *quoad hoc*. It was "a public war between the two nations," qualified in the manner prescribed by Congress. Marshall, C.J., cast doubts on the existence of war in the phrase, "Even if an actual and general war had existed between this country and France."[2] But Webster, in his speech on French spoliations, considered that the situation did not amount, at any rate, to open and public war. There was no public declaration of war; general reprisals were never authorized on French commerce; French citizens continued to sue in American Courts. The Act of Congress authorized the use of force under certain circumstances and for certain objects against French vessels. "Cases of this kind may occur under that practice of retorsion which is justified, when adopted for just cause by the laws and usages of nations, and which all the writers distinguish from general war."[3] Lord Stowell was not very definite in some of his references to the situation, and in *The Santa Cruz* in 1798[4] spoke of "the present state of hostility (if so it may be called) between America and France," and in *The Two Friends*:[5] "It is not for me to say whether America is at war with France or not,"

[1] (1800) 4 Dall, 37.
[2] *Hallet and Browne* v. *Jenks* (1805), 3 Cranch, 210. See also *Talbot* v. *Seeman* (1801), 1 Cranch, 1.
[3] J. B. Moore, *Digest of International Law*, vol. VII, § 1102, where the subject is discussed; see also an article by H. N. Stull on "Our partial war with France" in *Harper's Magazine*, December, 1915.
[4] 1 C. Rob. p. 64.   [5] *Ibid.* p. 276.

but he decreed salvage on recapture by the crew of an American vessel from the French. Whatever the position, whether war, partial war or war *sub modo*, as Professor Holland termed the so-called Pacific Blockade of Venezuela in 1902, the Government of the United States, by way of retaliation for the illegal treatment of American ships, cargoes and crews, authorized the latter to defend themselves, and the former to carry guns for the purpose of resisting visit and search. After nearly two years of "partial" war, France and the United States agreed to a settlement of their differences.

It would appear that some 40 years ago fears were entertained that the torpedo boat would act as the German submarines acted during the war of 1914–18 and sink enemy merchant ships at sight. The especial features which belong to submarines, their secret methods of attack and their vulnerability, were attributed to torpedo boats, and it was suggested that these afforded reasons why the prevailing rules of law should not apply to them. The answer given by the distinguished French officer, Admiral Bourgois, to such arguments is as true to-day as it was then. "The advent of the torpedo, whatever its influence on naval *matériel*, has in no way changed international treaties, the law of nations, or the moral laws which govern the world. It has not given the belligerent the right of life and death over the peaceful citizens of the enemy State or of neutral States."[1] Professor Dupuis, in discussing the question of sinking vessels without visit and search, points out that the indiscriminate destruction of enemy ships must necessarily, on occasion, involve the destruction of neutrals also. Visit and search are necessary to ascertain the nationality of a vessel, flags are no necessary criteria of nationality, the usages of the sea

[1] "Les torpilles et le droit des gens," *Nouvelle Revue*, 1886.

admit of enemy merchant ships flying neutral flags. The build of the ship is, again, no necessary criterion of its nationality, and even if a vessel should clearly appear to be of enemy build, hundreds of merchant ships are built in countries other than those whose nationality they possess. Then follows this passage in which is discussed the right of self-defence of all vessels, enemy or neutral, against a proceeding in all respects similar to that with which the shipping of the whole world was faced during the war of 1914–18.

Certainly if the aggressors contented themselves with data so doubtful (i.e., the flag or the build of the ships) every neutral ship would be justified in treating as pirates the torpedo boats which should dare to send a ship to the bottom on such feeble evidence; not only would it be justified in law, but the interest of its security would oblige it, provided it had a gun on board to aim it (*à le braquer*) without any hesitation at every torpedo boat heading for it. Enemy or neutral, cruiser or merchant vessel, every ship will have the right and the duty of treating as enemies the frail barks which have become a peril for all.[1]

For "torpedo boat" in this passage read "submarine" and the doctrine applies to the methods of the German submarines.

The continued attacks on neutral merchant vessels and the loss of many American ships by German submarines, notwithstanding the assurance given to the United States that merchant ships would not be sunk without warning, and the subsequent withdrawal of that assurance in January, 1917, caused the United States to sever diplomatic relations with Germany on February 3rd. On March 12th, 1917, the State Department issued a notice to all foreign missions in Washington that

in view of the announcement of the Imperial German Government on January 31, 1917, that all ships, those of neutrals included, met within certain zones of the high seas, would be sunk

[1] *Le Droit de la Guerre maritime* (1899), p. 350.

without any precautions being taken for the safety of the persons on board, and without the exercise of visit and search, the Government of the United States has determined to place upon all American merchant vessels sailing through the barred areas, an armed guard for the protection of the vessels and the lives of the persons on board.[1]

Not only armed guards but guns were also placed on American vessels and the procedure was continued after April 6th, 1917, when the United States declared war against Germany.

IX

The situation produced by the German methods of submarine warfare may, it is hoped, never recur; agreement as to the place of conversion of merchant ships into warships under the conditions of the Seventh Hague Convention, 1907, may be reached; but the legal right of merchant ships to carry arms and defend themselves from capture whenever there is a reasonable likelihood of success cannot be abandoned in the present condition of uncertainty on these points. Changes from sail to steam, from muzzle-loading guns to breech-loading, the invention of the torpedo and the introduction of the fast torpedo-boat all left the old rules unchanged, and they cannot be changed by the fiat of any one state. Instead of advocating the abolition of the right to carry defensive armament, or of placing defensively armed ships on the same footing as regards attack without warning as warships, it is surely more in accord with the principles of naval warfare to refuse to recognize the legitimacy of attack on merchant ships, armed or unarmed, unless the traditional methods of sea warfare are complied with. These were the principles which were enunciated by the Rules adopted

---

[1] *U.S. Naval War College, International Law Documents*, 1917, p. 225; C. C. Hyde, *International Law*, vol. II, §§ 750, 751.

at Washington in 1922, and which, though the treaty embodying them has failed to take effect, were recognized by all the signatory Powers as stating the recognized rules of the Law of Nations.[1]

In some future war there may be valid reasons of policy against arming merchant ships, and convoys may again be found to be the better protection for trading vessels, but from the standpoint of International Law the legality of defensively arming merchant ships as aids to their legitimate resistance to capture appears established. To say this is not to exclude the conclusion that it appears to be a regrettable necessity that states should be compelled to have recourse to this expedient. Everything which tends to obliterate in any way the line between combatants and non-combatants and which may produce a return to the days of privateering is a retrogression. It is to be hoped that the dangers which led to the arming of merchant ships in 1913 may be overcome by international co-operation.

[1] A similar rule was proposed by the Commission of Jurists at Rio de Janeiro in the session April–May, 1927, in Project No. ix, Section 111 (*American Journal of International Law*, Special Supplement, January, 1928, p. 259).

APPENDICES

TO DEFENSIVELY ARMED MERCHANT SHIPS

A

The United States Government's First Memorandum on the Status of Armed Merchant Vessels.[1]

A. A merchant vessel of belligerent nationality may carry an armament and ammunition for the sole purpose of defence without acquiring the character of a ship-of-war.

B. The presence of an armament and ammunition on board a merchant vessel creates a presumption that the armament is for offensive purposes, but the owners or agents may overcome this presumption by evidence showing that the vessel carries armament solely for defence.

C. Evidence necessary to establish the fact that the armament is solely for defence and will not be used offensively, whether the armament be mounted or stowed below, must be presented in each case independently at an official investigation. The result of the investigation must show conclusively that the armament is not intended for, and will not be used in, offensive operations.

Indications that the armament will not be used offensively are:

1. That the calibre of the guns carried does not exceed six inches.
2. That the guns and small arms carried are few in number.
3. That no guns are mounted on the forward part of the vessel.
4. That the quantity of ammunition carried is small.
5. That the vessel is manned by its usual crew, and the officers are the same as those on board before war was declared.
6. That the vessel intends to and actually does clear for a port lying in its usual trade route, or a port indicating its purpose to continue in the same trade in which it was engaged before war was declared.
7. That the vessel takes on board fuel and supplies sufficient only to carry it to its port of destination, or the same quantity substantially which it has been accustomed to take for a voyage before war was declared.

[1] *U.S. Naval War College, International Law Topics*, 1916, p. 93.

8. That the cargo of the vessel consists of articles of commerce unsuited for the use of a ship of war in operations against an enemy.

9. That the vessel carries passengers who are, as a whole, unfitted to enter the military or naval service of the belligerent whose flag the vessel flies, or of any of its allies, and particularly if the passenger list includes women and children.

10. That the speed of the ship is slow.

D. Port authorities, on the arrival in a port of the United States of an armed vessel of belligerent nationality claiming to be a merchant vessel, should immediately investigate and report to Washington on the foregoing indications as to the intended use of the armament, in order that it may be determined whether the evidence is sufficient to remove the presumption that the vessel is, and should be, treated as a ship of war. Clearance will not be granted until authorised from Washington, and the master will be so informed upon arrival.

E. The conversion of a merchant vessel into a ship of war is a question of fact which is to be established by direct or circumstantial evidence of intention to use the vessel as a ship of war.

DEPARTMENT OF STATE
September 19th, 1914

B

The United States Government's Second Memorandum on the Status of Armed Merchant Vessels.[1]

I

DEPARTMENT OF STATE

WASHINGTON

March 25th 1916

The status of an armed merchant vessel of a belligerent is to be considered from two points of view: First, from that of a neutral when the vessel enters its ports; and, second, from that of an enemy when the vessel is on the high seas.

[1] *U.S. Naval War College, International Law Topics*, 1916, p. 101.

First: An Armed Merchant Vessel in Neutral Ports.

(1) It is necessary for a neutral Government to determine the status of an armed merchant vessel of belligerent nationality which enters its jurisdiction, in order that the Government may protect itself from responsibility for the destruction of life and property by permitting its ports to be used as bases of hostile operations by belligerent warships.

(2) If the vessel carries a commission or orders issued by a belligerent Government and directing it under penalty to conduct aggressive operations, or if it is conclusively shown to have conducted such operations, it should be regarded and treated as a warship.

(3) If sufficient evidence is wanting, a neutral Government, in order to safeguard itself from liability for failure to preserve its neutrality, may reasonably presume from the facts the status of an armed merchant vessel which frequents its waters. There is no settled rule of international law as to the sufficiency of evidence to establish such a presumption. As a result, a neutral Government must decide for itself the sufficiency of the evidence which it requires to determine the character of the vessel. For the guidance of its port officers and other officials a neutral Government may, therefore, declare a standard of evidence, but such standard may be changed on account of the general conditions of naval warfare or modified on account of the circumstances of a particular case. These changes and modifications may be made at any time during the progress of the war, since the determination of the status of an armed merchant vessel in neutral waters may affect the liability of a neutral Government.

Second: An Armed Merchant Vessel on the High Seas.

(1) It is necessary for a belligerent warship to determine the status of an armed merchant vessel of an enemy encountered on the high seas, since the rights of life and property of belligerents and neutrals on board the vessel may be impaired if its status is that of an enemy warship.

(2) The determination of warlike character must rest in no case upon presumption but upon conclusive evidence, because the responsibility for the destruction of life and property depends on the actual facts of the case and cannot be avoided or lessened by a standard of evidence which a belligerent may announce as creating a presumption of hostile character. On the other hand, to safeguard himself from possible liability for unwarranted destruc-

tion of life and property the belligerent should, in the absence of conclusive evidence, act on the presumption that an armed merchantman is of peaceful character.

(3) A presumption based solely on the presence of an armament on a merchant vessel of an enemy is not a sufficient reason for a belligerent to declare it to be a warship and proceed to attack it without regard to the rights of the persons on board. Conclusive evidence of a purpose to use the armament for aggression is essential. Consequently, an armament which a neutral Government, seeking to perform its neutral duties, may presume to be intended for aggression might, in fact, on the high seas be used solely for protection. A neutral Government has no opportunity to determine the purpose of an armament on a merchant vessel, unless there is evidence in the ship's papers or other proof as to its previous use, so that the Government is justified in substituting an arbitrary rule of presumption in arriving at the status of the merchant vessel. On the other hand, a belligerent warship can on the high seas test by actual experience the purpose of an armament on an enemy merchant vessel, and so determine by direct evidence the status of the vessel.

SUMMARY

The status of an armed merchant vessel as a warship in neutral waters may be determined, in the absence of documentary proof or conclusive evidence of previous aggressive conduct, by presumption derived from all the circumstances of the case.

The status of such vessel as a warship on the high seas must be determined only upon conclusive evidence of aggressive purpose, in the absence of which it is to be presumed that the vessel has a private and peaceable character, and it should be so treated by an enemy warship.

In brief, a neutral Government may proceed upon the presumption that an armed merchant vessel of belligerent nationality is armed for aggression, while a belligerent should proceed on the presumption that the vessel is armed for protection. Both of these presumptions may be overcome by evidence—the first by secondary or collateral evidence, since the fact to be established is negative in character; the second by primary and direct evidence, since the fact to be established is positive in character.

II

The character of the evidence upon which the status of an armed merchant vessel of belligerent nationality is to be determined when visiting neutral waters and when traversing the high seas having been stated, it is important to consider the rights and duties of neutrals and belligerents as affected by the status of armed merchant vessels in neutral ports and on the high seas.

First: The Relations of Belligerents and Neutrals as Affected by the Status of Armed Merchant Vessels in Neutral Ports.

(1) It appears to be the established rule of international law that warships of a belligerent may enter neutral ports and accept limited hospitality there upon condition that they leave, as a rule, within 24 hours after their arrival.

(2) Belligerent warships are also entitled to take on fuel once in three months in ports of a neutral country.

(3) As a mode of enforcing these rules a neutral has the right to cause belligerent warships failing to comply with them, together with their officers and crews, to be interned during the remainder of the war.

(4) Merchantmen of belligerent nationality, armed only for purposes of protection against the enemy, are entitled to enter and leave neutral ports without hindrance in the course of legitimate trade.

(5) Armed merchantmen of belligerent nationality under a commission or orders of their Government to use, under penalty, their armament for aggressive purposes, or merchantmen which, without such commission or orders, have used their armaments for aggressive purposes, are not entitled to the same hospitality in neutral ports as peaceable armed merchantmen.

Second: The Relations of Belligerents and Neutrals as Affected by the Status of Armed Merchant Vessels on the High Seas.

(1) Innocent neutral property on the high seas cannot legally be confiscated, but is subject to inspection by a belligerent. Resistance to inspection removes this immunity and subjects the property to condemnation by a prize court, which is charged with the preservation of the legal rights of the owners of neutral property.

(2) Neutral property engaged in contraband trade, breach of blockade, or unneutral service obtains the character of enemy

property and is subject to seizure by a belligerent and condemnation by a prize court.

(3) When hostile and innocent property is mixed, as in the case of a neutral ship carrying a cargo which is entirely or partly contraband, this fact can only be determined by inspection. Such innocent property may be of uncertain character, as it has been frequently held that it is more or less contaminated by association with hostile property. For example, under the Declaration of London (which, so far as the provisions covering this subject are concerned, has been adopted by all the belligerents) the presence of a cargo which in bulk or value consists of 50 per cent. contraband articles impresses the ship with enemy character and subjects it to seizure and condemnation by a prize court.

(4) Enemy property, including ships and cargoes, is always subject to seizure and condemnation. Any enemy property taken by a belligerent on the high seas is a total loss to the owners. There is no redress in a prize court. The only means of avoiding loss is by flight or successful resistance. Enemy merchant ships have, therefore, the right to arm for the purpose of self-protection.

(5) A belligerent warship is any vessel which, under commission or orders of its Government imposing penalties or entitling it to prize money, is armed for the purpose of seeking and capturing or destroying enemy property or hostile neutral property on the seas. The size of the vessel, strength of armament, and its defensive or offensive force are immaterial.

(6) A belligerent warship has, incidental to the right of seizure, the right to visit and search all vessels on the high seas for the purpose of determining the hostile or innocent character of the vessels and their cargoes. If the hostile character of the property is known, however, the belligerent warship may seize the property without exercising the right of visit and search, which is solely for the purpose of obtaining knowledge as to the character of the property. The attacking vessel must display its colours before exercising belligerent rights.

(7) When a belligerent warship meets a merchantman on the high seas which is known to be enemy owned and attempts to capture the vessel, the latter may exercise its right of self-protection either by flight or by resistance. The right to capture and the right to prevent capture are recognised as equally justifiable.

(8) The exercise of the right of capture is limited, nevertheless, by certain accepted rules of conduct based on the principles of humanity and regard for innocent property, even if there is definite knowledge that some of the property, cargo as well as the

vessel, is of enemy character. As a consequence of these limitations, it has become the established practice for warships to give merchant vessels an opportunity to surrender or submit to visit and search before attempting to seize them by force. The observance of this rule of naval warfare tends to prevent the loss of life of non-combatants and the destruction of innocent neutral property which would result from sudden attack.

(9) If, however, before a summons to surrender is given, a merchantman of belligerent nationality, aware of the approach of an enemy warship, uses its armament to keep the enemy at a distance, or after it has been summoned to surrender it resists or flees, the warship may properly exercise force to compel surrender.

(10) If the merchantman finally surrenders, the belligerent warship may release it or take it into custody. In the case of an enemy merchantman it may be sunk, but only if it is impossible to take it into port, and provided always that the persons on board are put in a place of safety. In the case of a neutral merchantman, the right to sink it in any circumstances is doubtful.

(11) A merchantman entitled to exercise the right of self-protection may do so when certain of attack by an enemy warship, otherwise the exercise of the right would be so restricted as to render it ineffectual. There is a distinct difference, however, between the exercise of the right of self-protection and the act of cruising the seas in an armed vessel for the purpose of attacking enemy naval vessels.

(12) In the event that merchant ships of belligerent nationality are armed and under commission or orders to attack in all circumstances certain classes of enemy naval vessels for the purpose of destroying them, and are entitled to receive prize money for such service from their Government, or are liable to a penalty for failure to obey the orders given, such merchant ships lose their status as peaceable merchant ships and are to a limited extent incorporated in the naval forces of their Government, even though it is not their sole occupation to conduct hostile operations.

(13) A vessel engaged intermittently in commerce and under a commission or orders of its Government imposing a penalty, in pursuing and attacking enemy naval craft, possesses a status tainted with a hostile purpose which it cannot throw aside or assume at will. It should, therefore, be considered as an armed public vessel and receive the treatment of a warship by an enemy or by neutrals. Any person taking passage on such a vessel cannot expect immunity other than that accorded persons who are on board a warship. A private vessel engaged in seeking enemy naval craft

without such a commission or orders from its Government stands in a relation to the enemy similar to that of a civilian who fires upon the organised military forces of a belligerent, and is entitled to no more considerate treatment.

C

British Instructions for Defensively Armed Merchant Ships.

A. THE STATUS OF ARMED MERCHANT SHIPS

(1) The right of the crew of a merchant vessel forcibly to resist visit and search, and to fight in self-defence, is well recognised in international law, and is expressly admitted by the German prize regulations in an addendum issued in June, 1914, at a time when it was known that numerous merchant vessels were being armed in self-defence.

(2) The armament is supplied solely for the purpose of resisting attack by an armed vessel of the enemy. It must not be used for any other purpose whatsoever.

(3) An armed merchant vessel, therefore, must not in any circumstances interfere with or obstruct the free passage of other merchant vessels or fishing craft, whether these are friendly, neutral, or hostile.

(4) The status of a British armed merchant vessel cannot be changed upon the high seas.

B. RULES TO BE OBSERVED IN THE EXERCISE OF THE RIGHT OF SELF-DEFENCE

(1) The master or officer in command is responsible for opening and ceasing fire.

(2) Participation in armed resistance must be confined to persons acting under the orders of the master or officer in command.

(3) Before opening fire the British colours must be hoisted.

(4) Fire must not be opened or continued from a vessel which has stopped, hauled down her flag, or otherwise indicated her intention to surrender.

(5) The expression "armament" in these instructions includes not only cannon, but also rifles and machine guns in cases where those are supplied.

(6) The ammunition used in rifles and machine guns must conform to Article 23, Hague Convention IV, 1907; that is to say, the bullets must be cased in nickel or other hard substance and must not be split or cut in such a way as to cause them to expand or set up on striking a man. The use of explosive bullets is forbidden.

C. CIRCUMSTANCES UNDER WHICH THE ARMAMENT SHOULD BE EMPLOYED

(1) The armament is supplied for the purpose of defence only, and the object of the master should be to avoid action whenever possible.

(2) Experience has shown that hostile submarines and aircraft have frequently attacked merchant vessels without warning. It is important, therefore, that craft of this description should not be allowed to approach to a short range at which a torpedo or bomb launched without notice would almost certainly take effect.

British and Allied submarines and aircraft have orders not to approach merchant vessels. Consequently, it may be presumed that any submarine or aircraft which deliberately approaches or pursues a merchant vessel does so with hostile intention. In such cases fire may be opened in self-defence in order to prevent the hostile craft closing to a range at which resistance to a sudden attack with bomb or torpedo would be impossible.

(3) An armed merchant vessel proceeding to render assistance to the crew of a vessel in distress must not seek action with any hostile craft, though, if she is herself attacked while so doing, fire may be opened in self-defence.

(4) It should be remembered that the flag is no guide to nationality. German submarines and armed merchant vessels have frequently employed British, Allied, or neutral colours in order to approach undetected. Though, however, the use of disguise and false colours in order to escape capture is a legitimate *ruse de guerre*, its adoption by defensively armed merchant ships may easily lead to misconception. Such vessels, therefore, are forbidden to adopt any form of disguise which might cause them to be mistaken for neutral ships.

ADMIRALTY WAR STAFF
   TRADE DIVISION
      October 20th 1915

TABLE OF CASES

INDEX

Press, power of, in international affairs, 13
Private property on land and sea, 268
Privateers, 244; abolished by Declaration of Paris, 245
Prize, see Ships of war
Prize Act, 1708, 207, 210
Prize Court, British, and Orders in Council, 221

Racial discrimination, 29
Rebus sic stantibus, doctrine of, 139
Renault, M., on submarine cables, 201
Reprisals in war, see Retaliation
Requisition, meaning of, 179, 182
Resistance of neutral ships and enemy, 251, 289, 293
Retaliation, in war, a matter for executive, 177; in naval warfare, 213–238; affecting neutrals, 216; right of a belligerent, 228; comparison of British and German methods, 231; permissible within limitation of humanity, 232; suggested bases for future, 237; United States armed merchant ships in, 290, 293
Retaliatory Orders in Council, 1915, 1917, 220; upheld by Prize Court, 225, 227
Revenue cutters, 245
Roosevelt, President Theodore, on Internationalism, 13; and Monroe Doctrine, 72, 81; on enforcement of laws of war, 237
Root, Secretary Elihu, on Monroe Doctrine, 80, 84
Rush, Mr, and origins of Monroe Doctrine, 69, 76
Russia, disturbing factor internationally, 23; outside League of Nations, 24; and Great Britain, Persian policy, 34; Prize Regulations regarding captured warships, 205; Prize Regulations on defence by merchant ships, 254

St Bartholomew Island, cession of, 71, 73
Salisbury, Lord, and Venezuela boundary dispute, 79

Schramm, Dr G., 255, 256, 267
Scott, Dr James Brown, on defence of merchant ships, 269; on execution of Captain Fryatt, 269
Scott, Sir William (Lord Stowell), 219, 244, 251, 262, 263, 264, 266, 289, 291
"Scrap of paper," 128, 133
"Self-determination," ambiguous term, 16
"Self-preservation" in International Law, 127, 128
Serbia, Austria declared war against, 2
Ships, see also Merchant ships
Ships of war as prize, 202–212; ships pass to state on capture, 203; naval instructions of states regarding, 203; history of treatment in England, 205; dealt with in Naval Prize Acts, 206; necessity for prize procedure in England, due to grants of prize, 212
Snow, Professor Freeman, 250
Soviet ideals, 40
Spain, rules for admission of defensively armed merchant ships to ports, 277
State, the, and individuals, 20
States, duties of, 37–45, 100; equality of, 25, 100; backward, 26; need for efficient government, 41; and co-operation, 41
Statutes, 13 and 14 Car. II, c. 11, 246; 22 and 23 Car. II, c. 11, 246; 4 and 5 Will. and Mary, c. 25, 206; 5 and 6 Will. and Mary, c. 24, 247; 6 Anne, c. 13 (First Prize Act), 207; 5 Geo. II, c. 20, 247; 24 Geo. III, c. 4, 247; 34 Geo. III, c. 50, 247; 27 and 28 Vic. c. 25 (Naval Prize Act, 1864), 208, 209, 260; 4 and 5 Geo. V, c. 13, 209; 8 and 9 Geo. V, c. 30, 209
Stockton, Rear-Admiral, on submarine cables, 196
Story, Mr Justice, 262, 264
Stowell, Dr Ellery, 272, 274
Stowell, Lord, see Scott, Sir William
Stresemann, Herr, proposals to France, 1923, 106

Lightning Source UK Ltd.
Milton Keynes UK
UKOW02f1555231115

263336UK00001B/21/P

9 781107 586796